Research Methods for Social Work

Research Methods for Social Work

Editors
D.K. Lal Das
Vanila Bhaskaran

RAWAT PUBLICATIONS
Jaipur • New Delhi • Bangalore • Mumbai • Hyderabad • Guwahati

ISBN 978-81-316-0161-7

Reprinted, 2018

Published by
Prem Rawat for **Rawat Publications**
Satyam Apts, Sector 3, Jawahar Nagar, Jaipur 302 004 (India)
Phone: 0141 265 1748 / 7006 Fax: 0141 265 1748
E-mail: info@rawatbooks.com
Website: www.rawatbooks.com

New Delhi Office
4858/24, Ansari Road, Daryaganj, New Delhi 110 002
Phone: 011 2326 3290

Also at *Bangalore, Guwahati* and *Kolkata*

Typeset by Rawat Computers, Jaipur
Printed at Nice Printing Press, New Delhi

Contents

Preface

Research entails critical awareness, careful thinking and ability to view situations from new perspectives. It is in this perspective that social work research has a major role to play in the development of knowledge for social work theories and practice. Hence, research methodology useful for social work should reflect the theory, approach and processes that exist in social work practice.

There has been little growth and practically no developments in the field of social work research in India. This is evident from observations by social work educators at different points of time. This shows that there has been serious stagnation or at least very poor growth in social work research in our country.

There are a number of reasons for this neglected situation, the most important is the curriculum of research methods in social work. Most of the schools of social work are still following the hypothetico-deductive model of social science research. This is most probably the reason why research in many schools of social work is in no way different from the contents of social science research curriculum.

Social work research educators, in general, teach the research methods course independent of social work framework. This is most probably another important reason for this unfortunate situation.

Research methods for social work have undergone several changes in the recent past. Some significant changes have been brought about in the areas of Research Designs, Techniques of Data Collection, Analysis of Data and Computer Application in Social Work Research.

Against this background, a seminar was organized with a specific objective in view for social work educators, researchers and practitioners. The objective was to bring research closer to social work practice and to find from the research methodologies used by social scientists those methods which can be especially suitable for application in the context of social work.

In developing the focus of the seminar, we were, however, careful in finding a suitable nomenclature for research methods for social work and have scrupulously avoided the oft-repeated term 'social work research'. For, the type of research with which social work educators are to be now concerned belongs to a wider field of knowledge and represents an altogether different type of concern.

The papers are selected to cover four broad areas of research. While the first part has nine papers, which are descriptive accounts of research methods used with social work interventions, the second and third consist of two papers each on data analysis and interpretation, and fields of social work, respectively. The last part contains four papers dealing with different research strategies, e.g., qualitative research, case study method and action research.

In a nutshell, the papers discuss at length the following aspects of research methods:

1. Research Methods for Social Work
2. Single-Subject Design: AB Design
3. Evaluation Research: True Experiment
4. Evaluation Research: Quasi-Experiment
5. Qualitative Research in Social Work
6. Action Research in Social Work
7. Case Study Method in Social Work Research

8. Computer Assisted Quantitative Data Analysis
9. Content Analysis: A Method of Social Science Research
10. Research in Correctional Setting with Social Work Intervention
11. Research in Industrial Social Work
12. Social Work Research Ethics
13. Social Work Research Curriculum
14. Developing Research Interest among Social Work Trainees

One thing brought out in sharp focus is the recent shift that has taken place in the area of social work research. This includes the inclination of social work researchers towards intervention and evaluative research. It is still for us to appreciate that intervention and evaluative research need much more attention than what we have today.

The seminar's concern, as it is now evident, was primarily with substantive areas of research methods for social work. It is therefore imperative for social work educators to shift from depending entirely upon social research to intervention and evaluative research. This needs adaptations of various research methods for its effective use by social work educators.

We are delighted to bring out this Volume on research methods for social work with the major aim to cater to specific readers, who are either students or teachers of social work or researchers in the fields of social work, development sector and management. The editors acknowledge the contribution and involvement of many people without whose support this endeavour would not have been possible.

First of all, we wish to thank the University Grants Commission, New Delhi for having sponsored the seminar and providing aid for the publication of this book. Dr. S. Jelani, Deputy Secretary, South Eastern Regional Office (SERO), Hyderabad, has been very kind in having faith in us and supporting us in all our academic pursuits.

We are thankful to Mr. Rama Rao, Executive Secretary-Centre for World Solidarity for his support, and others who have very graciously contributed in different ways in organising the seminar.

We are grateful to the Board of Management of the College and its Chairman, Mr. Basheer Mohammad Khan for encouraging us in organising this seminar and always supporting us in our efforts. We thank Dr. Anna Mathew, Principal for her cooperation and encouragement in this endeavour.

We thank our colleagues Dr. (Mrs) Hanna Anandaraj, Dr. B.V. Jagadish, Mr. P. Narsimha Reddy and Mr. A. Ravindra Chary, who have contributed in different ways in accomplishing our tasks. Dr. Shashikala Singh has been extremely kind in proofreading and offering suggestions while reading through the manuscripts.

A special word of thanks goes to Mr. Naveen Kumar, faculty member, who had taken up large responsibility in organizing the seminar. Under his guidance and leadership, the student volunteers have done excellently in all their tasks and responsibilities; we thank each one of them.

Sr. Ancy, Research Scholar, deserves a special mention as she has worked unstintingly in organising the seminar from day one and has contributed immensely to its success and in the publication of this book.

No work of this nature will be complete without the help and contribution of the secretarial staff. We thank Mrs. Ayesha Vaseem and Ms. Saniya, who have worked tirelessly to complete the typing and other related work meticulously. We also acknowledge the help of administrative and support staff for their contribution in different ways.

We are indeed indebted to all the paper presenters who made the deliberations of the seminar of immense value and made this volume a reality. The participants of the seminar who have come from across the country, have contributed in making the seminar, a professionally useful and learning experience to all. We thank each one of them for their active participation.

D.K. Lal Das
Vanila Bhaskaran

Editorial Note

The seminar has evinced interest from many social work educators and researchers who have participated and presented papers. However, keeping in view the central theme of the seminar, the following papers have been included in this Volume:

The first paper on 'Research Methods for Social Work: Need for Paradigm Shift' by Murli Desai deals with the need for social work knowledge and examines the influence of programme ideologies on social work knowledge development. It is also concerned with the methodological development and the different types of progressive social work research methodologies, which emerged over a period of time. The author concludes with a note on the ethics of social work research, which is the foundation on which all research knowledge should base.

The second article on 'Dimensions of Research Methods for Social Work' by D.K. Lal Das, who is also co-editor, systematically presents the different research methods used in social work research, giving impetus to intervention research as being specific and exclusive to the practice. It also goes on to help the readers in understanding the need and to appreciate the growing recognition of social work research as different from social research. The article emphasises on integrating theory, practice and research in evolving intervention strategies and their note in creating a need-based methodology for social work.

The next paper presented by Sushma Batra and Tushti Bhardwaj on 'Social Work Intervention in Psychosomatic Pain Disorder, examines the effectiveness of social work intervention in the case of an adolescent with tension type headache. The authors have used the multimodel approach to treat somatoform disorder in adolescents. The study was carried out using the AB single-subject design as an effective tool of intervention in this case. Cognitive behavioural treatment and problem-solving skills formed the part of the treatment process.

The article on 'Clinical Social Work Research' by Anna Mathew explicitly describes the process of clinical social work research in a problem related to attempted suicide. Single-subject design is used in carrying out the study. The objective was to assess the effectiveness of an intervention package in dealing with suicidal tendencies in a young adult student. The intervention package consisted of crisis intervention cognitive therapy and problem solving skills, designed to bring improvement in the client. The results show that the effectiveness of the intervention is statistically significant.

The article by Kalpana Sampath entitled 'Effect of Value Clarifications on Orientation towards Vision and Values' reports the study undertaken by the author to assess the impact of value clarification as a process to enhance the level of orientation towards vision and values among students of management. True experimental research design was used in the study. An instrument consisting of five dimensions, viz., freedom, relationship, power and influence, learning and honesty was used. The findings corroborate the objective of the author in conducting the study.

The next paper by Mary Venus Joseph, based on her study on social work research in child welfare setting, used intervention research in training school teachers in child mental health. It was conducted using pre-test two-groups quasi-experimental research design. The author has reported the intervention package devised which consisted of the following: the developmental needs of the children, the mental health problems in children and the healthy disciplining practices of children. It was found that the intervention brought out significant improvements in the teacher's knowledge, leading to positive attitude and perception of healthy and constructive practices. These findings can be of immense help to practitioners in this field.

Every research needs to adopt and maintain ethical standards for research to follow. This is essential more so in researches involving people as subjects. The article on 'Social Work Research Ethics: Select Perspectives' by J.S. Gunavathy seeks to present select insights into social work research ethics. It has compiled some of the structures and mechanisms selected to be applied in researches prevailing in institutions abroad. The author concludes that social work research ethics must be addressed to the process of conducting research in order to add to the credibility of the findings and impact of interventions can be observed only if the research carried out is based on ethical principles.

The body of knowledge in social work draws heavily from social sciences and to a limited extent from other sciences. This interdisciplinary nature of social work knowledge makes it to adopt a multidisciplinary approach in its intervention and research. The essay on 'Social Work Research Curriculum in Select American Universities: A Review' by Sudershan Pasupuleti is a compilation of social work research curriculum from select universities in the United States to have an understanding of the research approach in the field of social work. The author has stated that social work research in the United States has set the trend of combining both qualitative and quantitative methods in their research known as mixed methods. A detailed description of the courses and the institutions offering and undertaking social work research has been given which makes it a good reading and useful information.

Research is a part of any curriculum, specially in social sciences. Teaching of research methodology courses and dissertations or research studies as compulsory or optional for students is found in many of the social work institutes. Nagmani Rao, in her article on 'Developing Research Interest Among Social Work Trainees: Problems and Challenges' has discussed the need and the efforts made in this direction by her institute in inculcating interest among their students. She has brought out a module for research, which can be adopted by other institutions as well. Nagmani concludes that if social work research as a method has to be practised and contributed to theory, it should start with students.

The next paper on 'Content Analysis: A Method of Social Science Research' by B. Devi Prasad has brought out the role of content analysis in social science research. It is of great significance, and it refers to the analysis of the meanings, references and intentions communicated therein. It is a method of observations made of communications and a technique for making inferences by systematically and objectively identifying specific characteristics of messages. The author has intended to describe the concept and identify the purposes and uses of content analysis. In his study on dowry-related violence, he has used content analysis to examine the characteristics of dowry, related news. The article carefully brings out the steps involved in this process.

Quantitative data analysis has been one of the widely used method employed by researchers in social sciences. Social work research has been one of the most important fields, which has used this method extensively, as its data can be put to rigorous means of analysis for ascertaining the reliability and generalisability of findings. In an article on 'Computer-Assisted Quantitative Data Analysis and Interpretation' T. Saraswati and D.K. Lal Das have described the different computer-assisted methods of data analysis and interpretation like univariate and bivariate models of analysis. It has referred to a study made by the authors in explaining the entire process of computer-assisted analysis. It makes a good reading for the understanding of statistical methods used in social work research data analysis and interpretation.

Social work research is effective in dealing with delinquency and crime. V.V. Devasia, in his paper on 'Research in Correctional Social Work with Social Work Intervention' has discussed the role of social work research in control, correction and prevention of delinquency and crime.

Social work in industrial settings has always been given a step-motherly treatment. In spite of its contribution to the field, it has more often been considered only in relation to welfare aspects. However, its role can be observed wherever human relations exist. As such, social work research in industrial settings has not been very encouraging. It has a vast scope and many areas to be explored. The article 'Significance of Social Work Training to Human Resource Personnel' by Ranjana Sehgal deals with the problems encountered by welfare functionaries and their practices in relation to their roles. The author concludes that social work training is of utmost importance for human resource functionaries. An alignment of social work with personnel management was considered a good combination and that training in the area of personnel management as a specialisation of social work is essential. Social workers in industries can help employees overcome their problems and aid in efficient functioning.

The article on 'Qualitative Research in Social Work: An Overview' by Surendra Singh has emphasized the strong footage gained by qualitative research among the other methods. It involves non-statistical methods of inquiry and analysis. The author has systematically brought out the importance and the areas of application of qualitative method of inquiry and analysis of social phenomenon. Some of the misconceptions about qualitative research, like lack of verifiable methods of testing objectivity, have been dealt with by the author and makes it an interesting reading.

In qualitative research the emphasis is on discovering the meaning of any occurrence rather than its frequency. The emphasis or meaning is important for social work as social work is involved in searching for solutions to problems. In the article titled 'Social Work and Qualitative Research: Natural Allies' the author Raja Samuel has brought out the close relationship between social work and qualitative research. In this article, he looks at the important features of qualitative research paradigm and examines how they are linked with social work. He further examines the advantages of using semi-structured interview methods in qualitative research.

The article on 'Case Study Method in Social Work Research' by B. Vijayalaxmi reports that the case study method has been used extensively in social work research. As the method aims to investigate into and develop an in-depth understanding of the subject studied, it adopts appropriate techniques. The author has described, in detail, case study as a method of social work research. She has dealt extensively with various aspects and steps involved and listed out the differences between the case study method and other methods.

The last article on 'Research and Action in Field Action Project: An Example of *Ankur*', by Anita Panot is concerned about change in contrast to other research methods. It is an option chosen by the practitioners engaged in development programmes. This is one option of bringing research and practice into closer alliances. In this article, the author has narrated the example of a field action research project undertaken by her college to work with children with mental retardation in state-run schools. The objective was to study the perception of teachers about the role played by parents and to identify the areas of social work interventions. The conclusions drawn by the author Editorial Note that some tangible outcomes have been observed as an outcome of the intervention and noted for implementation.

This crispy introduction about the paper included in this book will give the readers a bird's eye view of the contents of the book. The readers can have an insight into the various research methods used in different areas of social work and need for shift in focus.

D.K. Lal Das
Vanila Bhaskaran

Part I

Social Work Research

1

Research Methods for Social Work

Need for Paradigm Shift

Murli Desai

Institutions for social work education have a major role to play in development of social work knowledge. Social work educators are regularly in touch with the field as fieldwork instructors and also through their field action projects. However, the research methodologies useful for social work practice do not seem to have taken off in India. Social work educators, in most of the institutions for social work education, do not carry out research, for several reasons, such as research not being considered part of their workload, priority given to contribution to development of the field of practice, lack of infrastructural support and so on. Those who do carry out research seem to be more involved with research of the social phenomena that they are teaching and/or working with in the field. Citation and referencing are generally not given importance. As a result, researchers often do not disseminate their findings out of fear of plagiarism. The books that they publish are generally on the social phenomena rather than on methods and skills of practice.

Social work practitioners generally do not document their practice or undertake research, and if they do, they tend to carry out ad hoc studies, without linking these to the existing state of knowledge. Since they do not publish their findings, these do not become retrievable and are not utilized by other social work professionals. They thus do not add to the body of social work knowledge.

This article starts with the concept and need for social work knowledge. It then examines the influence of progressive ideologies on social work knowledge development and the methodological developments and types of progressive social work research. It concludes with the steps and ethics for such social work research.

Concept and Need for Social Work Knowledge

Concept of Social Work Knowledge

Mattaini (1995) made a case that professionals and non-professionals may share similar values, it is knowledge that is the most distinctive aspect of professional practice. Since 1915, when Abraham Flexner concluded that social work was not a profession because it does not have a knowledge base, pursuit for professionalism has led social workers to work hard for a scientific knowledge base as well as specialized skills, techniques and functions. In fact, leadership of caseworkers in knowledge development on specialized skills is one of the main reasons that led to their subsequent dominance in the profession (Hopps and Pinderhughes, 1987). The question to be addressed is what is social work knowledge.

In the *Encyclopaedia of Social Work in India*, Herlekar (1968) used the term 'social work literature' which is related to or useful to social work. She grouped social work knowledge into three areas. The first is knowledge provided by social sciences, an area which is concerned with the knowledge of human beings in society, human growth and behaviour and social problems. The second is knowledge of fields and programmes of social work, concerned with the organization, administration and operation of social welfare programmes. The third is knowledge of social work practice, concerning the methods, processes and professional skills.

In the *American Encyclopedia of Social Work*, Khinduka (1987: 686) defined the knowledge base of social work more specifically as follows:

> The knowledge base of social work is a composite of knowledge produced indigenously by social workers themselves and, predominantly, of that derived from other disciplines by analyzing and evaluating their own practice experiences and by selectively borrowing and adapting concepts from cognate disciplines and profession, social workers have developed various approaches (of intervention).

In my option, when various social sciences study social phenomena/issues/problems in their varied dimensions, it is imperative for a profession such as social work to 'base' its intervention on social science knowledge, and not just use it at the level of borrowing, However, if social work intervention is based on social science knowledge, the base knowledge cannot be conceptualized as comprising social work knowledge. On the other hand, if all knowledge produced by social workers is to be included into social work knowledge, the substantive definition of what comprises social work knowledge becomes less important. Another conceptual mistake that takes place, in the Indian context, is to assume that all that is published in the journals of social work is social work literature. A study of articles published in the *Indian Journal of Social Work* (IJSW) by Vijayalakshmi, Devi Prasad and Rao (1996) revealed that social work professionals (educators/practitioners) wrote less than a third of the articles published in the IJSW from 1970 to 1990.

Social work knowledge may be conceptualized as knowledge specific to the social work profession. It then covers various aspects of social work profession such as its origin and the history of development; its paradigms, values, goals and ethics; methods, practice and process of intervention; case records research and knowledge building; education and training; curriculum plans; field instruction; specializations; educators and students; employment and human power; professional associations; and so on. Thus defined, it may include literature developed by an author outside of the profession. On the other hand, literature developed on any social phenomenon by a social work professional, which does not draw any link with the profession, may not be considered social work literature.

According to Mattaini (1995), practice wisdom is knowledge passed on from generation to generation of social workers; sometimes as a form of oral tradition experienced social workers often have learned a tremendous amount that can be of value to others. He identifies two types of practice wisdom: (1) explicit rules that are handed down by experienced practitioners to others that appear to work; and (2) patterns of professional behaviour which may or may not be articulated, that have been shaped and refined over years of practice and serve as models for other workers. Social workers also base their work on their own life experiences – personal and professional.

Mattaini further warns that there are risks associated with a reliance on such rules. For example, accepted rules sometimes grow more from what works for the practitioner than what works for the client. It is, therefore, important for the social worker to constantly monitor whether approaches rooted in this body of knowledge contribute to meeting the client's goals.

Need for Social Work Knowledge

Social work profession needs different types of knowledge for its different functions, such as practice, policy planning and administration, research and education and training. Social work practitioners need transformative knowledge to understand exclusion and the knowledge domain of people they work with and knowledge needed for their inclusion. They need to update themselves with developments in the field that impinge upon their practice. Social work educators need to know the latest knowledge developed in order to update their curriculum and the recommended readings. Students need to know what to read for their assignments and prepare for the examination and social work researchers need to comprehensively know the state of art of research in the field. Thus, the needs for different types of social work knowledge are as follows:

- Information on social work, welfare and development;
- Social work research;
- Organized social work knowledge for practice, policy planning and administration, education and training and research; and
- Bibliographic resources on social science, development studies and social work literature.

Information on Social Work, Welfare and Development

The following may be the main types of information on social work, welfare and development that the social work professionals need to have access to:

- Directories of voluntary organizations, professional associations, international organizations and academic instutions.
- Newsletters of social work professional associations for updates and reviews of social work education and practice.
- Newsletters and bulletins for updates and reviews of voluntary work and government laws, policies and schemes and so on.

Organized Social Work Knowledge

Any literature can be considered knowledge only when it is cumulatively organized to link new literature to previous ones and to theories. This linkage could be in the form of application, adaptation, elaboration or critique. Social work profession has to base its work on the understanding of social phenomena as studied by various social sciences. Reality needs to be understood holistically in order to plan intervention. Multidisciplinary literature developed as applied social science on issues and problems is more directly useful for social work.

Social work educators need knowledge necessary for teaching and training. Such knowledge can be organized in the form of curriculum development, course compendia, teaching-learning resources, standards for social work education and so on. Encyclopedias and dictionaries are reference books, concisely prepared out of range of primary literature, most useful for any discipline or profession. Organizing social work knowledge is also essential for development of cumulative body of knowledge. Citations and referencing are, therefore, indispensable tasks in this process.

Bibliographic Resources on Social Science and Social Work Literature

The purpose of secondary literature is to 'filter' the primary information sources, usually by subject area, and provide the indicators to this literature in the form of reviews, abstracts, annotations and indexes. These act as a gateway to several attributes of primary literature: authors, subjects, publishers, dates (and languages) of publication, and citations (*Britannica*, 2001). Social work educators and researchers need bibliographic resources on social sciences and social work literature.

Progressive Ideologies and Social Work Knowledge

Modern ideologies of the western white world have considered science as the exemplar for discovering 'truth' and 'truth' (often described as reality) is equated only with the observable and measurable. Scientism rejects every method of inquiry other than scientific (Geiger, 1947). This ideology is challenged by emerging ideologies such as postmodernism, critical pedagogy and qualitative research.

The emerging ideology of postmodernism rejects attempts to apply the model of natural science inquiry in social sciences (Rosenau, 1992) and critiques totality, reason and universality (Nicholoson, 1990). Postmodernists recognize the highest ideals of modernity in the West as immanent to a specific historical time and geographical region and also associated with certain political baggage. Such a baggage included notions of the supremacy of the West (Nicholoson, 1990). In social work, high value has generally been attached to the American social work education model and American social work literature, which have now begun to be questioned. The American social work literature travels round the world fast, following the adoption of the American model for social work curriculum by different countries. Although there is value in learning from other countries, there are problems inherent in adopting knowledge developed in one country for use in social work practice in another country (Desai, 1997).

The ideology of postmodernism has brought about visibility to important ideological and structural forces, such as race, gender and class by acknowledging the question of power and value in the construction of knowledge and subjectivities. It has raised questions regarding how culture is inscribed in the production of centre/margin hierarchies and the reproduction of postcolonial forms of subjugation (Giroux, 1991). In modern society, knowledge, which sees truth as based in science, has been increasingly concentrated in the hands of 'experts' and the elite class they represent. The claim to truth gives rise to hierarchies of knowledge, which reinforce and legitimate the economic and social hierarchies. As Foucault put it, the truth claim and the procedures for gaining access to that truth have historically privileged the pronouncements of trained experts over the discourses of 'ordinary' people. Underlying these elements of the power of expertise is the expert's lack of any accountability to the ordinary people affected by his or her knowledge (Sohng, 1995).

The political nature of knowledge is well illustrated by the fact that each of these privileged truths is being challenged – not primarily by alternative theories from the sciences but by the socio-political movements that Foucault called the "insurrection of subjugated knowledge". It provides forms of historical knowledge as a way of reclaiming power and identity for subordinate groups (Hartman, 1992). Transformative knowledge represents quests for knowledge that take account of perspectives, experiences and wisdom of the marginalized groups and excavate historically subjugated knowledge. In order to organize transformative knowledge, there is a need to critically identify the ideological base of the literature, examine the process of exclusion and assure inclusion of the marginalized groups (www.classes.csumb.edu/MAE/MAE637-01/worls/elements/Transformative.html).

The postmodern understanding of knowledge-power linkage has brought about a painful paradox for social work professionals. As professionals, social workers possess knowledge and are experts because of their knowledge, but the power in their knowledge can disempower out clients. As Hartman (1992) suggested, they need to be open to local knowledge and participate with them in the insurrection of subjugated knowledge.

From a socially critical perspective, knowledge is constructed within our historical and cultural frameworks. Knowledge, according to the critical theorists, is historically, socially, economically and politically conditioned (Toohey, 1999). According to Giroux (1999), critical pedagogy attempts to do the following:

- Create new forms of knowledge through its emphasis on breaking down disciplines and creating interdisciplinary knowledge.
- Raise questions about the relationships between the margins and centres of power in schools and is concerned about how to provide a way of reading history as part of a

larger project of reclaiming power and identity, particularly as these are shaped around the categories of race, gender, class and ethnicity.

- Reject the distinction between high and popular culture so as to make curriculum knowledge responsive to the everyday knowledge that constitutes people's lived histories differently.
- Illuminate the primacy of the ethical in defining the language that teachers and others use to produce particular cultural practices.

The postmodern reaction to modern ethical theories recommends that moral thinkers should turn their attention away from the problematic to the person as a whole. People's goodness has to do, not with virtues, but with their integrated wholeness (Agarwal, 1998). The paradigm of qualitative research relies on such holistic analysis and detailed description derived from close contacts with the participants of the study. The qualitative methodology tends to focus on techniques such as participant observation, semi-structured interviews and hermeneutic analysis of texts. Moreover, techniques such as presenting extensive direct quotations to readers can make their own judgments and having several other researchers examine the raw data to ensure that the findings do not reflect a single researcher's biases, are critical (Mattaini, 1995). The qualitative approach is more suitable to social work as both have similar holistic and participatory philosophy. This approach is useful to synthesize social theory, practice and research (Ruckdeschel, 1985).

Methodological Developments in Social Work Research

Traditionally, the ideal in social work research has been empiricism. However, as Austin (1979) stated, the legitimating of social work profession has depended on social utility rather than on its scientific base. He concluded that social work is a profession based on organized practitioner wisdom and is not, and probably will not be, a truly science-based profession in the foreseeable future. Goldstein (1990) noted that by adopting the scientific emphasis, intuition and commonsense ways of understanding were discredited. Emphasizing the rigour of detached objectivity, scientism held little regard for subjective constructs such as morality, spirituality, and cultural or personal belief systems. Not the least, he says, a positivistic preoccupation with instrumental means tended to overlook the profession's commitment to certain social ends. Goldstein concluded that social work practice has to be an ever-changing and complex blend of theory, analogue, wisdom and art.

As education of social work research has traditionally been modelled on pure social research, students of the professional course are trained for research, which can tell one the state of things as they are, than research that aims at bettering them. Social work students, therefore, fail to see a direct link between research and practice. As a result of such training, most of the social workers think that they have nothing to do with research. Such training makes social workers poor researchers and poor users of research in the practice situation.

This explains why practitioners generally do not document their own work and analyze it. As a result, much of the contributions of social work practitioners to theory building remain irretrievable for the purpose of social work education.

Thomas (1979) observed that at best, social workers view the culmination of research as the drawing of conclusions from research findings that may have implications for social work, or be worthy of utilization research, rather than as the generation of interventional or other social innovating that director applications in the social technology of social work. He further noted that social work has been slow to recognize that its social technology is subject to systematic rather than incidental and haphazard alternating and that social work researcher and others in social work can participate actively in its generation.

Powers and others (1985) highlighted the need for a practitioner to make informed decisions. These decisions and subsequent practice behaviours are precisely the types of things that professionals should justify. They said that the ultimate test of effective knowledge building in any profession is the degree to which the body of knowledge is prescriptive. Social work profession thus requires knowledge-as-action. Such knowledge could be organized by linking social work practice wisdom with social science/work research/theories of drawing implications of social science/work research and theories for practice, towards development of praxis. Knowledge for practice, policy planning and administration may be organized in the forms of handbooks, manuals, standards for practice and so on.

Social intervention research, systematic review methods, research syntheses and meta-analysis, evidence-based practice and action and participatory research are important methodological developments in contemporary social work research that guides social work practice.

Social Intervention Research

Evaluation research gained increased importance in social work, in the 1970s, as a tool to ascertain accountability of social work organizations and programmes. Subsequently, single system design and developmental research, both of which contain the element of evaluation, developed as methodologies in social work research. Single system design facilitates a formative typed of evaluation of practice with a system – be it an individual, family, group, organization, community or other collectivity. The heart of single system design is collecting repeated information on the target problem a like time series research (Bloom and Fischer, 1982). Thomas (1979) developed the paradigm of development research, which is a combination of the models of research and development and research utilization. Analysis, development and evaluation comprise the phases of research utilization. As translated to social work research, this R & D approach becomes known as social intervention research. As a research and development methodology, social intervention research has provided the profession with a systematic, cumulative research methodology for developing, refining, testing and disseminating research-based social interventions. Accordingly, rather than wasting research resources on the evaluation of poorly conceptualized interventions, this methodology has contributed to the development and identification of interventions of proven effectiveness (Mullen, 2002).

In the early years of evaluation research, there were many flawed attempts to identify and measure social intervention outcomes. However, with experience and increased methodological prowess, the science of outcomes measurement has developed into a sophisticated specialization (Mullen, 2002).

Systematic Review Methods, Research Syntheses and Meta-Analysis

While the outcome of a single evaluation may be cause for attention, one study does not establish a foundation for decision-making. In the early 1970s social work researchers used narrative reviews to summaries findings from groups of evaluations, sometimes using systematic methods and sometimes not. When using systematic methods and sometimes not when few studies existed, this approach served the profession well. As studies increased, without explicit, systematic review methods such overviews were subject to unknown bias. Accordingly, the development of systematic review methods as well as sophisticated, quantitative meta-analytic procedures has made it possible to specify with greater confidence and precision the combined outcomes of many studies. The growth of methodology sophistication in the review and syntheses of outcomes from multiple studies has been a singularly important methodological development in the move towards evidence-based approaches (Mullen, 200).

Evidence-based Practice

Evidence-based practice is an emerging approach in the United Kingdom, which means any practice that has been established as effective through scientific research according to some set of explicit criteria (Mullen, 2002). According to Gambrill (2003), evidence-based practice suggests a philosophy of practice and policy designed to honour ethical obligations to clients and students and an evolving technology for helping us to do so. Professionals have an obligation to inform clients about services found to be effective and to avoid harm. Concerns that practitioners were continuing to use methods found to be harmful was a key reason for the development of evidence-based practice.

Evidence-based practice encourages transparency of what is done to what effect in all venues of interest including practice and policy, research and professional education. It is designed to make decisions and the reasons for them explicit. Evidence-based practice involves sharing responsibility for decision-making in a context of recognized uncertainly. It is this characteristic of transparency that is such a break with authority-based practice and policy, research and professional education (Gambrill, 2003).

Gambrill further states that evidence-based practice describes a process designed to encourage integration of ethical, evidentiary and application concerns. It involves a systemic approach to improving quality of services including the following:

- Efforts to educate professionals who are life-long learners;
- Involving clients as informed participants who take part in decisions made;
- Attending to management practices and policies that influence practice (that is, evidence-based purchase of services); and
- Attending to application challenges including the implications of scarce resources.

Evidence-based practice and social care are designed to maximize flow of accurate information concerning the evidentiary status or practice-related claims including information about harming in the name of helping.

Action and Participatory Research

O'Brien (1998) defined action research as aiming to contribute both to the practical concerns of people in an immediate problematic situation and to further the goals of social science simultaneously.

Thus, there is a dual commitment in action research to study a system and concurrently to collaborate with members of the system in changing it in what is together regarded as a desirable direction. Accomplishing this twin goal requires the active collaboration of researcher and client, and thus it stresses the importance of co-learning as a primary aspect of the research process. Several attributes separate action research from other types of research. Primary is its focus on turning the people involved into researchers, too – people learn best, and more willingly apply what they have learned, when they do it themselves. It also has a social dimension – the research takes place in real-world situations, and aims to solve real problems. Finally, the initiating researcher, unlike in other disciplines, makes no attempt to remain objective, but openly acknowledges their bias to the other participants (O'Brien, 1998).

Following are the six principles of action research identified by Winter (1989, cited from O'Brien, 1998):

- *Reflective critique*: The principle of reflective critique ensures people that reflect on issues and processes and makes explicit the interpretations, biases, assumptions and concerns upon which judgments are made. In this way, practical accounts can give rise to theoretical considerations.
- *Dialectical critique*: Reality, particularly social reality, is consensually validated, which is to say it is shared through language. Phenomena are conceptualized in dialogue.

- *Collaborative resource*: Participants in an action research project are co-researchers. The principle of collaborative resource presupposes that each person's ideas are equally significant as potential resources for crating interpretive categories of analysis, negotiated among the participants.
- *Risk*: the change process potentially threatens all previously established ways of doing things, thus creating psychic fears among the practitioners.
- *Plural structure*: The nature of the research embodies a multiplicity of views, commentaries and critiques, leading to multiple possible actions and interpretations. This plural structure of inquiry requires a plural text for reporting.
- *Theory, practice and transformation*: For action researchers, theory informs practice, practice refines theory, in a continuous transformation. In any setting, people's actions are based on implicitly held assumptions, theories and hypotheses, and with every observed result, theoretical knowledge is enhanced.

Originally designed to resist the intellectual colonialism of western social research into the Third World development process, participatory research developed a methodology for involving disenfranchised people as researchers in pursuit of answers to the questions of their daily struggle and survival. Based in Paulo Friere's ideology, participatory research is means of putting research capabilities in the hands of deprived and disenfranchised people so that they can identify themselves as knowing actors: defining their reality, shaping their new identity, naming their history, and transforming their lives for themselves (Sohng, 1995)

Finn (1994, cited from Sohng, 1995) outlined three key elements, namely, people, power and praxis, which distinguish participatory research from traditional approaches to social science:

- Participatory research is people-centred in the sense that the process of critical inquiry is informed by and responds to the experiences and needs of oppressed people.

- Participatory research is about power, which is crucial to the construction of reality, language, meanings and rituals of truth. Participatory research promotes empowerment through the development of common knowledge and critical awareness, which are suppressed by the dominant knowledge system.
- Participatory research is also about praxis. It recognizes the inseparability of theory and practice and critical awareness of the personal-political dialectic.

Participatory research is grounded in an explicit political stance and clearly articulated value base – social justice and the transformation of those contemporary socio-cultural structures and processes that support degeneration of participatory democracy, injustice and inequality.

Types of Social Work Research according to Stage of Practice

Desai (1992) has classified social work research according to the purpose it serves depending upon the stage of practice in which it is conducted, as discussed below:

Research in the Planning Stage of Practice

Research in the planning stage of practice may be carried out in order to plan or ascertain appropriateness of the plan for practice (Epstein and Tripodi, 1997).

Need Analysis

While studying the plan of practice, it is essential to ascertain that it is based on the actual and felt needs of the potential beneficiaries depending upon their situation. Such baseline data may be obtained through need analysis. Some objective criteria, to establish the need conditions for the specific intervention, will first have to be theoretically worked out, based on the expected outcome. All the individuals in an age group may need developmental intervention, whereas specific outcome may have to be laid down for need for remedial intervention. According to Carter (1960), the need conditions may be those expressed by clients and those unexpressed by clients. For the needs expressed by the clients, they may or may not be utilizing the services.

Survey of Similar Programmes

At the stage of initiating a programme, it is also important to carry out a survey of similar programmes that may exist in the city. Gaps in these services indicate the need for extension of new services. If similar programmes are available, the need survey may also examine whether the potential beneficiaries are using these services. If they are not, the reasons may be examined. A need analysis may be used in three major ways:

1. The scope of the programme may be planned according to the magnitude of people concluded as needing the intervention.
2. The characteristics of the people needing the intervention can be useful while planning the content of the intervention.
3. The difficulties people report in utilizing services of similar programmes are useful for planning the service delivery aspects of practice.

Resource Survey

At the stage of planning of practice, a resource survey may also be carried out in the defined locality in order to compile information needed for providing information and referral services to the beneficiaries. Such a survey may explore number and types of services available, and provided by originations as well as individuals to meet a particular need. Criteria for intake of clientele for these services are also important to examine in such a survey.

Research in the Implementation Stage of Practice

According to Morris and Fitz-Gibbon (1978), formative evaluation of programme implementation is known as programme monitoring and summative evaluation of the same is known as programme documentation. They further specify that monitoring often means assuming a role in the programme planning, development and refinement. It helps the staff and the planners to identify obstacles, implement changes and make additions to the programmes as it develops. Morris and Fitz-Gibbon describe programme documentation as useful for accountability, providing a lasting description of the programme and a list of the possible causes of the programmes effects.

Monitoring and documentation at the implementation stage may be carried out of the following:

1. Check the implementation of intervention with reference to the goals set and the plan formulated,
2. Examine its utilization by the designated population and satisfaction of the beneficiaries,
3. Analyze the problem,
4. Ascertain the process of change and the intermediate outcome of the intervention, and
5. Review the relevant theories.

Different types of organizational studies and studies of service delivery systems may be carried out in order to assess the implementation of an intervention.

Through a service utilization study, one can ascertain the extent to which the designated target population is being reached. Such a study may identify difficulties in service utilization by people, such as lack of awareness, cultural or personal obstacles, long distance, transportation difficulties, service insufficient, strict intake criteria, and so on.

Opinion/attitude studies for the intervention may assess service utilization as well as acceptance of the intervention. The targets for such studies may be the staff or the beneficiaries.

A periodic review of the case records of the agency is useful for several purposes. Some of these are:

1. It is another way to examine whether the programme reaches the designated target population.
2. It is useful to analyze the problems people come with.
3. It can show the trend in people's problem manifestations over a period of time.
4. The process of the practitioner's intervention can be examined through such a review.
5. The process of change and the intermediate outcome of the intervention can be analyzed through such a review.

Such an analysis feeds into the documentation of the programme efforts that helps to study what led to the final outcome of the programme. A valuable outcome of such a review is that it also helps in arriving at an improved case recording system.

Research in the Conclusion Stage of Practice

Research in the conclusion stage of practice is the same as summative evaluation with reference to effectiveness and efficiency. Such a study will be useful for making improvements in the intervention approach, reviewing the theories behind practice and repeating or replicating the practice.

Effectiveness of practices may be examined by comparing the outcome with the baseline data and the expected outcome.

Rosen and Proctor (1979) have classified outcome into three types:

1. *Intermediate outcomes*, which are presumed to contribute to or create a facilitative climate for continuation of the programme. Assessment of the intermediate outcome may be done at the implementation stage of the intervention.
2. *Instrumental outcomes*, which, when achieved, are assumed to lead necessarily to the achievement of the programme goals without the help of the programme.

3. *Ultimate outcomes* are indicators of achievement of the programme goals. The instrumental outcome may be assessed at the conclusion stage, whereas a follow-up study is needed to assess the ultimate outcome of practice. Efficiency of practice may be assessed by a cost-benefit analysis of the outcome with reference to the resources or efforts put in.

Ethics of Social Work Research

The Declaration of Ethics for Professional Social Workers by Bombay Association of Trained Social Workers (2002) lists the following ethical best practices for social work research:

- Carefully select the topic for research considering its possible consequences for those studied, when conducting a research.
- Do not cause the respondents any physical or mental discomfort, distress or harm, through research.
- Consider the informants of research as co-partners in understanding the phenomenon.
- Share their research objectives with them and get their informed and voluntary consent, respect their knowledge and attitude about their life situation, and share/interpret the findings with them.
- Protect the confidentiality of the information shared by them and use the findings for their benefit, by recommending and promoting policies and programmes concerning them.
- Provide information and referral services to them, as and when necessary, during the process of data collection.
- Dissociate from or do not engage in any research activity, which requires manipulation, distortion or falsification of data or findings.

References

Agarwal, M.M., 1998, *Ethics and Spirituality*, Shimla: Indian Institute of Advanced Study.

Austin, D.N., 1979, Research and Social Work: Educational Paradoxes and Possibilities, *Journal of Social Service Research*, 2(2), 159-176.

Bloom, M. and Fischer, J. 1982, *Evaluation Practice: Guidelines for the Accountable Professional*, New Jersey: Prentice Hall, Inc.

Desai, M. (ed.), 1997, "Social Work Literature", Special Issue of *The Indian Journal of Social Work*, 58(2).

Epstein, I. and Tripodi, 1979, Incorporating Research into Macro Social Work Practice and Education. In A. Rubbin and A. Rosenblatt (eds.), *Sourcebook on Research Utilisation*, New York: Council for Social Work Education, 121-131.

Gambrill, E.D., 2003, Evidence-Based Practice: Sea Change or the Emperor's New Clothes, *Journal of Social Work Education*, 39 (1)

Gay, G., 1989, *Curriculum Development. The International Encyclopedia of Educational Methodology*, Oxford: Pergamon Press, 467-476.

Geiger, G.R., 1947, *Philosophy and the Social Order: An Introductory Approach*, Boston; Houghton Mifflin Co.

Giroux, H.M., 1999, *What is Critical Pedagogy*? (www. perfectfit.org/CT/firoux2.html).

Goldstein, H., 1990, the Knowledge Base of Social Work Practice: Theory, Analogue, or Art? *Families in Society: the Journal of Contemporary Human Services.*

Harman, A., 1992, In Search of Subjugated Knowledge, *Social Work*, 37(6).

Herlekar, A., 1968, Literature of Social Work. In *Encyclopedia of Social Work in India*, Volume 2, New Delhi: Planning Commission.

Hopps, J.G. and Pinderhughes, E.B., 1987, Profession of Social Work Contemporary Characteristics. In *Encyclopedia of Social Work*, Silver Spring, Maryland: National Association of Social Workers, 351-366.

Kearl, M.C., 2004, *Sociology of Knowledge*, Department of Sociology and Anthropology, University of Colorado at Denver (www.trinity.edu/-mkearl/knowledg.html).

Khinduka, S.K., 1987, Social Work and the Human Services. In *Encyclopedia of Social Work*, Silver Spring: National Association of Social Workers.

Mattaini, M.A., 1995, Knowledge for Practice. In C.H., Meyer and M.A. Mattaini (eds.), *The Foundations of Social Work Practice: A Graduate Text*, Washington, D.C.: National Association of Social Workers, 59-85.

Mullen, E.J., 2002, Evidence-Based Social Work Theory and Practice: Historical and Reflective Perspective. Paper presented at the 4th International Conference on Evaluation for Practice, University of Tampere, Finland.

Nicholoson, L.J., 1990, Introduction. In L.J., Nicholson (ed.), *Feminism/Postmodernism*, New York: Routledge.

O'Brien, R., 1998, *An Overview of the Methodological Approach of Action Research.*

Powers, G.T., Meenaghan, T.M. and Toomey, B.G., 1985, *Practice-focused Research: Integrating Human Service Practice and Research*, New Jersey: Prentice hall, Inc.

Rosen, A. and Proctor, E.K. 1979, Specifying the Treatment Process: The Basis for Effectiveness Research, *Journal of Social Service Research*, 2(1), 25- 43.

Rosenau, P.M., 1992, *Postmodernism and the Social Sciences: Insights, Inroads and Intrusions,* Princeton, New Jersey: Princeton University press.

Ruckdeschel, R.A., 1985, Qualitative Research as a Perspective, *Social Work Research and Abstract*, 21(2), 17-21.

Sohng, S.S.L., 1995, Participatory Research and Community Organizing. A Working Paper presented at the New Social Movement and Community Organizing Conference, University of Washington, Seattle, W.A., November 1-3.

Thomas, E.J., 1979, Generating Innovations in Social Work: The Paradigm of Developmental Research, *Journal of Social Service Research*, 2, 95-116.

Toohey, S., 1999, *Designing Courses for Higher Education,* Buckingham: Open University Press.

Vijayalakshmi, B., Rao, K.V. and Devi Prasad, B., Trends in articles published in The Indian Journal of Social Work, 1971-1990, *The Indian Journal of Social Work*, 56(3), 442-460.

2

Dimensions of Research Methods for Social Work

D.K. Lal Das

In a very broad sense, the term 'Research Methods for Social Work', popularly labelled as 'Social Work Research' by Schools of Social Work, connotes research strategies to meet the specific and peculiar needs of social work theory and practice. Thus, research methods that are available in the general armory of social science research may need to be modified when applied to social work research so that the research becomes relevant.

Research methods have two major dimensions to it. One is the substantive area in which research is done. The other dimension pertains to the methodological issues. From the substantive viewpoint we talk of sociological research, political science research, research in social work or social work research.

Substantive Area

Substantive area in which social work research is done can be classified in two major categories:

1. Research pertaining to social work interventions, and
2. Research pertaining to the knowledge base of social work.

Research Pertaining to Social Work Interventions

Research pertaining to social work interventions, also known as intervention research or evaluative research, includes researches undertaken to assess the effectiveness of social work interventions with individuals, family, groups and community, to assess the effectiveness of interventions, to suggest alternate intervention and to innovate interventions. Various intervention research designs can be grouped into following two categories:

1. Single-Subject Designs
2. Group Designs

Single-Subject Designs

Single-subject research designs are used to assess the effectiveness of social casework intervention. The essence of single-subject design is to measure effectiveness of intervention by subjects as their own control and multiple data sets before and after the intervention.

Single-subject designs are basically quasi-experimental research designs, which use time series analysis technique of social research to the evaluation of the impact of interventions on individual cases. Such designs involve repeated measure of the dependent variable before and after a particular intervention, to see if a sustained pattern of change in the dependent variable commences shortly after the onset of intervention (Rubin and Babbie, 1989).

Prior to single-subject designs, social work researchers had no alternative other than to use conventional experimental research designs such as comparison of experimental group with control group. Such experimental researches, however, were often inappropriate or impossible to conduct in social work practice settings. It was often too time-consuming and expensive to identify clients with similar problems and randomly assign some to treatment and others to control groups.

In such experiments the results were an average of the whole group's response, obscuring individual reactions which are significant to social work practitioners. For example, knowing that a given intervention was effective on majority in an experimental group may be interesting, but it does not help at all in inferring about a particular client (Monette et al.,1986)

As with advances in other areas of social research, interest in single-subject designs based on time series research design grew out of problems faced by social work researchers with existing techniques of social research.

In a nutshell, single-subject designs aim at the systematic evaluation of social work practice through the use of scientific research techniques. It must be kept in mind, however, that this research design does not reject conventional large-group experimental researches. Such researches are necessary for evaluating complete programmes and for confirming the generalisability of programme effectiveness.

Use of Single-Subject Designs in Social Work Practice

Single-subject designs can be used in social case work practice in different situations and in different ways. A few social work situations where this research design will be appropriate are illustrated in the following sections. Social case work practitioner as part of their own practice, can use single-subject designs in studying their clients, diagnosing the target problem and selecting the appropriate treatment. They can also use it in monitoring the client's progress.

For example, suppose, a child in a special school is being treated for aggressive behaviour, and further that the problematic behaviour occurs shortly before the child is about to enter the classroom. Repeated measures of the target behaviour might help the social worker chronologically identify this coincidence during the initial stages of service delivery, which in turn would help better understand the causes of the target problem and develop an appropriate strategy to deal with it. Social workers who spend considerable amounts of time systematically attempting to record and evaluate their practices may find conducting single-subject design research to be one way to make that effort more systematic and valid. The very use of such research designs helps case workers to become scientific practitioners.

As another example, let us consider the following illustration. Suppose, a school social worker seeking to enhance the self-esteem and social functioning of a group of school students who are at high risk of dropping out of school and monitors the students' disciplinary referrals and administers a standardized self-esteem scale on a weekly basis. Suppose further that the social worker requests the school authorities to suspend disciplinary actions for a specified period to see whether self-esteem improves. If the students' self-esteem scores improve then the social worker would have reasonable grounds for inferring that it was probably the intervention, and not history, that accounted for the students' improved functioning.

There are, however, some practical problems in using single-subject design research in social work practice. Many a time, the situation needs immediate intervention and hence does not allow social workers enough time to take repeated measures to identify baseline trends prior to implementing the intervention. In some situations social workers are heavily loaded with cases which reduce the amount of time they have to plan or conduct single-subject design studies. Despite these problems, social work practitioners should make efforts to use single-subject designs whenever they can. Social work practice or services have not yet received adequate scientific testing concerning their effects on clients. In the light of this, the question is not whether cases need immediate intervention or can we afford the time needed to use single-subject design research as part of our practices, but can we afford to use untested interventions to see whether they help the clients or harm them.

By using single-subject designs as part of our practice, we can get immediate feedback that would help us to modify the service or chose other alternative intervention for our client.

Apparently, it looks simple and easy to implement single-subject research designs. It also gives an impression that single-subject researches would clear all the doubts about the effectiveness of social work interventions. In practice, however, conducting repeated measures of target problems to provide reliable and valid data is not always a simple task. It is easy to introduce intervention only when the baseline is established, but it is rather difficult in situations where cases are in dire need of treatment. Nevertheless, barring a few situations, the technique of single-subject designs is very useful for social work researchers.

Types of Single-Subject Designs

Although there are numerous types of single-subject designs, all involve repeated measurements during baseline and intervention phases and a comparison across phases as evidence of intervention effects. The designs differ in the number of phases involved, the number of interventions applied, and the number of baselines employed. Perhaps, the most important differences are in the internal validity of the designs. Some are more capable of providing evidence for the effect of an intervention when such an effect actually exists. Ideally, of course, social work researchers should select the most valid design that fits their particular case.

There are three alternative single-subject designs:

- AB: The Basic Single-Subject Design
- ABAB: Withdrawal/Reversal Design
- ABCD: Multiple Component Design

(i) AB: The Basic Single-Subject Design

The basic single-subject design, as the name suggests, is the simplest single-subject design and most popular design among researchers mainly because it involves only one baseline phase (A) and one intervention phase (B) as illustrated below in Figure 1:

Figure 1

Hypothetical Baseline followed by Successful Intervention

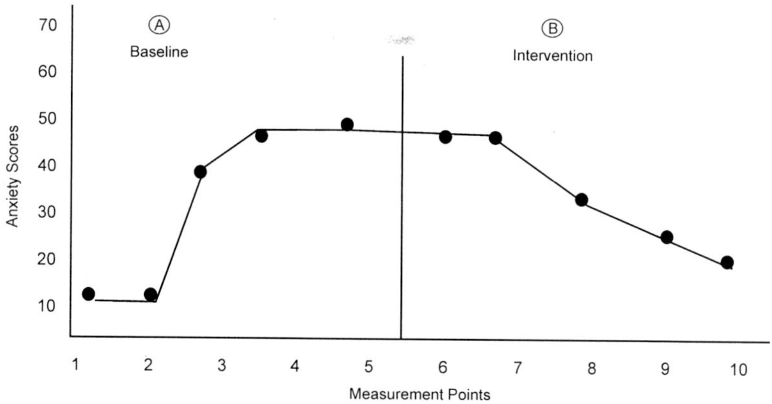

This design is more commonly known as AB design. The letter 'A' signifies baseline phase and the letter 'B' indicates an intervention phase in which some specific intervention is introduced.

In this research design the effects of intervention is ascertained by comparing the client's condition during intervention phase with that of the baseline phase.

Since this design involves one baseline assessment and one intervention phase, its validity is threatened by history: events other than the intervention could be responsible for the change in the client's behaviour.

Despite the limitations of the AB design, it provides better evidence of intervention effects than non-experimental case study. It also has the advantage of being applicable to most clinical situations, especially in cases where more rigorous designs might be precluded. With enough repeated observations, this design can provide valid and reliable evidence concerning the effectiveness of interventions.

(ii) ABAB: Withdrawal/Reversal Design

In order to have better control over extraneous factors withdrawal/reversal design is used. It has two baseline phases and two intervention phases. In this research design, after the first intervention is over, it is withdrawn and the second base line phase is established. Once the second baseline is stable, the intervention is reintroduced. This design is based on the logic that if there is improvement in the problem by the first intervention, then the target problem will go back to its original baseline level during the second baseline if the intervention is withdrawn and the target problem should improve when intervention is reintroduced.

The AB design can be strengthened substantially by moving to a reversal design so called because, after one intervention phase, the intervention is withdrawn for a period of time. There are basically two versions of the reversal design: ABA and ABAB. The two versions differ only in that the ABA design ends in a no intervention phase whereas, in the ABAB design, the intervention is reintroduced a second time (see Figure 2).

Figure 2
Hypothetical Example of ABAB Design

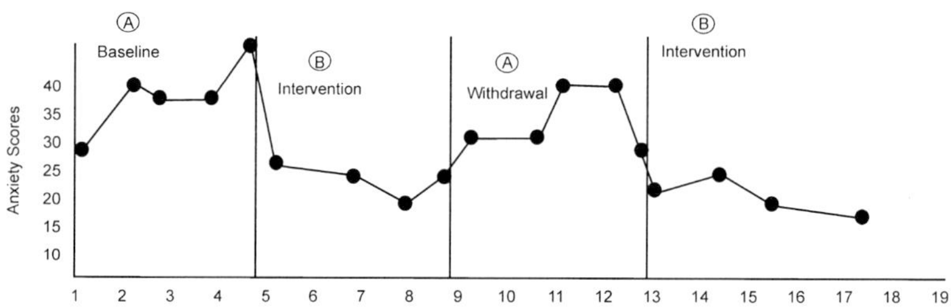

The value of the reversal designs stems from their ability to demonstrate more conclusively that it is the intervention and not some extraneous factor that is producing change in the client's condition. If the client's condition deteriorates when the intervention is withdrawn, we have evidence that the intervention is the controlling factor. Even more evidence is provided with the ABAB design if the reintroduction of the intervention coincides with renewed improvement of the client. Although it is possible for a set of extraneous factors to produce the first client improvement, it is likely that the same set of factors would recur at precisely the right time to produce improvement on reintroduction of the intervention. Especially with the ABAB design, we would have great confidence in the efficacy of an intervention that produced similar real-life results.

This research design has higher strengths on internal validity when compared with the AB design. However, there are practical problems that restrict the use of ABAB designs. First, the changes in client's condition due to first intervention which are more or less, permanent in nature, cannot be put in reverse order. Second, putting clients to their baseline is not only unwise but it is also unethical.

(iii) ABCD: Multiple Component Design

The multiple component designs are devised to handle special problems in varied situations. These are commonly known as specialized designs and symbolised as ABCD design where B, C, D stand for alternative interventions. These designs are basically used to evaluate the impact of changes in the intervention and modify the intervention that does not appear to be effective. Conversely, the researcher seeks to determine which intervention package is really responsible for the improvement in the target problem. Let us consider the problem of a client who is an alcoholic. Say, for example, first we introduce problem experiencing in relation to drinking behaviour as a treatment (B) and find that it is not effective. Then, we try the costs and benefits of drinking behaviour as a treatment (C) in its place. Suppose, there still is no improvement, then, the method of counselling is applied. The process describes a typical ABCD design:

A→Baseline

Interventions:

B→ Problems experienced in relation to drinking behaviours
C→ Costs and benefits of drinking behaviours
D→ Methods for resolving drinking problems

Figure 4
Hypothetical Example of the Multiple Component Design

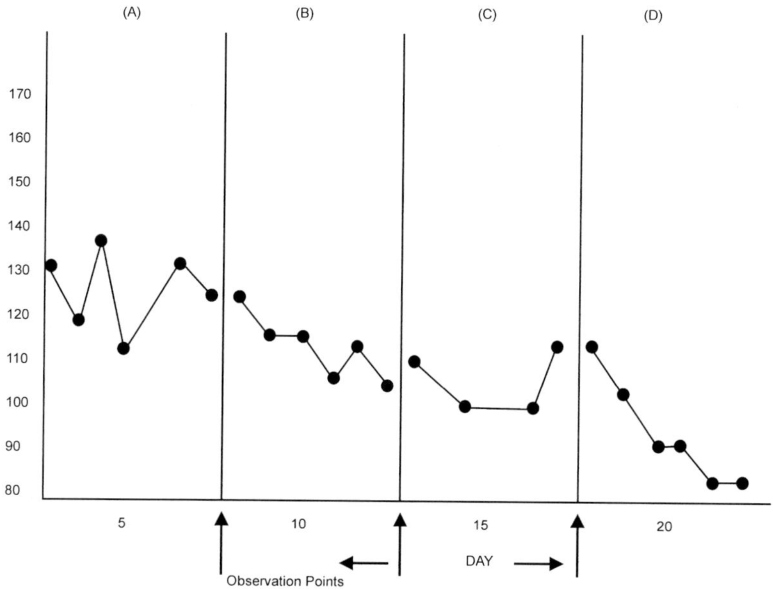

Generalisability of Single-Subject Designs

The ultimate goal of a scientific research is the generalizability of the findings of the study. In social work research, findings which are generalizable to a considerably large number of situations and cases can only contribute to the knowledge base of social work practice.

Interestingly, in single-subject design research, even if it is proved that the interventions were effective, there is no guarantee that the same intervention would be effective on other clients in different settings. This limitation of single-subject designs research, however, does not discourage social work researcher because generalizability of findings can be achieved through repeating the study by taking more measurements.

Group Designs

Group design research, also known as evaluative research, includes researches undertaken to assess the effectiveness of social work interventions with groups and community.

Evaluative research is an area of social work research and implies the use of conventional research designs with a view to measure the contribution of the interventions/programmes towards the changes brought in relation to the social conditions. Evaluative research uses different social research designs to study the contribution of the programmes.

In general, any of the conventional research designs can be used for the purpose of evaluation research with some modifications. Group designs or evaluation research designs are basically experimental research designs with some modifications. Some of the evaluation research designs are discussed below:

Experimental Research Designs

There are a large number of experimental designs. Various authors have grouped experimental designs into certain categories based on the extent of control. Most common grouping comprises:

- True experimental designs
- Pre-experimental designs (no random assignments)
- Quasi-experimental designs (no random assignments)

True Experimental Designs

True experimental designs use the process of randomization to control the validity threats that can lead to false causal inferences. The two very commonly used true experimental designs are described as follows:

(i) Evaluation research designs using experimental research designs

True experimental designs have maximum control and hence highest degree of internal validity. The essential components of an experimental research design involve (a) random assignments of subjects to experimental and control groups, (b) introducing the stimulus (independent variable) to the experimental group while withholding it from the control group, and (c) comparing the amount of change in dependent variable in experimental and control groups.

(ii) Pre-test-post-test control group design

The classic experimental design, which is also known as pre-test-post-test control group design, can be shown in shorthand notation as under:

$$E \longrightarrow R \longrightarrow Y_1 \longrightarrow X \longrightarrow Y_2$$

$$C \longrightarrow R \longrightarrow Y'_1 \longrightarrow \text{Non-X} \longrightarrow Y'_2$$

E and C represent experimental group and control group respectively. R stands for random assignments of subjects to either experimental group or the control group. The notation X represents the introduction of a stimulus, Y_1's represent pre-test and the Y_2's represent post-test. In this design, experimental group and the control group subjects are measured on a dependent variable before and after the introduction of stimulus.

This experimental design is frequently used as evaluation research design in social work research, especially in social group work/community organization practice. Suppose, for example, a social work researcher working in a school social work setting and wishes to test a hypothesis that punishments lead to low self-esteem using pre-test-post-test control group design. To test the hypothesis, first, he/she has to select a sample of students preferably from one particular class, say, 10th standard. Then, he/she has to randomly assign the subjects to either the experimental group (E) or the control group (C). Now, both the groups are measured for their self-esteem (Y_1, Y'_1). Punishments (X) are withheld for students who are in control group. Later, both the groups are measured and compared for self-esteem (Y_2, Y'_2). If there is a significant difference in the pre- and post- self-esteem scores, it can be concluded that suspension of punishment had an effect on self-esteem. Further, if it is observed that the average post-self-esteem scores of students in group E is comparatively lower than the students in group C, then, the hypothesis that punishments lead to low self-esteem will be accepted.

Pre-test-post-test control group design is diagrammed as shown in Figure 5:

Effects on Experimental Group (D1) = $Y_2 - Y_1$

Effects on Control Group (D2) = $Y'_2 - Y'_1$

Net Effects = D2 – D1

Figure 5

Pre-test-Post-test Control Group Design

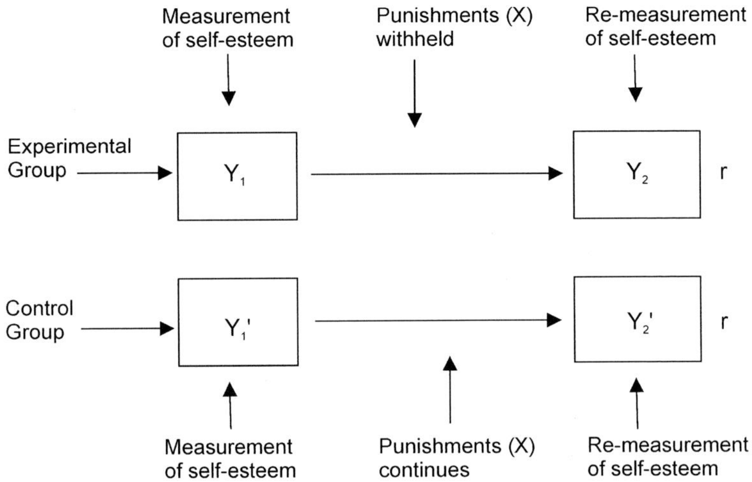

Though it sounds as the most appropriate research design for evaluation research, there are many practical difficulties in using randomized experimental research designs which compare experimental group with control group such as finding two exactly similar groups, pre-conditions and assumptions of statistical analysis of data, etc.

Moreover, the use of control groups, to whom intervention is withheld, has been a source of ethical concern to social work researchers. Thus, although conventional experimental researches are appropriate for some purposes, the drawbacks associated with the method have led social work researchers to find an alternative design for evaluating the effects of interventions based on experimental research designs with some modifications.

Pre-Experimental Designs

Research designs in which most of the sources of internal and external validity are not controlled, are termed as pre-experimental research designs. The two very commonly used pre-experimental designs are:

- One group pre-test-post-test design (no comparison group)
- The post-test comparison group design (no pre-measurement)

(i) One group pre-test-post-test design

Suppose, we wish to assess the effect of cognitive behaviour intervention on abusive parents and decide to undertake the study using one group pre-test-post-test design. The shorthand notation for this design may be diagrammed as shown in diagram.

To conduct the study, first, we select a group of abusive parents and measure their parenting skills and cognition about childhood behaviours. The test is followed by introduction of cognitive behavioural intervention with the abusive parents. After a specified period of intervention its effects on parental skills are assessed. If it is found that there is significant increase

$$E \longrightarrow Y_1 \longrightarrow X \longrightarrow Y_2$$

where:

$E \longrightarrow$ Experimental group

$X \longrightarrow$ Independent variable (social work intervention)

$Y_{1,} \longrightarrow$ Dependent Variable before introduction of X (pre-test)

$Y_2 \longrightarrow$ Dependent variable after introduction of X (post-test)

in the parental skills score of the abusive parents, we may infer that the change in the score is due to the intervention.

(ii) The post-test comparison group design

Another commonly used pre-experimental research design involves post-test measurement only but does employ a comparison group. The term 'comparison group' denotes a group which is not formed by random selection of subjects and on whom experimental manipulation is not performed.

In example mentioned above, if we compare the parenting skills and cognition about childhood behaviours of the group of abusive parents who participated in experiment with the parenting skills and cognition about childhood behaviours of a group of abusive parents who did not it exactly demonstrates the post-test comparison group design of research. The comparison group is usually chosen to be as similar as possible to the group that was introduced to the intervention. The example may be shown diagrammatically as:

$$E \longrightarrow X \longrightarrow Y_1$$

$$C \longrightarrow \text{Non-X} \longrightarrow Y_1$$

where:

$X \longrightarrow$ Independent variable (cognitive behaviour Intervention)

$Y_1 \longrightarrow$ Dependent variable (parental skills) before introduction of X (pre-test)

$E \longrightarrow$ Experimental group

$C \longrightarrow$ Comparison group

One serious disadvantage of this design is that the groups were not equivalent before introduction of the stimulus (intervention). In other words, it is possible that the subjects in the two groups might have differed initially with respect to the dependent variable measured (parenting skills and cognition about childhood behaviours).

The internal validity of the pre-experimental research designs is weak. Hence, causal inferences drawn from pre-experimental research designs are generally inconclusive.

Quasi-Experimental Research Designs

In quasi-experimental designs subjects are not assigned to experimental and control groups randomly. A very commonly quasi-experimental design is pre-test post-test non-equivalent control group design when it is not possible to divide subjects into experimental and control groups by random assignments, we try to get an existing control group (comparison group) that appears to be similar to experimental group.

Suppose, we wish to evaluate the effects of an intervention (say, counselling) on the level of loneliness of the inmates of a Home for the Aged. It is unlikely that we would be permitted to select randomly in any Home for the Aged those inmates who will be given counselling and those who will not be given. As an alternative, we may find two Homes for the Aged that agree to participate in our research study and which appear to be very similar in all respects. That is, we make sure that the inmates in two homes are very similar in terms of age, socio-economic status, mental and physical disabilities, psychological functioning, and so on. We can introduce the intervention in one home, and use the other as a comparison group. The two homes could be compared by a pret-est measurement to make sure that they really are equivalent on the dependent variable before introducing the intervention (independent variable). If their average loneliness scores are approximately same, then it would be reasonable to infer that differences in post-test scores are due to the effects of intervention. The example may be shown diagrammatically as under:

E ⟶ Y_1 ⟶ X ⟶ Y_1

C ⟶ Y'_1 ⟶ Non-X ⟶ Y'_2

where:

X ⟶ Independent variable (intervention: counselling)
Y_1 Dependent variable before introduction of X (pre-test)
Y_2 ⟶ Dependent variable after introduction of X
⟶ (post-test)
E ⟶ Experimental group
C ⟶ Comparison group

Research Pertaining to the Knowledge Base of Social Work

Social work research deals with the application of research methods in social work theory and practice. In other words, social work research aims at enhancing the knowledge base of social work and making the social work practice a scientific practice by using various research methods, tools and techniques.

As such, another major objective of social work research is enhancement of the knowledge base of social work. Social work profession has a scientific base, which consists of a special body of knowledge — tested knowledge, hypothetical knowledge and assumptive knowledge. Assumptive knowledge requires transformation into hypothetical knowledge, which in turn needs transformation into tested knowledge. Social work research has significant role in transforming the hypothetical and assumptive to tested knowledge.

Concepts are the building blocks of social work knowledge base. Social work has been using concepts derived from other social sciences. They should be verified and integrated into a system. Social work research should focus on this area.

Not all concepts or theories that are used by professional social workers have been tested and validated. Many social work concepts have roots in American culture and when applying to Indian conditions, we need to know how the values and social philosophy of India are suited to their transplantation.

The concepts are the constituents of knowledge and therefore are basic to the practice. Hence, concepts used in social work are the core of practice of social work.

Concerted efforts through social work research are very much required to conceptually articulate and validate the concepts and theories, which in turn will strengthen the scientific base of professional social work.

Research in social work values and goals in India has been almost negligible. Research in this area means identification of the motives, goals and values which guide social work practice.

Social work tradition in India, motives in helping others and the philosophy of individual-community relationships in the context of the practice of social work need to be studied.

We have accepted social work as a technique, like the acceptance of industrial techniques, without assessing the philosophical and cultural implications of its practice and the need for adapting it (Goyal, 1967).

It is therefore imperative for social work educators, schools of social work, social work researchers, practitioners and planners to concentrate on research in social work.

Methodological Issues

Methodological issues include specific research strategies to be adopted in fulfilling the objectives of social work research. Thus, such specific issues as qualitative versus quantitative approach, experimental (true experiments, quasi-experiment and pre-experiment, evaluation research designs, etc.) versus non-experimental research designs(survey research, etc.), probability versus non-probability sampling, combination of probability and non-probability sampling, data analysis and interpretation, etc., are all methodological issues.

Qualitative versus Quantitative Approach

The qualitative versus-quantitative debate has persisted in the field of social science research since a long time. It has been more of a philosophical debate than that of research practices. Qualitative researches have also been the subject of considerable controversy among social work researchers.

The philosophical roots of qualitative research emphasize the importance of understanding the meanings of human behaviour and the socio-cultural context of social interaction. This method estimates validity, reliability and objectivity of a social situation and tries to picture the empirical social world as it actually exists to those under investigation, rather than as the researcher imagines it to be.

While in qualitative research a researcher takes the phenomenon as a whole and describes it as it exists whereas in quantitative research a phenomenon is analyzed into various components or variables which can be measured in quantified terms. The researcher takes into consideration the phenomenon as a whole and assumes that there is some quality in the phenomenon in its entirety. When the researcher attempts to retain the totality of a phenomenon while verifying propositions regarding it, he/she adopts a qualitative research approach.

Quantitative research uses standardized measures that fit diverse opinions and experiences into predetermined response categories. This approach measures the reactions of a large number of individuals to a limited set of questions, thus facilitating comparison and analysis of the data with the help of close-ended questionnaires, attitude scales, rating scales and postal surveys.

These diverse approaches have created many doubts among social researchers such as the problems of trustworthiness, subjectivity, individualistic generalizations etc.

In recent years, the debate has softened. A consensus has gradually emerged that the important challenge is to match appropriate approach of research to research questions and not to advocate any single methodological approach for all research situations. Both qualitative and quantitative data can be collected for/under the same study.

Experimental versus Non-Experimental Research Designs

Experimental researches are designed for testing causal relationships. A causal relationship refers to a relationship between two variables where one variable (characteristic or occurrence) X determines another variable (characteristic or occurrence) Y. For example, if a researcher wishes to test a causal relationship that punishments (X) cause low self-esteem (Y) by comparing a group of students who have been exposed to punishments (X) with one that has not been exposed, he/she has to measure the two groups with respect of Y, either during or after exposure to X.

In the words of J.S. Mill (1930), "a cause which is itself a phenomenon without reference to the ultimate cause of any thing". He further says, "causation is simply uniform antecedence. Though this explanation of the concept of 'cause' and 'causation' is more or less accepted by sciences including social sciences, there are still ambiguities about the concepts specially when one thinks of a first cause and subsequent cause and a final cause. As a result, 'even in a scientific' explanation, the different measures of the term 'cause' are frequently confused.

A cause may act by impelling or by releasing or by unwinding. Let us consider an example. In the game of snooker a ball is impelled to strike another ball which may in turn strike on a number of balls. In this case, the first impulsion is the cause of movements of the second ball and the subsequent balls. The movements of second and subsequent balls are the effect of the cause induced by the impulsion. In other words, the event in question is shown to be determined by the preceding events.

In short, the investigation of preceding event (the cause) and successive events (the effects) caused by the preceding event constitutes causal relationships. Scientific research is mainly concerned with discovering necessary and sufficient conditions for an effect. While common sense leads one to expect that one cause may provide a complete explanation for the effect, the researcher 'rarely expects to find a single cause or condition that is both necessary and sufficient to bring about an effect. Rather, he is interested in finding out multiplicity of 'effects' or 'events'.

It is rather impossible, however, to demonstrate directly that a given variable 'X' either by itself or in conjunction with other variables causes 'Y'. Hence, we prefer to infer from the data that the causal relationship (hypothesis) that 'X' is a cause for the occurrence of 'Y' is tenable only with some level of confidence.

The Logic of Causal Inference

To clarify the issues raised above, we have to understand the logic of causal inference. The three conditions that have to be fulfilled to draw a causal inference are:

1. if the cause precedes the effect in time,
2. there is an empirical correlation between them, and
3. the relationship is not found to be the result of the effects of some third variable on each of the two initially observed.

The first condition in a causal relationship is that the cause precedes the effect in time. For example, in the game of snooker, the first impulsion is the cause of movements of the second ball and the subsequent balls. The movements of second and subsequent balls are the effect of the cause induced by the impulsion.

The second condition in a causal relationship is that the two variables should be empirically correlated with one another. For example, if a researcher wishes to examine if there is cause-effect relationship between gender and achievement, he or she has to use correlational technique to assess the magnitude of the relationship. It is also required that the coefficient of correlation is substantial.

The third condition for a causal relationship is that the observed empirical correlation between two variables cannot be explained away as being due to the influence of some third variable that causes both of them. For example, it may be observed that there is a strong correlation between 'knee joint pain' and 'amount of rainfall' but this does not mean that joints pain effect rainfall. A third variable, relative humidity is the cause of both knee joint pain and rainfall. Any relationship satisfying all these conditions is causal, and these are the only conditions of cause-effect relationship.

In a typical experimental study two groups are chosen such that they do not differ significantly from each other except by chance. One of the groups is exposed to the independent variable (known as 'experimental group'). The two groups are then compared in terms of the effects. Research design, which involves comparison of two or more groups of subjects, who have been exposed to an experiment, there is an underlying assumption that the groups being compared were similar before the introduction of experiment. To ensure this the techniques such as 'randomization' or 'matching' are utilized. The technique of randomization involves assignment of members of a group of subjects to experimental and control group. The procedure of assignment must give each member equal chance of being assigned to any of the groups. The technique of matching involves putting the subjects for assignment to the experimental or control group in a manner that a particular type of the experimental group is balanced by assigning his an exact counterpart in the control group.

Non-experimental research or survey research method is used to collect detailed descriptions of existing phenomena and with the aim of examining the data to justify current conditions or practices or to make plans to improving them. The objective may not only be to ascertain status, but also to determine the adequacy of status by comparing it with selected or established norms. Survey is probably the most widely used method for obtaining descriptive and evaluative information.

Surveys are appropriate for research questions about self-reported beliefs or behaviours. Surveys are considered as most appropriate method in case of measuring variables through answers of questions.

Though, appropriate methodology depends on the nature of research question, survey research utilizing questionnaires or scales may be used to assess staff, client or community attitudes that effect programme implementation decisions. Participant observation might be used to assess how staff relates to clients or to one another. Available records might be analyzed to assess whether the attributes of clients beings served match programme priorities.

Correlational Studies

The methodology of social research is based on its basic presumption that in human relations as much as in natural phenomena, a large degree of measurable and even predictable sets of associations occur. Hence, social research seeks to establish, measure, analyze and predict these associations in all their variety and intensity. Data collected through survey method are analyzed keeping this presumption in mind. This design of survey research is commonly known as correlational studies.

Much of the social researches establish interrelationships among variables as its first step. Correlational studies are concerned with determining the extent of relationship existing between variables. They enable us to measure the extent to which variations in one variable are associated with variations in another. We may wish to know, for example, how delinquency is related to social background or whether a relationship exists between the number of years spent in full time education and subsequent annual income, or whether there is a relation between gender and achievement.

By and large, correlational studies intend to answer the following questions:

1. Is there a relationship between two variables?
2. What is the direction of the relationship?
3. What is the magnitude of the relationship?

For example, if a researcher wishes to test a hypothesis that there is a relationship between gender and achievement, he or she has to use correlational technique to test his/her hypothesis about the relationship between the two variables by assessing the magnitude and direction of the relationship.

It also needs to be stressed that a high correlation among two variables does not in itself constitute a proof that they are causally related. A significant correlation between variables, for example, between income and size of family or the size of an educational institution and the performance of the students, is hardly any indication of a causal relationship. Suppose, we were to find that higher income is inversely correlated with the number of children, i.e., higher the income of parents, the lesser their number of children (the coefficient of correlation is, say–0.8, which is statistically quite high), we shall be wrong and unjustified saying that higher income is the cause of lower fertility. It was pointed out earlier that an inference of causality is warranted only if three kinds of proof, viz., concomitant variation, time order and elimination of any other variable as the determining condition of the hypothesized effect can be secured. In this case, following inferences may possibly be drawn in full consideration of the pronounced correlation evident among the variables of income and number of children: (a) one might be causing the other, (b) both the variables might be the effects of some other cause or causes, and (c) the association may be a mere chance occurrence. Casual inferences can obviously be very surely established in an experimental situation. We have considered this when dealing with experimental designs. In social sciences, it is very difficult to set up experiments, so most of the studies are non-experimental ones. Analytical procedures have, however, been devised to draw inferences about causal relationship in non-experimental studies.

Coefficient of correlation is calculated to identify the extent or degree of correlation between two variables. It does not mean that their relationship is functional or constant. In other words, correlation in two sets of data need not always be the result of mutual interdependence. Changes in one set of data may be the cause of changes in the other set (of data) and there may be a cause and effect relationship between these two sets. But it is also equally possible that the changes in the two sets of data are the effects of some third factors, which affects both these sets of data.

In such situations researcher needs to control the effect of a third variable on the bivariate relationship by cross-tabulation or partial table method which is quite common in the empirical research. However, the method has a serious drawback that limits its use when the number of cases are relatively small. The partial cross-tabulation involves sub-division of the sample into gradually smaller sub-groups. This reduces the size of cell frequency, thus its reliability and validity is questionable.

An alternative to method of control is the partial correlation. This is a mathematical process of adjustment of the bivariate correlation, deemed to nullify the effect of third variable (control variable) on the independent and dependent variables.

However, there is hardly any situation where one independent variable determines the dependent variable. Often we have situations where a set of independent variables is associated with another set of dependent variables. In other words, more often several independent variables contribute to the prediction of the dependent variables. Multiple regression is commonly used to estimate the effect of multiple independent variables.

Unobtrusive Research Analysis of Available Data

Data collected by some one other than the researcher for purposes that differ from the researcher are referred to as available data or secondary data. A wide range of such data is available for analysis. For example, governmental as well as non-governmental organizations collect a large amount of statistical data about crime, health, birth rates, death rates and the like. Another form of secondary data is documents in different forms of communication in qualitative format. This form of data includes articles of journals, books, magazines, letters, memoranda, diaries etc. Social work case records and fieldwork records are a rich source of secondary data for social work research. These data in combination with data collected from other sources can make significant contribution to the knowledge base of social work.

Probability and Non-Probability Sampling

The essential characteristic of probability sampling is that one can specify for each element of the population the chance of being included in the sample. In the simplest case, each of the elements has the same probability of being included, but this is not a necessary condition. What is necessary is that for each element there must be some specific chance that it will be included.

Based on this assumption probability sampling makes it possible to select a sample which will be representative. This helps researchers to estimate the extent to which the sample statistics are likely to differ from population parameters.

This means, if probability sampling method is used, it is possible to ascertain the size of the sample that will be needed if we want to have a given degree of certainty that their sample results do not differ by more than a specified value from those of the population parameters.

In non-probability sampling, there is no way of estimating the probability that each element has of being included in the sample and no assurance that every element has some chance of being included (Wilkinson and Bhandarkar, 1977).

In general, the major advantages of non-probability sampling are convenience and economy. However, in social work research, most often, we have no option other than non-probability sampling. For example, a social worker who is interested to study why cancer out-patients are not regular in reporting to the doctor or what are the problems of the parents of the mentally challenged children and the like, will have to use any one of the non-probability sampling plans. It is likely, therefore, that many sampling operations in social work research will be conducted according to non-probability principles. Social work researchers are convinced that these sampling procedures work reasonably well, despite the fact that they do not provide any basis for estimating how far the sample results are likely to deviate from the true population figures. Social work researchers, in other words, will continue to use non-probability methods and to justify their use on the grounds of practical experience, even while conceding the representativeness in principle of probability sampling. Moreover, many researchers argue that, many a time, this so-called representativeness exists only on paper. They believe that there is a difference between the sampling plan and its actual implementation; there can be many a slip in the implementation of the plan, which would nullify its theoretical merits.

For example, in situations where investigators may fail to follow the instructions in selecting respondents, or some of the selected respondents may refuse to be interviewed or not be available, investigators are allowed to substitute other respondents when those selected for the sample are not available for interview. Truly speaking, the sample thus obtained may, hence, not be the probability sample as it was planned to be.

In fact, there are situations in social work practice, in which probability sampling is unnecessary or inappropriate.

One such situation arises from the fact that many a time social work researchers do not necessarily carry out studies of samples only for the purpose of generalization to the populations from which samples have been drawn. If samples are used for other reasons, ability to evaluate the likelihood of deviations from the population values is irrelevant.

For example, a social worker who wants to study the problems of parents of mentally challenged children would be interested in obtaining ideas, good insights and critical appraisals rather than assessing the status of opinion among the parents. In this situation he/she has to select a non-probability sample, most probably a purposive sample. The situation is almost exactly analogous to one in which a social worker tries to evaluate the effectiveness of a new technique of educating alcoholic patients. The alcoholics — also a purposive sample — are not called in order to get an average opinion that would correspond to the average opinion of the entire alcoholic population. They are called in precisely because of their special problems.

Another example of sampling for diagnosing the problems of a group of delinquent children rather than for the estimation of population values is provided by the single-subject research, also known as evaluative research. The typical problem of evaluative research is to find out something about motives, attitudes and associations that are evoked by certain social conditions, but that may not be obvious even to the respondents themselves. The results of such studies are reported to agencies, which make use of them in developing treatment plans for their inmates. Interestingly, the evaluative researchers are quite happy with accidental samples, or with purposive samples selected in such a way as to maximize the likelihood of differences among the elements in the sample. They are looking for causative factors to transmit to the agency people, not for correct estimates of population distributions.

Sampling in Single-Subject Designs

The sample in this design of social work research is one ($\overline{N} = 1$), irrespective of whether the unit of analysis is individual, family, community, or organization. As such, one of the major limitations of these designs is their dubious external validity. But, we should not forget that single-subject experiments can identify with a high degree of internal validity in those interventions that seem to work in one, perhaps idiosyncratic context and can be tested for generalizability in subsequent studies. These subsequent studies might include large-scale experiments utilizing control groups, or they might be additional single-subject experiments that attempt to approximate replications of the original single-subject experiment in other contexts (Rubin and Babbie, 1989)

Analysis and Interpretation of Data

One of the most important stages of the research process is processing, analysis and interpretation of data. For many social work researchers processing, analysis and interpretation of data is not a very serious activity. They feel that data processing and analysis is a job of computer assistants. As a consequence, most of the research reports end up only with univariate/percentage analysis of data. Though, some researchers do attempt bivariate analysis but essentially fail to substantiate its inferences because most of them are either unaware of trivariate analysis for establishing the cause-effect relationship or have no access to advance computer software like SPSS.

The purpose of data processing is to prepare data as a model where relationships between the variables can be studied. Analysis of data is made with reference to the objectives of the study and research questions with a view to examine association/relationship between variables. It is also designed to test the hypothesis. Interpretation of data pertains to further analysis of data to establish cause-effect relation between variables and to draw causal inferences.

To achieve these objectives researchers need to make a perfect plan of processing, analysis and interpretation of data in advance. They are further required to instruct computer assistants accordingly.

A plan of processing, analysis and interpretation of data is discussed below:

Re-classification and Re-categorization of Data

The first step is re-classification/re-categorization of responses. Most of the times researchers do not use statistical techniques for re-categorization or re-classification of data. The reason could be, researchers do not use statistical techniques for re-categorization or re-classification of data because, researchers while preparing their questionnaires, use closed-ended questions for collecting 'factual data' like age, income, number of children, etc. In making the questions 'closed-ended' generally they use simple and convenient groupings (arbitrarily). For example, for age of respondents, very 'popular' response provided in questionnaires is 20-30, 30-40. Arbitrary classification adversely affects the normal distribution of data leading to unreliable research results. Re-classification/re-categorization of data is a process to re-arrange data with the help of statistical techniques/reasoning to justify further analysis/interpretation of data.

Say, for example, responses to a statement which are assigned scores can be summated on the bases of quartile values and re-classified as high, medium and low. The basic principle in the process of re-categorization of qualitative responses is that the categories thus obtained must be exhaustive and mutually exclusive in other words the categories have to be independent and not overlapping.

Setting up the Analytic Model

The next step in the process of data analysis is to set up analytic models. For this we need to look back to research questions, objectives and hypotheses of the study. Analytic models are diagrammatic presentation of variables and their interrelationships.

To illustrate the process of making analytical models we will consider a study on 'life satisfaction of elderly persons'. For example, say, the major objectives and hypotheses of the study are:

Objectives

1. To assess the extent of life satisfaction among older adults, and the factors determining it.
2. To find out how social support effect the association between physical and psychological health and life satisfaction among older adults.

Hypothesis

"There may be a direct association between physical and psychological health and life satisfaction of older adults."

From the proposed hypothesis it is very clear that the life satisfaction among older adults is the dependent variable in the study. Further, say, for example, the researcher wishes to examine the associations among independent variables — physical and psychological health, social support - and the dependent variable - life satisfaction. The bivariate associations among dependent and independent variables can be diagrammatically presented by Bivariate Analytical Model as follows:

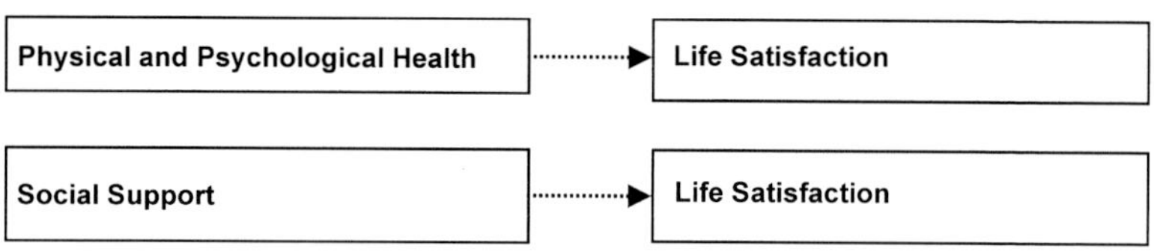

The bivariate associations between dependent and independent variables are required to be substantiated by examining cause-effect relationship by introducing third variable as control. This can be diagrammatically presented by Trivariate Analytical Model as follows:

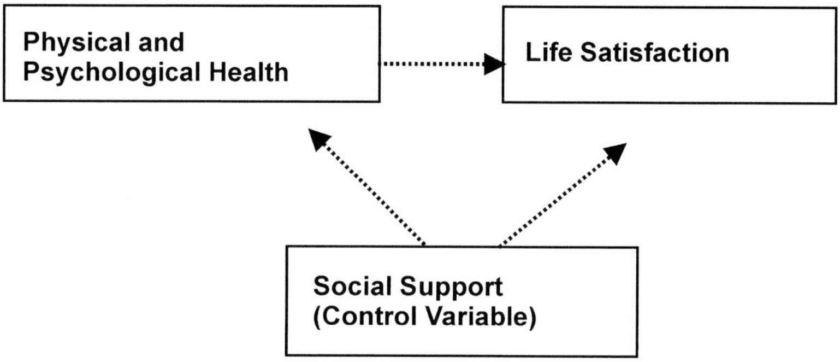

Data Analysis and Data Interpretation

Data can be analyzed at various levels depending upon the research questions, objectives and hypotheses of the study. Each level of analysis has its very specific purpose and limitations. It is the researcher who has to select the level of analysis because he/she only knows what results he/she is expecting. A brief discussion of various levels of data analysis is presented below:

Univariate Analysis

Univariate analysis refers to tables, which give data relating to one variable. Univariate tables, which are more commonly known as frequency distribution tables, show how frequently an item repeats. The characteristics of the sample can be explained by examining the percentages. Further properties of a distribution, can be found out by various measures of central tendencies. However, researcher is required to decide which is most suited for a particular analysis. To know how much is the variation, the researcher has to calculate measures of dispersion.

Univariate tables are basically prepared for describing the independent and dependent variables. Many a time it is found that researchers, usually amateur, tend to jump to conclusion about the association of the two variables by comparing two univariate tables. It is not acceptable as scientific finding.

Bivariate Analysis

To know the association between independent variable and dependent variable bivariate analysis is undertaken. For this the data pertaining to these variables are cross-tabulated. A bivariate table presents data of two variables with row or column percentages.

The association between two variables can be explained either by comparing the percentages of respondents column-wise or row-wise depending upon the computation of percentages. If the percentages are calculated row-wise we compare data column-wise. The association between the variables can also be examined by various statistical techniques depending upon the level of measurement of the data.

In bivariate analysis the researcher also explains the nature and the degree of association. That is whether the relationship is positive or negative and it also indicates the degree of association in terms of high, moderate or low.

Trivariate Analysis

If the two variables are associated it is not necessary that there is cause and effect relationship between the two variables. It is essential that the effects of other variables are ruled out as alternative explanation of the relationship. For example, a relationship between 'knee joint pain' and 'amount of rainfall' can probably be accounted for by the variable 'humidity'. 'Humidity' is related to both 'knee joint pain' and 'amount of rainfall' and this joint relationship produces a statistical relationship that has no causal significance. The original bivariate relationship between 'knee joint pain' and 'amount of rainfall' is called spurious. It is mandatory for a researcher to reveal such variables and substantiate the bivariate relationship. It is the basic principle of all research designs and is achieved by a process called 'control'.

Bivariate analysis of data is the initial step of cause-effect analysis. It is followed by trivariate analysis of data. The purpose of trivariate analysis is to substantiate the findings of bivariate analysis. The bivariate analysis establishes covariation and its direction. To draw the causal inference one has to re-examine the bivariate association by controlling the effect of third variables into the analysis.

Bivariate relationship may be observed because of two reasons: it may be observed just due to chance, or it may exist due to a third variable which is yet to be revealed. Above all, the change in the dependent variable may be explained by more than one single independent variable. In both the cases, re-examination of the bivariate association by controlling the effect of third variable serves the purpose of clarifying and elaborating the original relationship. It plays a very significant role in drawing inferences.

Multivariate Analysis

In rarity, particularly in social sciences, however, there is hardly any situation where one independent variable determines the dependent variable. Often, we have situations where a set of independent variables is associated with another set of dependent variables. In other words, more often, several independent variables contribute to the prediction of the dependent variable. Multiple regression is commonly used to estimate the effect of multiple independent variables.

In case a bivariate association is confirmed, the researcher may proceed to a more advanced stage of analysis and elaborate the bivariate association. Elaboration usually involves the introduction of other variables to determine the links between the independent and dependent variables or the specification of the conditions under which the association takes place (Nachmias, 1981).

Trivariate and multivariate analyses serve three important functions in social research: control, elaboration and prediction. Firstly, whenever the experimental control is not possible, trivariate analysis is used to examine the bivariate relationship to see if the relationship is due to the third variable.

Secondly, bivariate relationship is clarified by introducing a third variable. Finally, trivariate analysis helps to identify more independent variables to account for the variation in the dependent variables.

The Emerging Need

Redesigning Social Work Research Curriculum

It is evident from the above discussion that the curriculum of research methods for social work needs change in its focus. Research methods curriculum in social work education has traditionally been following hypothetico-deductive model of social science research. This is most probably the reason why research in many schools of social work is in no way different from the contents of social science research curriculum.

This dominant paradigm mainly focuses on quantitative measurement, experimental design, and probability sampling and multivariate parametric statistical analysis. As such, social work students largely view the culmination of research as the drawing of conclusions from the research findings through the process of deductive reasoning. These conclusions, obviously, contributed neither to knowledge base of social work nor to the social work practice. Seldom do they try to test the interventions or evaluate the outcome of their interventions. The research course offered to social work students has hardly any relevance to practice. As a consequence, social work students fail to establish the link between research and practice. Most of them develop a notion that they have nothing to do with research.

Against this background, research curriculum in social work needs to be redesigned to make it more relevant to social work. While redesigning the curriculum, research and practice should be perceived as allied aspects of social work and bound by the common goal of advancing and consolidating the theory and practice of social work. As such, the focus of research methods should be on practice-based research/evaluative research methodology, namely, single-subject research, programme/project evaluation research, experimental research, cost-benefit analysis, social impact analysis, etc.

Interlinking research with practice/practice-based social work research offers an opportunity for social workers to make significant difference in their professional standards and accountability to their interventions. Common areas need to be identified to merge research with theory and practice emphasizing on combining research training with field work (Monette, 1986).

Social work research, by and large, calls for non-probability sampling because it is often impossible to develop an exhaustive sampling frame. For example, convenience or accidental sampling is probably one of the more common forms of sampling in social work research. Hence, it is imperative for social work researcher to deal with topics such as representativeness of sample, generalizability of findings, sampling error and finally internal/external validity in much greater detail than in the case of non-probability sampling.

Though non-probability samples are very useful, they do have some important limitations. First, no real claims of representativeness can be made. This greatly limits the generalizability of findings beyond the level of the sampling error which remains unknown. One of the chief limitations of non-probability sampling is its dubious external validity. Consequently, researcher has to take utmost precaution in generalizing the conclusions.

However, regardless of limitations due to sample size or selection procedure, these researches can identify with high degree of internal validity and can be tested for generalizability in subsequent studies. The generalizability of these studies can be improved by replication of experiments and generalization on the bases of accumulation of facts. Emphasis on these methodologies/techniques as a way to integrate research and practice will increase the amount of social work research being produced and ultimately advance the empirical base of social work practice.

The final step in research is drawing conclusions based on analysis and interpretation of data. Unfortunately, data analysis and interpretation is one of the most neglected areas in research. This area needs special emphasis in the curriculum of social work research. Preparation of analytical models, bivariate and trivariate analyses including cause-effect relationship, and multivariate analysis are some of the topics, which need to be dealt with in detail so that researchers could be able to draw conclusions on scientific lines.

Statistics are needed in social work research to analyze and interpret the data. We need to emphasize the application of non-parametric statistical analysis like Kolmogorov-Smirnov Test, Sign Test, Wilcoxon Test, Mann-Whitney U-Test, etc., because many a time we are not in a position to fulfil the assumptions of parametric tests like t-test, F-test etc.

Teaching of Research Methods

Most of the knowledge used by social work educators lacks a strong empirical basis – an unavoidable limitation of profession that deals with the elusive complexities of psychological and social phenomena. Social work educators can make use of scientific orientation in motivating social work students to go for empirical testing of the various knowledge base of social work – theories, principles and concepts taught in the theory classes. Research will provide empirically grounded knowledge, which in turn can make a significant change in the attitude of the students and educators towards the profession.

The present practice of teaching research methods for social work as an independent course must be dispensed with. Suitable adjustments need to be made in the social work curriculum to enable social work educators to relate research with other courses in social work.

The teachers must teach the research methods course in the framework of social work practice and not, as is now the unfortunate situation, independent of social work framework.

When the social work research methods course is taught independent of social work framework, it is most probable that the class is taught social science research methodology and not social work research. It is a fact that most social work students study research for only one reason — it is a compulsory requirement for the degree. Many students wonder why research courses are required for social work when there is so much to learn about how to help people.

Most of the research educators, who teach research methods, do not have practice-based research experience, hence, knowledge used by them lacks empirical basis. As a result, research methods are taught like any other theory paper/course.

Some major objectives of research methods course are to acquire skills in conducting research, learn to prepare tools, collect data, analyze and interpret data, etc. As such, it is necessary that course relating to skill development must be taught using "Learning through Doing" approach. That is, process like formulation of hypothesis, preparation of tools, collection, analysis and interpretation of data, writing research reports, etc. needs to be taught through organizing workshops, group exercises, demonstrations etc.

Practice and research are treated independently at the training level, and the approach, therefore, continues in the post-training careers of social workers. The gulf between researchers and practitioners over the years has widened. Researchers frequently complain that practitioners ignore their pertinent and important findings. Practitioners consider much of the university stimulated research irrelevant and express their inability to use it. Such gaps have been widened by the belief that the same person cannot be both a good researcher and a practitioner (Fansel, 1980). Such beliefs have been substantiated by the facts that social work researchers hardly find time to practice.

Conversely, the practitioners, due to their preoccupation with service delivery systems, are least concerned about research. Both the contentions underscore the need to solidify the relationship between schools and agencies by integrating research and practice (Reid, 1978).

Thus, as research and practice have existed as parallel to each other, most of the time research is not practice-oriented and as such the findings do not affect social work knowledge and practice.

Statistics has to be taught to social work students avoiding mathematical derivations and minimizing the use of formulas by using words and visual imagery introducing formulas only after they have been explained in detail in narrative form as far as possible. The teachers have to cite examples of primary interest to social workers, which show the relevance of statistics.

The rationale to motivate social work educators, practitioners and students to study statistics is that there has been very rapid growth in the field of social work profession in the recent years and growing recognition of the need for research and statistics to enhance practice. It is for this reason that social work educators and students must be well versed with the use of statistical methods and tools. Courses on general statistical methods and specially sampling techniques, tests of significance, measurement of relationship should be adapted for use in social work.

Courses in the methodology of social work research, research designs, single-subject design research, evaluation research, integrating research and practice, practice-based research, and statistics need to be organized periodically.

Conclusions

There has been little growth and practically no development in social work research front in India. This is evident from observations by social work educationors at different points of time in India. These show that there has been serious stagnation or at least very poor growth in research in India (Ramachandran, 1987).

Social work research offers an opportunity for social workers to make a significant difference in their professional standards and accountability to their interventions. Research has multifaceted role to play in this direction. There is no doubt about the fact that social worker will be more effective practitioner guided by the findings of social work research.

Steps like redesigning the research curriculum for social work, integration of research, theory and practice, stimulating research in social work and emphasis on need-based research methodology have to be taken to demonstrate the role of research in social work education.

References

Bloom, M., 1978 "Challenges to Helping Profession and the Responses of Scientific Practice", *Social Service Review*, 52, 584-595.

Dasgupta, Sugata, 1977, "Social Work Research" in *Encyclopaedia of Social Work*, New Delhi: Government of India.

Epstein, I. and Tripodi, T., 1973, *Research Techniques for Program Planning, Monitoring and Evaluation*, New York: Columbia University Program.

Fansel, David, 1980, "Services to and by the Real People", *Social Work*, 34, 195-196.

Goyal, C.P., 1967, Social Work Research in India, in Dasgupta, Sugata (ed.), *Methodology of Social Science Research*, New Delhi: Impex India.

House, E.R., 1980, *Evaluating with Validity*, Beverly Hills, California, Sage.

Herlekar, A., 1964, Research in Social Work, *The IJSW*, Bombay, July.

Jacob, K.K., 1965, *Methods and Fields of Social Work in India*, Bombay: Asia Publishing.

Khinduka, S.K., 1965, *Social Work in India*, Allahabad: Kitab Mahal.

Levin. M.H., 1985, *Costeffectiveness: A Primer*, New Delhi: Sage.

Lynn, Lvons. V. and Morris (ed.), 1978, *Programme Evaluation*, London: Sage.

Micheal, J. et al., 1982, *Evaluating Your Agency's Programme*, London: Sage.

Mishan, E.J., 1971, *Cost-Benefit Analysis: An Informal Introduction*, London: George Allen and Unwin Ltd.

Monette, Duane R. et. al., 1986, *Applied Social Research: Tool for the Human Services*, Chicago: Holt.

Posova, E.J. and Carey R.G., 1985, *Programme Evaluation: Methods and Case Studies*, Englewood Cliffs, NJ: Prentice Hall.

Polansky, N.A. (ed.), 1975, *Social Work Research*, Chicago: The University of Chicago Press.

Reid, W., 1978, "The Social Agency as a Research Machine", *Journal of Service Research*, 2, 11-23.

Rubin, Allen and Babbie E., 1989, *Research Methods for Social Work*, Belmont, California, Wadsworth, 1989.

Rossi. H.P. and Williams. W. (ed.), 1972, *Evaluating Social Programs: Theory, Practice and Politics*, New York: Seminar Press.

Ramachandran. P., 1968, "Social Work Research and Statistics" in *History and Philosophy of Social Work in India*, Bombay: Allied Publishers.

Ramchandran, P., 1987, "Research in Social Work" in A.B. Bose (ed.) *Encyclopaedia of Social Work in India*, New Delhi: Government of India, p. 386.

Reid, William J., 1987, "Research in Social Work" in *Encyclopaedia of Social Work*, Silver Spring, Maryland.

Rossi, P. and H. Freeman, 1982, *Evaluation: A Systematic Approach*, Beverly Hills, Sage.

Schneirer, M.A., 1979, *Programme Evaluation: The Organizational Context* Beverly Hills, California, Sage.

Thomas, P.T., 1968, "Social Research" in M.S. Gore (ed.) *Encyclopaedia of Social Work in India*, New Delhi: Government of India, p. 204.

Wienback, R.W. and Rubin, A. (ed.), 1980, *Teaching Social Work Research: Alternative Programs and Strategies*, New York: Council on Social Work Education.

Weiss, Carol., 1972, *Evaluation Research*, Englewood Cliffs, NJ: Prentice Hall.

Werner, W.B., 1959, *Objectives of Social Curriculum of the Future*, New York: Council of Social Work Education.

3

Social Work Intervention in Psychosomatic Pain Disorder

Sushma Batra and Tushti Bhardwaj

Stress has become one of the biggest killers in today's world, especially among adolescents. All of us respond differently if the life gets tough and complicated. Under conditions of overwhelming stress, any individual is likely to develop psychological problems, i.e., he/she may experience a lowering or breakdown of integral, adaptive functioning. This breakdown may be sudden as in the case of an individual who has gone through a severe accident or fire, or it may be gradual, as for a person who has been subjected to prolonged periods of tension and self-esteem loss. Usually, a person recovers once a stressful situation is over, although in some cases there may be long-lasting damage to his/her self-concept and an increased vulnerability to psychosomatic disorders.

Psychosomatic disorder is a condition in which psychological stress adversely affects physiological (somatic) functioning to the point of distress. Psychosomatic disorders are described in DSM-IV as the presence of physical symptoms suggesting an underlying medical condition, but the medical condition is neither found nor fully accounts for the level of functional impairment.

Disorders become diagnosable conditions when such impairment causes significant disturbances in school, work or home-life. The common feature of somatoform disorders is the presence of physical symptoms that suggest a medical condition. Among children and adolescents somatic symptoms are common but diagnosable conditions are rare.

Psychosomatic disorders resulting from stress may include hypertension, respiratory ailments, gastrointestinal disturbances, migraine and tension headache. The present article examines the effectiveness of social work intervention in case of an adolescent having tension-type headache. In this, we present multimodal approach used to treat somatoform disorder (headache) in adolescent. We designed our therapeutic approach based on the hypothesis that the fundamental struggle for adolescents is in part familial in origin; it is related with their social environment and involves difficulty in resolving adolescents' process of identity, individualization and independence.

Problem Description

Psychosomatic disorders may affect almost any part of the body, though they are usually found in system not under voluntary control. Theoretical development and burgeoning research on stress and illness in the mid-20th century yielded the foundations necessary to conceptualize headache as a psycho-physiological (psychosomatic) disorder. Various forms of headache, properly called headache disorders, are among the most common disorders of the nervous system. Historically, headaches have been classified as either migraine or tension based on the presence of autonomic nervous system symptoms (e.g., nausea, and/or vomiting, photophobia and/or phonophobia) and the quality of pain (e.g., pulsatile versus squeezing/band like) (AdHoc Committee on the Classification of Headache, 1962).

Mechanism of 'tension-type headache' is poorly understood although it has long been regarded as a headache with muscular origin. It may be stress-related or associated with musculo-skeletal problems in the neck. As documented in literature, 'episodic tension-type headache' occurs like migraine in varying episodes. These usually last no longer than a few hours, but can persist for several days. 'Chronic tension-type headache', one of the chronic daily headache syndromes, is less common than 'episodic tension-type headache' but presents most of the time, and can be unremitting over long periods. Headache in either case is usually mild or moderate and generalized, though it can be one-sided. It is described as pressure or tightness like a band around the neck. It lacks specific features and associated symptoms of migraine.

Tension-type headache begins during the teenage years, affecting three women every two men and reaches peak levels in the 30s. Episodic tension-type headache is most common headache disorder reported by over 70 per cent of the same population (WHO, 2004).

Headache itself is a painful condition and often disabling even though it continues to be underestimated in frequency and scale, and headache disorders remain underrecognized and undertreated throughout the world. Although the epidemiology of headache disorder is only partly documented taken together headache disorders are extraordinarily common. Population-based studies have mostly focused on migraine, which although the most frequently studied, is not the most common headache disorder. Other types of headache, such as the more prevalent tension-type headache and sub-types of more disabling chronic daily headache, have received less attention. In developing countries like India a large number of tension-type headaches go unreported because of ignorance among population and their attitude of not recognizing it as a serious ailment. Headache disorders are not perceived by the public as serious since they are mostly episodic, do not cause death and are not contagious. Moreover, limited funding also prevents proper documentation of headache disorders.

Headache disorders impose recognizable burden on sufferers including substantial personal suffering, impaired quality of life and financial cost. Repeated headache attacks and often the constant fear of next one damages family life, social life and employment. For example, social activity and work capacity are reduced in almost all migraine sufferers and in 60 per cent of tension-type headache sufferers (WHO, 2004).The long-term effect of coping with a chronic headache disorder may also predispose the individual to other illnesses. For example, depression is three times more common in people with migraine or severe headache than in healthy individuals.

Theoretical Framework

Research by psychiatrist Franz and his colleagues at the Chicago Institute of Psychoanalysis in the 1950s and 1960s suggested that specific personality traits and specific conflicts may create particular psychosomatic illness, but it is generally believed that the form a disorder takes is due to individual vulnerability. Emotional stress is assumed to aggravate existing illnesses (www.britannica.com).

The psychological and interpersonal causal factors predispose the individual to develop the specific maladaptive behaviour. Freud considered anxiety to be the central problem in psychosomatic disorders — a conclusion echoed over the years by many writers of widely differing theoretical persuasions. According to the "anxiety defense view", threats stemming from internal and external sources elicit intense anxiety, which in turn leads to the exaggerated use of various ego defense mechanisms and to maladaptive behaviours.

"Faulty learning", a major focus of the behavioural perspective, has become the most widely used explanation for both the development and the maintenance of psychosomatic disorder. Faulty learning is seen in the acquisition of maladaptive anxiety response and modes of coping with stressful situations.

"Humanistic perspective" placed emphasis on values, meaning, personal growth and self-fulfilment. Lack of meaning and blocked personal growth often appear to stem from a lack of needed competencies and resources or a feeling that duty requires one to remain in a self-stiffing role. According to the humanistic perspective, such a lifestyle can ultimately bring feelings of anxiety, hostility and futility – feelings that may inspire psycho-somatic symptoms.

According to "pathogenic interpersonal relationships view" certain interactions within families and other early relationships can set the stage for children or adolescents to develop somatic lifestyles in later life. For example, the parents who overprotect or indulge their children may prevent them from developing the independent, effective coping techniques required in their adult years. Insecure parents may instil their own excessive concerns with ailments into their children, which is a common background in somatoform disorders (Keller, 1985). Much of what a person becomes in later life – attitudes, values, and often even particular symptoms – can be traced to interactions within the family during the formative years.

The precise role of genetic and constitutional factors in psychosomatic disorder has not been delineated. But ample evidence from army records and civilian studies indicates that the incidence of psychosomatic disorder is much higher in the family history of neurotic individuals than general population (Carson, Butcher and Mineka, 1995). Etiology of recurrent headache in both pediatric and adult is not completely understood. A complex set of genetic factors appears to be involved at least with headaches that have a strong autonomic nervous system component (Scheller, 1995). Recent twin studies have reported a significant genetic basis for both migraine and tension headaches that are stronger for women than men (Honkasalo et al., 1995; Larsson, Bille and Pederson, 1995).

More general models of headache etiology propose an inherited headache predisposition triggered by a wide range of biological (e.g., menarche) or psychosocial factors (e.g., stress) with the course moderated by multiple individual difference variables. Some individuals are more prone biologically to experience the physiological disruption underlying the anxiety experience.

A comprehensive functional model of the psychological factors involved in recurrent headache was recently presented by Martin, Milech and Nathan (1993). The basic assumption underlying this model is that environmental and individual subjective events occurring prior to, during and following pain episode have a significant influence on the course and outcomes associated with recurrent headache syndromes. Within this model antecedent, characteristics of headache episodes and associated individual as well as interpersonal consequences are specified as targets for therapeutic intervention.

Review of Literature

Over three decades of research have shown the effectiveness of a number of behavioural treatments, chiefly relaxation, biofeedback and cognitive behaviour therapy for uncomplicated forms of migraine and tension-type headache (Jeanetta et al., 2005).

Polmer and Scher (2001), in their study, described the assessment and treatment of severe functional impairment in a young female adolescent with somatoform pain disorder. Standardized assessment of functional impairment and health-related quality of life was performed at baseline and follow-up. The most effective treatment included an in-patient hospital admission using a rehabilitative approach and behaviour modification programme.

Bogardus et al. (1994) reported that cognitive behavioural therapy brought greater improvement in the frequency of tension-headache. It was also found that stress management significantly reduced the headache score. Interventions, including relaxation training, self-hypnosis, autogenic training and guided imagery, contains some of the more common clinical approaches used to treat recurrent headaches (Harsen and Bellack, 1985).

Family pathology is difficult to address in conventional therapeutic approaches because of high degree of family chaos, enmeshment and psychological denial found in the families of adolescents with somatoform disorders (DeGray et al., 1989). In addition studies suggests that defense styles of children and adolescents with somatoform disorder appear to be primarily structured so that denial and dissociation are often predominant, making insight-oriented therapy difficult to employ (Atlas, Wolfson and Lipschitz, 1999). Hence, there is a need for an approach that allows gradual confrontation of the somatic symptomatic presentation both in individuals and family therapeutic activities (Fritsch and Hagine, 1997).

Majority of the treatment reports in literature are single case reports or anecdotal and controlled trial using psychotherapy for the treatment are very rare. This is true in part firstly, because the condition is rare and moreover these patients are difficult to engage in psychiatric treatment because of their psychological investment in a physical explanation for their difficulties. It is therefore unlikely that many randomized trials will be successfully mounted to explore treatment for these patients. A case series therefore is still a valuable addition to the literature on care of somatoform disorders.

In general, most treatment approaches to somatoform disorders attempt to decrease symptoms expression through encouragement or suggestion. A rehabilitative approach that emphasizes a return to usual activities, the use of physical therapy and the use of active coping strategies have been recommended. Behavioural methods, self-management techniques, medication trials and family treatments have been employed in a large majority of studies. Standardized headache diaries have been used in majority of studies for evaluating outcomes.

Our literature review suggests that a method to address individual and familial psychopathology in adolescents with somatoform disorder should use an indirect approach. A multimodal approach is likely to be effective in working with such individuals because it addresses many of the issues at individual, familial and interpersonal levels and brings early improvement. Frequent rehabilitative sessions, individualized treatment plans and close monitoring provide the patient with ways to focus on symptom reduction.

Nature of the Study

The present study was carried out using AB Single-Subject Design. Single-subject design relates to clinical practice. While the unit of analysis in single-subject designs is usually an individual, it can also be a family, a group, a community or an organization. Single-subject designs are 'within subject design' (each participant is his/her own control). Using single-subject designs to evaluate social work practice has been around (in western world) since the late 1960s, when they were borrowed from behavioural therapy analysis. Although these designs can be used with a range of different treatment approaches, including psycho-dynamic, they are closely associated with behavioural and cognitive approaches, where the goals of intervention are often more discrete and unambiguous. Keeping this in view, cognitive and behavioural therapeutic approaches were used in the present case.

The single-subject design applies the logic of time-series designs to the evaluation of the effect of intervention on client system. Such designs involve obtaining repeated measures of a client system. With regard to particular outcome indicators of a target problem, repeated measures of the trend in the target problem are obtained before a particular intervention is introduced, i.e., baseline phase (control phase). These measures are again repeated after the intervention is introduced (experimental phase). The data then compared in order to infer if a particular intervention is effective.

Case Profile

Identifying Mark	:	X
Age	:	18 years
Gender	:	Female
Education	:	Pursuing Graduation
Residence (local)	:	College Hostel
Residence (permanent)	:	Gurgaon, NCR of Delhi
Father's occupation	:	Private Building Contractor
Mother's occupation	:	Teacher in Private School

Family Details

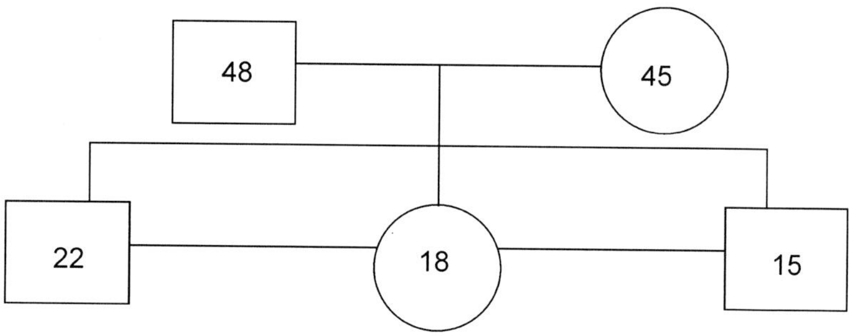

Reported Problem

Consistent headache and low mood.

Psychosocial Study

The client, an eighteen years old girl, came to meet the social worker for complaints of headache after a long-term treatment with medication had produced only slight improvement. She is an undergraduate student in Delhi University. She stays in hostel and visits her home only at weekend. She does not have close friends with whom she can share her personal matters. She feels lonely and rejected by the fellow mates. She is a normal looking girl with dusky complexion and not able to keep pace with the fashion styles as her other batchmates. She is an academic-oriented girl and prefers to devote her time in studies than in physical grooming which is one of the reasons she feels contributing to her feeling of 'rejection' by her friends. She is the second child among the three siblings.

Excerpt from the First Interview

Since the client is a hostler and spends most of the time with co-friends, so the first interview was directed to know about her relations with peer group.

Worker: How do you feel when you are in company of your close friends?

Client: I do not have as such 'close friends'. I don't feel comfortable interacting with my hostel mates. At times, I meet one of my school friends "A" and like spending some time with him. But for the last few months, I find him also irritating and he talks in very sarcastic way.

Worker: Can you recall any pleasant moment in the company of your hostel mates?

Client: I do not think I have ever had any pleasant and memorable experience with my hostel mates. But there are many unpleasant instances each day with them. Worst among them is facing all those faces in mess. I hate going to mess for food. So at times I miss my food totally or else I finish it soon or leave the mess before the hostel friends join the mess.

Worker: Are you having the same relations since you joined hostel?

Client: No, initially I used to enjoy the company of my next door neighbour and classmate ("Y"). But gradually I find her cunning, selfish and opportunistic, so now I avoid meeting her.

Worker: Would you like to share any unpleasant episode with her (friend "Y").

Client: Last week, we both were in the same group for class presentation. I was absent the day groups were formed and individual member's responsibilities were distributed. In the evening she told me the topic of my presentation. I felt very bad as I was given a topic, which was totally irrelevant and which required a lot of exploration. She got a very clear-cut topic of presenting on all the models. At the dinner table I came to know that she also arranged for getting her Curriculum Vitae forwarded to the place where I wanted to do my internship. Our placement teacher also gives favours to her favourite students and she is one of them. I could not sleep the whole night. She is very opportunistic. I felt like leaving that group but then it was matter of marks. The whole evening I was feeling dizziness and severe headache.

Worker: How do you spend most of your time?

Client: I like either sitting in library or surfing Internet. In the evening I either listen to my favourite radio jockey if I am not having headache otherwise I go to bed.

The client visits her home at every weekend. The session scheduled in the next week was directed to know about her relationship with family members as she is just back from her house.

Worker: How was your weekend? Would you like to share?

Client: I went to my house.

Worker: So, you had a great time with your parents and siblings.

Client: Oh! No, gone are the days when I used to be crazy for visiting my home. Now none of them are welcoming to me and moreover they don't have time for me.

Worker: What happened this weekend? Would you like to share?

Client: While I was working on my brother's laptop he shouted at me for not handling that properly. I felt really bad and then I cried. I thought one should be financially independent. He is always very possessive about his things.

My mother is also very disturbing to me. Whenever I am at home, time and again, she asks me to help her out in the kitchen. When I am having headache, how can I help her? She does not like seeing me resting even if I am having severe headache. She rather comments, "I am making excuse". Last evening she scolded me badly before our guests just because I forgot to switch off the booster pump. This happened only because I was having severe headache otherwise I was not so forgetful. After this episode my headache became worse I had to go to bed.

Assessment and Tools

During the intake interview elements of conflict and adjustment problems with family members were observed. Her mother is very demanding and expects her to contribute to household chores whenever she visits her home. She is often condemned by her mother as "good for nothing". The client is also not able to make adjustment with her friends and developed negative attitude. She expects others to contribute in relationship whereas she herself is not making efforts towards the same. She has developed avoidance coping strategy in situations of threat and used projections in order to alleviate her anxiety.

Since the client was being followed by a physician for her headache problem for the last 10 months, her medical reports were obtained including the neurological records in order to rule out organic cause of her headache. Intake interview identified the following components of the problem:

- Consistent headache across her forehead or around the top of his head without any sign of nausea, vomiting promodal symptoms.
- Signs of anxiety and depressed mood.
- Low self-esteem.
- Negativity and impaired problem-solving abilities.

In case of single-subject research design, we follow the principle of triangulation, i.e., as a general rule of thumb, two or three indicators are generally considered appropriate. Triangulation does not mean that more than one indicator of the same target problem is to be measured (Rubin & Babbie, 1993).

Three standardized instruments, namely, Hamilton Anxiety Scale (HAS), Beck Depression Inventory (BDI), and

Rosenberg Self-Esteem Scale (RSES) were used to supplement the information collected through interview. These instruments were consciously selected firstly because of being short and brief; and secondly these can be easily administered in interview setting even after a short interval of time.

Hamilton Anxiety Scale (HAS): The Hamilton Anxiety Scale is a 14-item test measuring the severity of anxiety symptoms. It is also sometimes called the Hamilton Anxiety Rating Scale (HARS). The HAS is used to assess the severity of anxiety symptoms present in children and adults. It is administered by an interviewer who administers a semi-structured series of questions related to symptoms of anxiety. The interviewer then rates the individuals on a five-point scale for each of the 14 items. Seven of the items specifically address psychic anxiety and the remaining seven items address somatic anxiety. For the 14 items, the values on the scale range from zero to four: zero means that there is no anxiety, one indicates severe anxiety, and any four indicates very severe or grossly disabling anxiety. The total anxiety score ranges from 0 to 56.

Rosenberg Self-Esteem Scale (RSES): The scale is a 10-item Likert Scale with items answered on a four-point scale – from strongly agree to strongly disagree. The scores range from 0 to 30.

Beck Depression Inventory (BDI): The BDI is a self-report inventory. The scale consists of 21 items and measures the mood profile in the recent past (within last week). Each item is scored on a scale from 0 to 3 and the possible sum range from 0 to 63.

In order to collect daily information concerning headache activity the client was instructed to fill up the "Pain Assessment Form" daily for a week. It was used to examine the antecedent, behaviour and consequences factors regarding headache episode. This form was used to trace the situational factors, and what happens when client gets pain. The client was required to indicate when she had headache in what situation and how she behaved or thought in that situation.

To assess pain intensity the client was asked to rate her pain intensity on a five-point scale:

0 = No pain.
1 = Pain present, but can be ignored.
2 = Pain present with everyday activities.
3 = Pain present, cannot be ignored, interferes with concentration.
4 = Pain present, cannot be ignored, interferes with all tasks except taking care of basic needs (eating, toilet visits).
5 = Pain preset, cannot be ignored, rest or bed rest required.

Most of the time the client rated her pain intensity on '3', however once she rated it on '2' point.

Baseline Measurement

The scales (HAS, BDI, and RESE) were administered before the intervention till we got a consistent baseline. Scores obtained were recorded and presented in Table 1. In order to establish the baseline, the measurement of each instrument was repeated five times over a week period.

Description of Intervention

The therapeutic intervention was planned at three levels:

- Individual (client) level
- Family level
- Peer group level

Intervention at family level and with friends was necessary as elements of adjustment problems were observed in the family system as well as with friend circle.

Client Level

The specific treatment plan at the individual level (to the client) included two sessions per week for the first month, followed by a second month of only one meeting each week and two fortnightly sessions in the third month.

At the individual level a multimodal treatment package consisting of cognitive behaviour therapy and problem-solving skills was given to the client.

Cognitive-behavioural treatment: The most structured cognitive-behavioural treatment programme for headache has been described by Bakal (1981). The objectives of this programme are two-folds:

1. Education of patients in the psychobiology of headaches
2. Development of strategies to regulate headaches

The process of treatment is conducted in three phases, consisting of observation, education and acquisition of skills. The observation phase is for the collection of headache activity. In present case the data was collected through headache diary or pain assessment from ABC chart. During the education phase a rational of the problem identified through ABC chart and treatment process was presented to the client. During the last phase, client learns to change her behaviours or thoughts that facilitate headache. In the present case the client was helped to acquire such skills through cognitive procedures.

In the treatment of headache, cognitive procedures are used to train or educate the client in behaviours facilitating coping skills. As noted by Lake (1983) cognitive procedures emphasize more adaptive thinking patterns, including the recognition of connections between thought, emotion, behaviour and headache, as well as the identification of thoughts and assumptions that may trigger or sustain headache activity. Thus, as the same line, cognitive restructuring was used to modify maladaptive cognitions of the client which were creating problems in client's interpersonal relationship ties. Positive self-statements were also used to enhance the self-esteem of the client.

Development of new skills, e.g., communication skills, interpersonal skills and changes in "Type A" personality styles were planned through skill-building programmes during counselling session.

Stress management sessions were given to client in one to one setting. The client was also given training for progressive muscular relaxation (PMR) based on the principle of Dr. Jacobson. This exercise consists of instructions to tense then relax different muscle groups of the body.

Guided imagery and visualization techniques were also used for relaxation.

Problem-solving skills: The client was helped to enhance her problem-solving skills through activities designed around techniques like analogies, imaginary brainstorming, causal mapping, potential problem analysis and SWOT analysis.

- The causal mapping, also known as cognitive mapping, helps one create a structure for messy or complex data and hence something can be discussed and shared.
- Potential problems-solving: Its aim is to provide a challenging analysis of an idea being developed or an action plan so that one can determine ways in which it may go wrong.
- SWOT (Strength, Weakness, Opportunity and Threat) analysis: A successful technique for identifying one's strengths and weaknesses and study opportunities and threats one faces. The SWOT analysis requires one to write down answers to the following questions:
    1. *Strengths:* What do one do well? What are one's advantages? This has to be considered from one's own point of view and that of others. One has to be realistic but not modest, a list of one's characteristics are required to be added, some of these will be strengths.
    2. *Weaknesses:* What is done badly? What could be improved? What should be avoided? This has to be considered from internal and external perspectives: Is it possible for others to see weaknesses but I do not? Are my competitors doing better?
    3. *Opportunities:* What are the interesting trends? Where are the opportunities available to me?
    4. *Threats:* What obstacles do I face? How are my competitors fairing?

Family Level

Intervention at family level was directed to mobilize family as a support system for the client. Initially, two sessions were held with the mother in order to educate her about the nature of client's psychosomatic problem. Two home visits were also made whereby the client's interaction with family members was observed. To break the ice of being a stranger to the family, the worker made a point to take a meal with the family. This enabled the worker to develop a healthy rapport with the client and also provided an opportunity to observe the client in her natural setting. So, she used her skills of interpersonal relationship and confronted the client for her problematic behaviour and unrealistic expectations. The family members were also educated to minimize the stress inducing factors for the client so as to facilitate better adjustment of family system and reduce client's headache episode triggered through family conflict. An additional home visit was made for the follow up of the case.

Peer Group Level

The client has shared with the worker that she has one of her school friends (Mr. A) with whom she likes to share few things. Keeping the same resource in mind, he was approached with due consent of the client. A joint session was planned whereby Mr. A was requested to give caring and understanding approach to the client so that the client can share her feelings with him and the suppressed emotions can be brought out from time to time. The client was made clear about her roles and responsibilities in the relationship and a working contract was agreed among the worker, client and her friend to facilitate the healthy interpersonal relationship. The client was also encouraged to carry forward her relationship with her hostel mates in the same cooperative manner. She was encouraged to participate in the extra-curricular activities being organized in the hostel so as to enhance her acceptance by hostel mates.

Post-Intervention Measurement

After the completion of the intervention, the instruments (HAS, BDI and RSES) were administered again to the subject and the scores of the post-intervention measurement were recorded. To ensure the reliability of the information collected during post-intervention measurement, each instrument was administered and it was repeated on weekly basis. This was purposefully done to ensure that the change should be near permanent. The intervention in this particular phase was continued for a period of three to four months before administering the single-subject design.

Findings

The findings were derived using both quantitative and qualitative methods of assessment. The pain assessment form or ABC chart helped the client to identify the antecedents which were triggering the headache episodes. She could reflect on her behaviour and analyzed the consequences related to the same. A conscious reflection on such consequences helped the client to improve her maladaptive behaviour.

The scores of the pre-and post-intervention measures (as reflected in Table 2) showed an overall improvement in each dimension of the problem as stated in the assessment phase, i.e., anxiety, depression and poor self-esteem.

Table 1

Pre- and Post-Intervention Scores

Measurement	*HAS*		*BDI*		*RSES*	
	Pre	*Post*	*Pre*	*Post*	*Pre*	*Post*
1	25	16	26	10	12	18
2	29	15	27	9	14	18
3	28	17	28	11	13	20
4	29	15	27	10	13	20
5	29	16	27	10	12	19

Table 3 shows that with the introduction of therapeutic treatment the scores of Hamilton Anxiety Scale (HAS) and Beck Depression Inventory (BDI) were found to be on the declining trend which reflected a noticeable change. While the mean and standard deviation of the self-esteem scores increased reflecting the improvement in the self-esteem of the client.

Table 2

Analysis of Pre- and Post-Intervention Scores

Intervention	*N*	*Mean*	*SD*	*Min Value*	*Max*
HAS Pre	5	28	1.58	25	29
BDI Pre	5	27	0.63	26	28
RSES Pre	5	12.8	0.74	12	14
HAS Post	5	15.8	0.74	15	17
BDI Post	5	10.0	0.63	9	17
RSES Post	5	19.0	0.89	18	20

To know whether there is a significant difference in the means and standard deviations of scores in the pre– and post-intervention phase of the HAS, BDI and RESE, the Wilcoxon Test was done. This test was done keeping in view the assumption that the sample is drawn from population whose parameters are not known. The results are presented in Table 3.

Table 3

Wilcoxon Test Results

	HAS	*BDI*	*RSES*
Z	–2.032	–2.060	–2.060
P (Level of Significance)	0.042	0.032	0.039

Figure 1

HAS Score for Pre- and Post-Intervention Measures

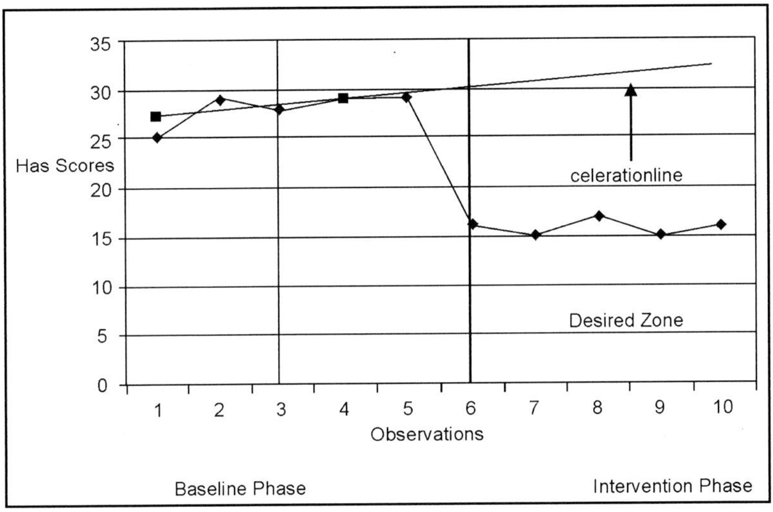

Figure 2

BDI Scores for Pre- and Post-Intervention Measures

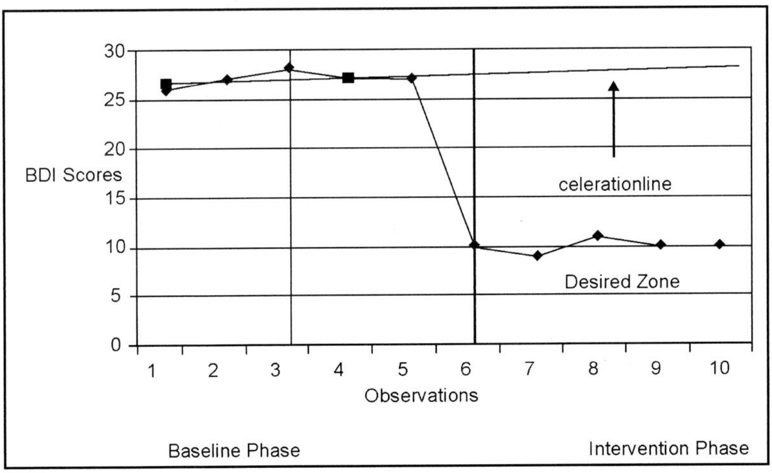

Figure 3

RSES Score for Pre- and Post-Intervention Measures

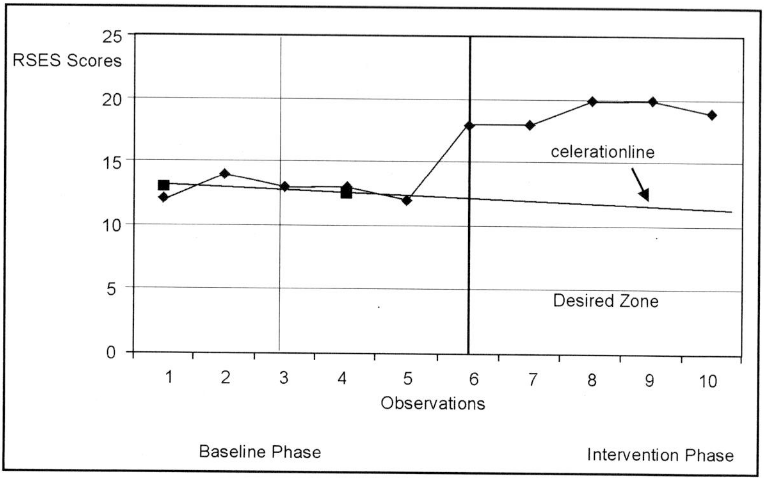

Results show that the differences between the pre- and post-intervention scores were statistically significant.

Further, to assess whether the intervention was statistically significant, Celeration Line Approach method was used. Celeration lines (Figures 1, 2 and 3) were drawn to take into account the specific direction in which the baseline data were moving, that is the slope or trend of the baseline in the determination of statistical significance (Lal Das, 2005). It was significant to note that all the scores after intervention were lying in the desired zone.

Discussion and Implication for Social Work Practice

The statistically significant results of the intervention suggest that the client showed the considerable improvement. It is clear from the findings that cognitive behavioural approach, coupled with problem-solving skills and applied in systems perspective, is the effective programme to deal with psychosomatic pain disorder (Tension-headache specifically). The findings also reflect that to get the effective results, we need to focus our intervention at different levels, where problematic elements were observed, e.g., in the present case intervention was directed at client level, family level and also at peers level. However, the findings of the study need to be considered in context of several methodological limitations. The study, being a single-subject research design, has limited generalizability. But, this is also true that it will be of great help to practitioners to apply the same intervention package with other such cases. It will also help them maintain data to evaluate practice with each client.

References

Adhoc Committee on Classification of Headache (1962): *Journal of American Medical Association*, Vol. 79, pp. 717-718.

Allpsychonline: Research methods – single subject design. Available at http://allpsych.com/researchmethods/singlesubjectconclusion.htm, surferd on June 3, 2006. American Psychiatric Association (1987): *Diagnostic and Statistical Manual of Mental Disorders – IV*, Washington, D.C.

Atlas, J.A., Wolfson, M.A. and Lipschitz, D.S. (1993): Dissociation and somatization in adolescent patients with and without history of abuse. *Psychological Reports*, Vol. 76, pp. 1101-1102.

Bakal, D.A., Demjen, S., and Kaganov, J.A. (1981): Cognitive behavioural treatment of chronic headache. *Headache*, Vol. 21, pp. 81-86.

Beck, A.T. (1973): *The Diagnosis and Management of Depression*. Philadelphia, University of Pennsylvania Press.

Bogardus, M.C. Moniek, M., and Ter, K.M. (1994): Treatment of recurrent tension type headache: a meta-analysis review. *Clinical Journal of Pain*, Vol. 21, pp. 174-190.

Carson, R.C., Butcher, J.M. and Mineka, S. (1995): *Abnormal Psychology and Modern Life*, 10th ed. New York, Harper Collins college Publishers.

Das Lal, D.K., (2001): *Practice of Social Research: Social Work Perspective*. Jaipur, Rawat Publications.

Das Lal, D.K., (2005): *Designs of Social Research*. Jaipur, Rawat Publications.

DeGray, et al. (1989): The families of patients with somatization disorder. *Family Medicine,* Vol. 21, pp. 438-442.

Encyclopedia of Britannica online: *Psychosomatic Disorder.* Available at http://www.britannica.com, surferd on June 10, 2006.

Foreyt, J.P. and Rathjen, D.P. (1978): *Cognitive Behaviour Therapy.* New York and London, Plenum Press.

Fritz, G.K., Fritson, S. and Hagine. O. (1997): Somatoform disorder in children and adolescents: A review of the past 10 years. *Journal of American Academy of Child and Adolescent Psychiatry,* Vol. 36, pp. 1329-338.

Hamilton, M. (1959): Hamilton anxiety rating scale. *British Journal of Medical Psychology,* Vol. 32, pp. 50-55.

Herson, M. and Bellack, A.S., (1985): *Handbook of Clinical Behaviour Therapy with Adults.* New York and London, Plenum Press.

Holden, W.E. and Deichmann, M.M. (1999): Empirically supported treatments in pediatric psychology: Recurrent Pediatric headache. *Journal of Pediatric Psychology,* Vol. 24, No. 2, pp. 91-109.

Honkasalo, M.L. et al. (1995): Migraine and concommitant symptoms among 8167 adult twin pairs. *Headache,* Vol. 35, pp. 70-78.

Jacobson, E. (1929): *Progressive Relaxation,* Chicago, University of Chicago.

Janosky, J.E. (2005): Use of the single subject design for practice based primary care research. *Journal of Postgraduate Medicine,* Vol. 81, pp. 549-551.

Jeanetta et al. (2005): Behavioural headache treatment: history review of the empirical literature and methodological critique. *Headache,* Vol. 45, p. 592.

Kazdin (1982): *Essential features of single subject designs.* Available at http://curry.edschool.virginia.edu/class/ed1f/733/acts/basics/essen tia l.html surfed on June 3, 2006.

Keable, D. (1997): *The Management of Anxiety: A Guide for Therapist.* New Delhi, B.I. Churchill Livingstone Pvt. Ltd.

Keller, M.B. (1985): Chronic and recurrent affective disorders: Incidence, course and influencing factors. *Advances in Bio-Chemical Psychopharmacology,* Vol. 40, pp 11-120.

Lake, A.E., (1983): Cognitive - behaviour therapy for headache: Assessment and treatment considerations. In J. R. Saper (ed.). *Headache Disorders,* pp. 233-251, Boston, John Wright.

Larsson, B., Bille, B., and Pederso, N.L. (1995): Genetic influence in headaches: A Swedish twin study. *Headache.* Vol. 35, pp. 513-519.

Maguire, A. (2002): *Clinical Social Work.* USA, Brooks/Cole Publishing Co. Ltd.

Martin, P.R., Milech, D., and Nathan, P.R. (1993): Towards a functional model of chronic headaches: Investigating of antecedents and consequences. *Headache,* Vol. 33, pp. 461-470.

Polmer, T.M. and Scher, M.S. (2001): Treatment of functional impairment in severe somatoform pain disorder: A case example. *Journal of Pediatric Psychology,* Vol. 26, No. 7, pp. 429-434.

Rosenberg, M. (1965): *Rosenberg Self-esteem Scale.* The Morris Rosenberg Foundation, University of Maryland.

Rubin, A. and Babbie, E. (1993): *Research Methodology for Social Work.* California, Brooks/Cole Publishing Company.

Scheller, J.M. (1995): The history, epidemiology and classification of headaches in childhood. *Seminars in Pediatric Neurology,* Vol. 2, pp. 101-108.

Schram, S. (2001): *Research and Evaluation for Social Work Practice.* Avaolable http://www.brynmawr.edu/Acads/GSSW/schram/sw132firsex.html, surfed on May 3, 2006.

Wasson, J.B. (2003): *Single Subject Design.* Available at http://www.practicalpress.net/updatenovo5/singlesubject.html surfed on June 6, 2006.

WHO (2004): *Headache Disorders.* Available at http://.who.int/mediacentre/factsheets/fs277/en, surfed on May 3, 2006.

4

Clinical Social Work Research Process

Anna Mathew

The clinical research process is not a radically new approach to intervention. Many researchers in the 19th century and early 20th century, such as Hermann Ebbinghaus and Ivan Pavlov, utilized data on individuals collected repeatedly across time as the basis for their research. Skinner (1938) outlined his Operant Theory of Behaviourism based on this model of inquiry (Feldman, 1985). This actually laid the foundation for many subsequent single subject writings. In fact, there are many parallels between this model and traditional practice.

This model injects greater specificity, objectivity and empiricism into the clinical process. By following the model, researchers are in a position to know precisely what treatment was applied and how much effect was produced and to have supporting data for proof. The model links research and practice by putting the researcher in an enviable position of not only bringing about change but also having valid evidence as to why the change occurred.

The process of clinical social work research is described below citing a clinical research study conducted by the author.

Identification and Assessment of the Problem

As in all practice approaches, the clinical research models began with the identification of the problem. Subsequently, the assessment of the client's problem was made. Typically, the problem involved some aspect of the client's functioning behaviour, perceptions, attitudes or feelings. During this stage, the practitioner strived to obtain as clear and specific an understanding of the problem as possible, using assessment strategies such as interviewing or paper and pencil assessment tools such as a brief scale commonly used by practitioners. To decide the specific indicator of a particular problem, the practitioner relied on the client's complaints of a particular problem, which were as follows:

- Observation of the extent of the client's expressed difficulty or dissatisfaction with the problem.
- Negative and positive indicators. Positive indicator representing the absence of the problem. Negative indicator signified the presence of the problem.
- Operational indicator occurred frequently were measured on a regular basis. There was no strict rule concerning how many operational indicators one should measure. The fewer one measures, the greater the risk of failing to detect client improvement.
- As a general rule of thumb two to three indicators were generally considered to be appropriate. It meets the criterion of triangulation (Rubin and Babbie,1993: 302-3) – it meant more than one indicator of the same target problem. For the case illustration of suicide attempt, depression, low self-esteem, feelings of hopelessness and uselessness, and sense of despair in the client were indicators of the crisis.

A theoretical framework was thus envisaged. For a case illustration of a problem related to attempting suicide, the various theories of suicide were examined. These were psychoanalytical theory (Freud, 1949; Menninger, 1938), behavioural theory (Stillion and others, 1989; Paulson and Stone, 1974) and cognitive behavioural theory (Fareberow and Shneidman, 1961). Hypothetical propositions were drawn out of these theories.

Review of Literature

From a review of several studies and literature (Beck, 1967; Berman and Carroll, 1984; American Psychiatric Association, 1987) the indicators that signified the presence of the problem of attempted suicide were found to be:

- signs of depression and low self-esteem;
- feelings of hopelessness and uselessness;
- engaging in and de-emphasizing what is positive; and
- impaired problem-solving techniques.

Beck's Depression Inventory (BDI), Global Assessment of Functioning (GAF)and Hudson's Self-Esteem Scale (SES) were used to measure the indicators of the target problem. These instruments were used in conjunction with converging information from interviews, direct observations and collateral others.

Study Design

The study was carried out using a single-subject design. Such designs involve obtaining repeated measures of the client with regard to particular outcome indicators of the target problem before and after the intervention is introduced to see if there is improvement in the target problem. The repeated measures before intervention is called the baseline, which serves the same function as control groups do in experiments. The data collected during the baseline are compared to the data collected after the intervention in order to infer that an intervention is effective. Among several single-subject designs, Multiple Component Design was found to be most appropriate for the study.

Establishment of the Baseline

The instruments (BDI, GAF and SES) were administered to the subject and the total scores obtained by the client were recorded. To establish the baseline, the measurement of each instrument was repeated seven times with a one-week interval between the readings and also between the administration of each instrument to assess the stable pattern of no constant change in the target problem. Table 1 shows the obtained score range of the baseline for BDI:30 to 44, GAF:41 to 20 and SES:80 to 98.

Table 1

Pre-Intervention Scores of BDI, GAF and SES

Observations	*BDI*	*GAF*	*SES*
First	30.00	41.00	80.00
Second	37.00	30.00	85.00
Third	30.00	25.00	89.00
Fourth	34.00	25.00	92.00
Fifth	44.00	25.00	92.00
Sixth	44.00	25.00	92.00
Seventh	44.00	20.00	98.00

- The phase of repeated measures that occurs before intervention (through standardized tools like scales on Depression, General Assessment of Functioning and Self-Esteem).
- They served the same function as control/comparison groups as in group experiment.
- A stable pattern of no constant change in the target problem.
- The ideal number of baseline measurement points needed varied depending on how soon a stable trend appeared.
- It is reasonable to plan for somewhere between 7-15 baseline measures.

- These baseline measurements are used as a basis from which to compare the individual behaviour/condition after the intervention is introduced.
- By comparing measurements after intervention with those of the baseline period, the researcher can trace the effects of the intervention.

Intervention

The objective of the study was to assess the effectiveness of an intervention package in dealing with suicidal tendencies accompanied by the prevalence of suicidal ideation in a young adult studying in an educational institution. The study conducted evaluated the effectiveness of social work intervention on the case of attempted suicide expressing chronic depression with low self-esteem and impaired general functioning.

An intervention package, consisting of crisis intervention, cognitive therapy and problem-solving skills, was designed to bring improvement in the target problem.

Engaging the individual meaningfully and purposefully began at this stage. The individual made the important decision of whether to enter into treatment (Skidmore and Thackeray, 1988). The initial contacts should be constructive and not diminishing experiences if the decision of the client was to be made to accept the service. The worker's attitude was an important controlling factor in what the client decided (Golan, 1986). Respect for the worth and dignity of the client and his or her right to self-determination were communicated by using the skill of responsiveness and listening to the problem stated by the individual (Hollis and Woods, 1981).

Guided by social work values in this stage of the process, the worker developed a helping relationship.

Post-intervention Measurement

After the completion of the intervention, the instruments (BDI, GAF and SES) were administered again to the subject and the total scores of the post-intervention measurement were obtained and recorded. To establish the post-intervention measurement, each instrument was administered seven times with one-week interval between the readings and one-day interval between the administration of each instrument to assess the improvement in the target problem. The range of the post-intervention scores obtained were for BDI 35 to 10, for GAF 40 to 82 and for SES 87 to 35.

Findings

Table 1 shows an overall difference in the pre- and post-intervention scores of each instrument. These findings reflect the efficacy of intervention in reducing depression, enhancing the general functioning and the self esteem of the client. Analyzing the pattern during the pre- intervention level separately for depression reveals that the scores had steadily increased till they remained stable in the last three measures. This indicates the intensity of the problem of depression that existed in the client before the intervention was introduced. Such was the trend found in GAF and SES also.

Table 2

Post-intervention Scores of BDI, GAF and SES

Observations	*BDI*	*GAF*	*SES*
First	35.00	40.00	87.00
Second	25.00	51.00	76.00
Third	20.00	62.00	69.00
Fourth	17.00	75.00	63.00
Fifth	16.00	80.00	57.00
Sixth	12.00	80.00	50.00
Seventh	10.00	82.00	35.00

Data in Table 3 show that with the introduction of the intervention, the mean and standard deviations of scores of the BDI and SES instruments had decreased while the scores of GAF as expected had increased.

Table 3

Analysis of Pre- and Post-intervention Scores of BDI, GAF and SES

Intervention	*N*	*Mean*	*Std. Deviation*	*Minimum*	*Maximum*
BDI-Pre	7	37.57	6.47	30.00	44.00
GAF-Pre	7	27.28	6.70	20.00	41.00
SES-Pre	7	89.71	5.79	80.00	98.00
BDI-Post	7	19.28	8.51	10.00	35.00
GAF-Post	7	67.14	16.51	40.00	82.00
SES-Post	7	62.42	17.16	35.00	87.00

To know whether there is a significant difference in the means and standard deviations of scores in the pre- and post-intervention of the GAF, BDI and SES, the Wilcoxon Sign Test was used. The results show that the difference between the pre- and post-intervention scores were statistically significant (BDI: 2.197, p. < .05; GAF: 2.201, p. < .05; SES: 2.197, p. < .05).

Further, to assess whether the intervention was statistically significant the Celeration Line Approach method was used. Celeration lines (Figures 1, 2 and 3) were drawn to take into account the specific direction in which the baseline data were moving, that is, the slope or trend of the baseline in the determination of statistical significance (Rubin and Babbie, 1993:520).

Figure 1

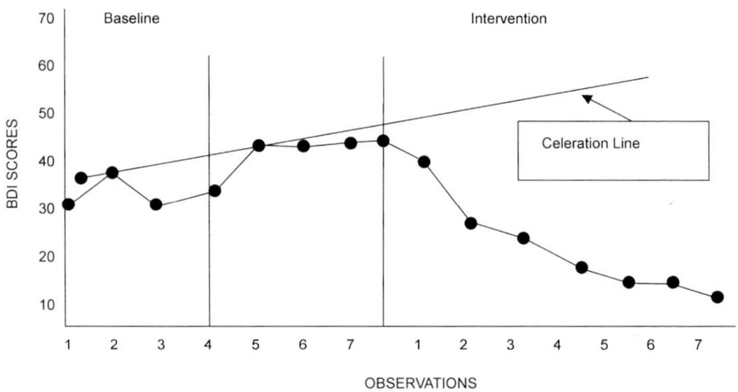

Figure 2

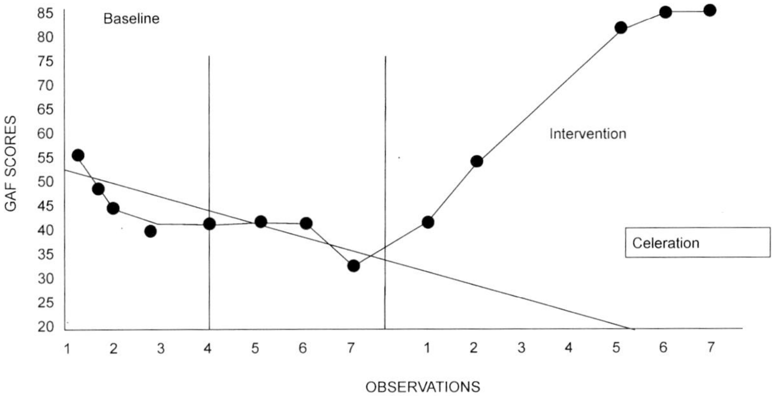

Figure 3

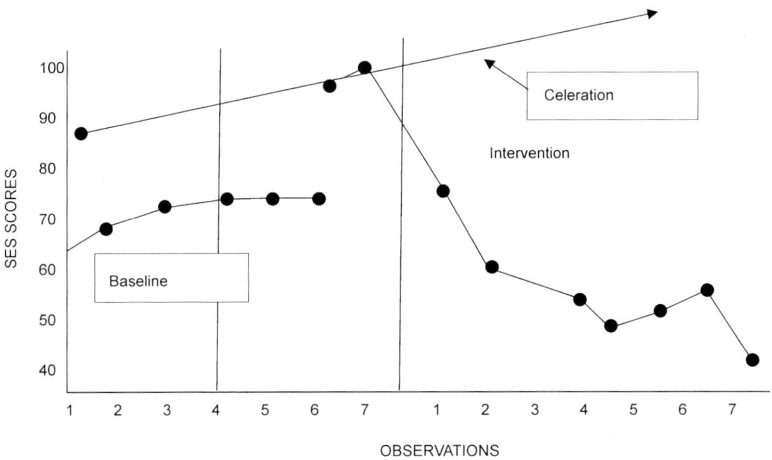

To test whether the effectiveness of interventions was statistically significant, we refer to the statistical table showing the number of observations during the intervention period that are necessary to represent a significant increase at the 0.05 level over the proportion of observations during the baseline period

(Rubin and Babbie, 1993: 520). Data show that the number of observations during the intervention periods are 8, 7 and 7 for BDI, GAF and SES respectively. All the numbers are more than the critical number 3 (Rubin and Babbie, 1993: 520). Hence, it can be inferred that the effectiveness of intervention was statistically significant.

Discussions and Implication for Social Work Practice

The statistically significant results of the intervention suggest that the client showed considerable amount of improvement in his condition. The results also showed that a focused cognitive approach, coupled with social work counselling, is an intervention package for effectively addressing and alleviating the problems of suicide attempters.

The study used both quantitative and qualitative measures to analyze the outcome of a combined intervention approach. The Multiple Component Design had a significant role to play. It was basically used to evaluate the impact of changes in the intervention.

It was sought to determine which intervention was really responsible for the improvement of the target problem. From the Celeration Line Approach, it can be inferred that cognitive therapy appeared to be most effective in reducing the suicidal ideation and depression in the client.

The Multiple Component Design typically resembled the way intervention would naturally be implemented. The client could not be helped with numerous problems simultaneously, but repeated measures of the relevant behaviours could be seen and observed when they changed. The predictable and orderly changes related to where and when the intervention was used, were seen and concluded that the intervention was causing the change.

Visual significance was ascertained by eyeballing the data pattern to the extent that we could see the shifts in the level or trend of the target problem coinciding with the introduction of the intervention (Rubin and Babbie, 1993: 323-24).

The results of the study need to be considered in the context of several methodological limitations. This study, being a single-subject design study, has limited generalizations. As such, the generalizability of these findings to other populations may be limited. However, the study can be replicated using the same design and intervention package for a similar condition. It may help social work practitioners to understand the importance of maintaining outcome data on an ongoing basis to evaluate practice with each client. The intervention described in the study may also be an efficient mechanism for social workers working in crisis management centres.

Above all, the study also indicates that it is essentially important to understand that social work research and practice are complementary and social work intervention research is complete only when it is integrated into practice.

References

American Psychiatric Association (1987), *Diagnostic and Statistical Manual of Mental Disorders* (Revised Edition 3), Washington, D.C.

Beck, A. (1967), *Depression: Clinical, Experimental and Theoretical Aspects*, New York: Hoeber, pp. 50-51.

Berman, A. and Carroll, T. (1984), *Adolescent Suicide: A Critical Review Death Education*, 8, in M. Stillion, E. McDowell and H. May (eds.), *Suicide Across the Life Span, Premature Exits*, New York: Hemisphere Publishers, pp. 97-98.

Fareberow, N.L. (1961), *The Cry for Help*, New York: McGraw Hill Book Co.?

Feldman, R.S. (1985), *Social Psychology*, New York: McGraw Hill Book Co.

Freud, S. (1949), *An Outline of Psychoanalysis*, New York: Norton.

Golan, N. (1986), *Crisis Theory*, in Turner's, *Social Work Treatment* (3rd ed.) *Interlocking Theoretical Approaches*, New York: The Free Press, pp. 303-317.

Hollis, F. and Woods, M. (1979), *Case Work: A Psychosocial Therapy*, in *Social Work Treatment: Interlocking Theoretical Approaches* (3rd ed.), New York: Random House, p. 323.

Hudson, W. (1982), *The Clinical Measurement Package: A Field Manual*, Belmont, C.A.: Dorsey.

Menninger, K. (1938), *Man against Himself*, New York: Harcourt, Brace and Company, pp. 24-25.

Paulson, J. and Stone, D. (1974), Suicidal Behaviours of latency-age children, *Journal of Clinical Child Psychology*, pp. 350-53.

Rubin, A. and Babbie E. (1993), *Research Methods for Social Work*, California.

Skidmore, R. and Thackeray, M. (1988), *Introduction to Social Work*, New Jersey: Prentice Hall, p. 58.

Stillion, M., McDowell, E. and May, H. (1989), *Suicide Across the Life Span, Premature Exits*, New York: Hemisphere Publishers.

5

Effect of Value Clarification on Orientation towards Vision and Values

Kalpana Sampath

Social work researchers have eluded experimental studies in general and true experiments in particular due to its complexity. True experimental designs have maximum control and hence highest degree of internal validity. The essential components of an experimental research design involve (a) random assignments of subjects to experimental and control groups, (b) introducing the stimulus (independent variable) to the experimental group while withholding it from the control group, and (c) comparing the amount of change in dependent variable in experimental and control groups.

True experimental designs use the process of randomization and matching to control the validity threats that can lead to false causal inferences. In this research design most of the threats to internal and external validity (history, maturation, etc.) are controlled.

True experimental researches are designed for testing causal relationships. A causal relationship refers to relationship between two variables where one variable (characteristic or occurrence) X determines another variable (characteristic or occurrence) Y.

A study was undertaken by the author to test a causal relationship that value clarification (X) causes change in orientation towards vision and values (Y) by comparing a group of students who have been exposed to values clarification process (X) with one that has not been exposed, we have to measure the two groups with respect of Y, after exposure to X.

This paper reports the study and attempts to assess the impact of value clarification as a process to enhance the level of orientation towards vision and values amongst students of management. The findings indicate significant changes in the experimental group in orientation towards vision and values.

Research Methodology

Research Design

In order to ascertain the impact of values clarification process (intervention) on orientation towards value and vision this study was conducted using Pre-Post Two Groups True Experimental Research Design (Rubin and Babbie, 2001). In this design subjects are matched and randomly assigned to the experimental (intervention) group (E) or to a no intervention control group (C). The experimental design was easier to adopt due to the admission policy being controlled in the institution. The research design of this study can be illustrated as follows:

E ⟶ R+M ⟶ Y_1 ⟶ X ⟶ Y_2

C ⟶ R+M ⟶ Y'_1 ⟶ Non-X ⟶ Y'_2

E ⟶ Experimental Group
C ⟶ Comparison Group
R ⟶ Random Assignments
M ⟶ Matched Groups
X ⟶ Value Clarification Workshop
Y_1 ⟶ Pre-Test Clarity on Vision-Value Scores for E Group

Y_2 ⟶ Post-Test Clarity on Vision-Value Scores for E Group

Y'_1 ⟶ Pre-Test Clarity on Vision-Value Scores for C Group

Y'_2 ⟶ Post-Test Clarity on Vision-Value Scores for C Group

Sampling

The study was conducted in a business school of Bangalore city. There were 48 students enrolled for MBA, who were divided into two groups — control and experimental — by simple random selection using student roll numbers, matched by age, gender and past educational qualification to maintain the variables. Out of the 24 subjects of the experimental group, five dropped out of the programme due to ill-health, marriage and job offer. One met with death. Consequently, five equivalent subjects were dropped from the comparison group. Hence, the sample of this study consists of 38 students. On average subjects in experimental and control groups were 22 years of age. The subjects were matched by gender and level of education. The personal characteristics of subjects in experimental group (E) and control group (C) are presented in Table 1.

Table 1

Personal Characteristics of the Subjects

Criteria	*Experimental Group (E)*	*Control Group (C)*
Age	Mean = 22.42 yrs	Mean =22.09
	S.D. = 1.57 yrs	S.D. = 1.07
Gender	Male = 8 (42.1%)	Male = 8 (42.1%)
	Female = 11 (57.9%)	Female = 11 (57.9%)
Education	B.A.= 2 members	B.A.= 2 members
	B.Sc. = 5 members	B.Sc. = 5 members
	B.B.M. = 3 members	B.B.M. = 3 members
	B.Com = 9 members	B.Com = 9 members

Measurement Instruments Used

Vision-Values Instrument (Version-2)

The instrument, Vision-Values Instrument (Version-2), developed by J.M. Sampath,[1] has been used in this study to measure the change in the ethical behaviour of students. In developing the instrument the author has used the method of Summated Rating Scales developed by Rensis Likert (1932). The instrument is built on the premise that excellence springs from the ability to be aligned in one's vision and values. To test the reliability of the instrument Split-Half (Spearman-Brown and Guttman) coefficients were calculated, and the results are given in Table 2.

Table 2

Reliability Index of Vision-Values Instrument

Tests Used	*Reliability Index*	
	Clarity on Vision	*Clarity on Value*
Spearman-Brown Split-Half	0.7412	0.8055
Guttman Split-Half	0.7212	0.8055

The face validity of the instrument appears to be fairly high, as only those items for which there was a high degree of agreement between the author (who has been assessing the clarity on values for last 15 years), executives and research experts have been selected. Further, content and face validity were established by the author using the method of known groups validated against ratings by self and others. This has given high consensual validity to the instrument. The uniqueness of the instrument is the ability to assess the extent of clarity on vision and values covering various dimensions. While administering the instrument the subjects are asked to respond to each of the statements on a seven-point scale. The responses to various items are scored and total scores of each subject are computed. The total scores depict the extent of clarity on vision and values.

Value Profile Instrument

The instrument has been used as a part of the values clarification process to evaluate an individual on five critical dimensions, namely, freedom (achievement orientation), relationship (sociability orientation), power and influence (leadership orientation), learning (learning orientation) and honesty (integrity orientation). The instrument is built on the premise that "no single value by itself is valuable. Values are interdependent. One needs to understand this interdependence to understand one's own behaviour". This is a 30-item instrument using a nine-point scale. The uniqueness of the tool is the ability to arrive at interdependence in five dimensions after converting the points obtained through rating scale into quantitative measures. The reliability coefficients of the instrument and the sub-scales are given in Table 3 and 4 respectively.

Table 3

Reliability Index of Value Profile Instrument

Tests Used	*Reliability Index*	
	Self	*Others*
Correlation between forms	0.8256	0.9163
Equal length Spearman Brown	0.9045	0.9563
Unequal length Spearman Brown	0.9045	0.9563
Guttman Split-half	0.9026	0.9554

Table 4

Reliability Index of The Sub-scales

Sub-scales	*Reliability Index*	
	Alpha	*Split-half*
Achievement orientation	0.9156	0.9161
Sociability orientation	0.7606	0.8502
Leadership orientation	0.8217	0.8090
Learning orientation	0.8970	0.8457
Integrity orientation	0.5575	0.7566

Development of the Intervention Strategy

For this study values are defined as those "beliefs that one holds within oneself, which governs one's behaviour in any given context". Therefore, clarification of values is focused on understanding one's beliefs and their implication in the real-life context. Our beliefs are formed based on what we have learnt over the years predominantly from experiences, education, family, society and religion. An individual is not all the time aware of why he/she behaves the way he/she does, though he/she is actually governed by his/her own beliefs.

Values clarification is a process that provides insights to an individual into why one behaves the way one does and what are the implications of the same. It allows the individual to recognize that his/her behaviour is an outcome of the beliefs he/she holds. When an individual is not comfortable with his/her own behaviour, values clarification facilitates discovering the beliefs that cause the behaviour and modify the same to achieve the behaviour as desired by the individual. The values clarification process enhances clarity, thereby causing a change arising out of realization than out of control or conformity or preaching.

Values clarification provides clarity on choices, their implications and the beliefs that govern them. It allows for change without waiting for events to bring in the change.

The role of values is based on the leadership development module that proposes organizations need to have three critical pillars, viz, values, vision and learning culture, to excel. The basic competencies that connect these pillars are innovation, farsightedness, focus, clarity, conviction and alignment. The outcomes would be value-addition, quality and leadership evolution (Sampath, 2003).

While values relate to process, vision relates to purpose and values clarification should enable the students to align their vision and values. Vision without values is risky; values without vision go nowhere; values with vision are evolution. Vision provides the direction while values provide the path of the journey. An effective methodology in teaching business ethics should include clarity on vision and values.

Pre-intervention Score

The Vision Value Instrument and Value profile Instrument were administered to the entire class to collect data on students orientation towards vision and values and their value profile before intervention.

The t-test results on the pre-intervention scores on the clarity of vision-value of both the groups showed vision 0.864 and values 0.853, which indicated that there was no significant difference in their orientation before the intervention.

Intervention

The entire intervention was split into two phases, viz., 'Alignment of Vision and Values' and 'Integration through Learning for Nurturing Excellence'. There was a time gap of one month in between the phases. In the intervening time the students worked on their identified areas of concern in their value profile. This was done by enabling them in the workshop to learn on identifying their restrictive beliefs and formulate modified facilitative beliefs.

Phase 1: Alignment of Vision and Values

A four-day workshop with the following objectives:

- To understand the importance of vision and values.
- To understand the need to be a high vision-high values individual.
- To understand what values are and learn how to work with causes than effects to bring about deep change.

- To understand one's orientation towards freedom, relationship, power and influence, learning, honesty and integrity.
- To gain clarity on one's own style of functioning and its implication in the context of organization and life.
- To understand the paradigms one is living by and gain clarity on the need to make shift in the same.
- To understand what prevents one from changing.
- To understand the ability to risk and accept challenges.
- To understand the source of conflict and learning how to deal with it.

Phase 2: Learning for Nurturing Excellence

This module focuses to build the capability of "learning to learn" in students. The objectives of the workshop were:

- To understand the business context and see the implications of one's own frame of reference.
- To understand how competition is handled in most competitive context.
- To understand learning and learn how to learn a skill critical for every leader today.
- To understand what it means to learn to learn.
- To gain clarity on the process of learning.
- To understand the distinction between mindless and mindful learning.
- To facilitate the movement from being a knowledgeable person to a wise person.
- To understand the need for a continuous clarification process to orient towards ethical leadership.

While Phase 1 enables the students to understand the process to align their vision and values, the Phase 2 helps them to be learners to keep the process of clarification ongoing.

The methodology of the workshop allows human processes to emerge. It is interspersed with small and large group activities, simulated exercises, reflection processes and lectures. Small group activities and individual reflection are designed to enable the students to look into their own self and realize the need for change. There is a flow in the whole structure and various events that happen during the course of the workshop are guided by this underlying structure.

Research Findings

The results of the pre-intervention scores analysis of the vision and values are presented in Table 5 and the results of the post-intervention scores analysis are presented in Table 6. The results of both pre and post analyses are given in Table 7.

Table 5

Score Analysis of Pre-intervention Clarity on Vision-Values

Pre-interven-tion Scores	*Experimental Group (E)*				*Control Group (C)*			
	Min	*Max*	*Mean*	*S.D.*	*Min*	*Max*	*Mean*	*S.D.*
Clarity on vision	169(38)	232(266)	195.95	15.15	151 (38)	231 (266)	196.37	20.47
Clarity on values	103(27)	139(189)	128.68	9.94	104 (27)	147 (189)	129.00	10.23

Table 6

Score Analysis of Post-intervention Clarity on Vision-Values

Post-interven-tion Scores	*Experimental Group (E)*				*Control Group (C)*			
	Min	*Max*	*Mean*	*S.D.*	*Min*	*Max*	*Mean*	*S.D.*
Clarity on vision	183(38)	239(266)	210.16	14.06	168 (38)	237 (266)	194.11	15.80
Clarity on values	114(27)	159(189)	140.89	9.95	114 (27)	148 (189)	131.79	8.00

Table 7

Score Analysis of Pre and Post Analysis of Value Profile

Groups	*Mean*	*S.D*	*df.*	*P*	*Significance*
Group E	–19.21	24.5	18	–003	Significant
Group C	2.50	22.7	18	0.637	Not-Significant

Effect of the Value Clarification Process

The main objective of the study was to the impact of values clarification as a process to enhance the level of orientation towards vision and values amongst students. It is evident from the results that there is a significant difference in the pre- and post-intervention clarity on vision-values scores. However, to know whether the difference is statically significant, t-test statistics was used. The results of the tests are presented in Table 8.

Table 8

T-Test Results of Pre-Post Intervention Clarity on Vision-Values Scores

S. No		Experimental Group (E)				Control Group (C)			
		t-Value	*df.*	*P*	*Significance*	*t-Value*	*df.*	*P*	*Significance*
1.	Pre-intervention and post-intervention clarity on vision scores	3.626	18	.002	Significant	.760	18	.457	Not Significant
2.	Pre-intervention and post-intervention clarity on values scores	5.010	18	.000	Significant	1.789	18	.09	Not significant

Results show that pre-intervention clarity on vision-values scores and post-intervention clarity on vision-values scores of the experimental group differ significantly, while the difference in the scores of the control group was statistically insignificant. In a study like this, it is important to probe the extent of impact of the values clarification process. Table 8, further shows the extent of impact on the clarity on vision-values. Analysis of scores on clarity on vision before intervention shows that on average the experimental group obtained a score of 196, which is 74 per cent of the maximum theoretical scores. After the intervention the scores moved up to a little over 210, that is, 81 per cent of the maximum theoretical scores. In case of clarity on values, the subjects obtained on average a score of nearly 129, which nearly 68 per cent of the maximum theoretical scores before the intervention and 141, which almost 75 per cent of the maximum theoretical scores after intervention. Therefore, it may be concluded that, comparatively, the extent of impact of values clarification process is higher on clarity of vision than the clarity on values.

The impact also differed by personal characteristics; for example, it was found that there was a significant difference in the impact on clarity on vision-values by age ($t=2.521$, df. $=17$, $p=.022$), comparatively, the extent of impact was higher on older subjects than younger ones. There was no significant difference in the impact on clarity on vision-values by gender or level of education of the subjects. This enhances the module usability.

Conclusion

The study confirms that the values clarification process has a significant impact on enhancing the value profile of the students. When students have clarity, their decisions and their ability to deal with conflicts are better. Values clarification enables them to understand their beliefs, resulting in changes at a causal level.

The study has a significant relevance to human resource development. The quality of human resource depends on its ability to bring synergy and optimize the available resources. Leadership in the corporate world can be simplified as the ability to make appropriate choices under constraints to achieve organizational goals. Values clarification, as a process, believes in enhancing the quality of decisions leaders can make under constraints and build an organization that will last.

The study also highlights the possibility of true experimental design in the behavioural science context. The process of research needs to have the vigour of constant follow-up and close monitoring to obtain the same subjects in the pre- and post-intervention data collections. It also requires extensive planning with the coordinators to ensure that the intervention methodology is well understood. Experimental research provides higher clarity on the findings and is more objective in the interpretation of the findings.

Notes

1. This Instrument is available with Arpitha Associates Pvt Ltd. 302, II Floor, Santoj Cottage, 107, Surveyor Street, Basavanagudi, Bangalore 560019. E-mail: info@arpitha.com

References

Brookfield, S.D. (1995). *Becoming a Critically Reflective Teacher*. San Francisco: Jossey-Bass.

Collins, J.C., and Porras, J.I. (1994). *Build to Last: Successful Habits of Visionary Companies*. New York: Harper Business.

Crainer S. and Dearlove D. (1998). *Gravy Training: Inside the Shadowy World of Business Schools*. Capstone, p. 260.

Crain, W.C. (1985). *Theories of Development*. Prentice-Hall., pp. 118-136.

Durkheim, E. (1925). "Education morale". Paris: Alcan.

Explored Through Five Perspectives. A. Monograph for ERIC – Clearinghouse on Adult, Career and Vocational Education. (ERIC order no: IN 385).

Fenwick, T.J., (2001). *Experiential Learning: A Theoretical Critique*.

Friedman, D. (2003, February 21). Has business ethics teaching and research had any discernible impact on business practice in the US and around the world? Transcription of a debate and discussion held at Santa Clara University. Retrieved 9/6/2004 from www.scu.edu/ethics/publications/submitted/debate/-

Gentile, M. (2003, February 21). Has business ethics teaching and research had any discernible impact on business practice in the US and around the world? Transcription of a debate and discussion held at Santa Clara University. Retrieved 9/6/2004 from www.scu.edu/ethics/publications/submitted/debate/-

Gilligan, C. (1989). *In a Different Voice: Psychological Theory and Women's Development*. Cambridge: Harvard University Press.

Harmin, R.L. and Simon, S.B. (1966). *Values and Teaching*. Columbus, Ohio: Charles, E. Merrill.

Harmin, M. Kirschenbann, H. and Simon, S.B. (1973). *Clarifying Values Through Subject Matter*. Minneapolis: Winston Press.

Howard R. (1990). Values make the company: An interview with Robert Haas. *Harvard Business Review*, September-October, pp. 133-144.

Kohlberg, L. and Turiel, E. (1971). Moral development and moral education. In G. Lesser (ed.), *Psychology and Educational Practice*. Scott Foresman.

Lal Das, D.K. (2005). *Designs of Social Research*. India, Jaipur: Rawat publications.

Machan, Tibor R. (1991). *Teaching Business Ethics in an Environment of Mistrust*. The Freeman: Ideas on Liberty.

Murphy, Patrick E. (1995). Corporate Ethics Statements: Current status and future prospects, *Journal of Business Ethics*, 14, pp. 727-740.

Murray, Mary Elizabeth & Nucci, Larry. An overview of Moral Development and Moral Education. Retrieved 11/11/2004 from http://tigger.uic.edu/~lnucci/MoralEd/overview.html

Paine, Lynn, S. (2003). *The Value Shift*. New York: Tata Mc Graw-Hill. pp. 23-27.

Piaget, J. (1965). *The Moral Judgement of the Child*. New York: The Free Press.

Rokeach M. (1973). *The Nature of Human Values*. San Francisco: Jossey-Bass.

Rubin, Allen and Babbie, E. (1989). *Research Methodology for Social Work*. Belmohf, California: Wadsworth.

— (2001). *Research Methods for Social Work*. California: Wadsworth.

Sampath J.M. (1999). A sociological study of values clarification process in the development of organization culture. Unpublished doctoral dissertation, Gujarat University.

— (2004). *Inner Realities: Notes from the School of Life*. Bangalore, India: Insight Publishers. p. 160.

Schon, D.A. (1983). *The Reflective Practitioner*. New York: Basic Books.

Singer, Paul. (2002, August 16). Business Schools add ethics in wake of corporate scandals. Associated Press state and local wire. Retrieved 10/6/2004 from www.kellogg.northwestern.edu/news/hits/020816ap.htm

Velasquez, Manuel. (2003, February 21). Has business ethics teaching and Research had any discernible impact on business practice in the US and around the world? Transcription of a debate and discussion held at Santa Clara University. Retrieved 9/6/2004 from www.scu.edu/ethics/publications/submitted/debate/-

Weisman, Robert. (2003, December 30). Harvard raises its hand on ethics. 1st year MBA students must take new course. Retrieved 9/6/2004 from www.boston.com/business/globe/articles/2003/12/30/harvard_raises_its_hand_on_ethics? mode=PF

Zapata, G. Roberto. An Evaluation of Cognitive Development and Moral Education. Retrieved 11/1104 from http://www.crvp.org/book/series05/V-4/ chapter_xiv.htm

6

Impact of Child Mental Health Orientation on School Teachers

Mary Venus Joseph

Experiments in social sciences have been effectively used as a method of evaluating the effectiveness of an intervention strategy by many researchers. In the present paper the quasi-experimental research design is discussed in detail with its advantages and limitations. The author shares her experience of the intervention research used in the training of school teachers in child mental health in the state of Kerala. The author concludes by pointing out the need for extensive need for family intervention programmes leading to family research and family policy in India.

Experiments have always been used in everyday life. This everyday method was adopted and improved by physical scientists and it became the standard method of discovery of knowledge. From the physical sciences experiments moved to psychology, where they are still utilized today. They were introduced by Wilhelm Wundt (1832-1920), a German psychologist. Although experimentation is more common in psychology than in other social sciences, it is currently used by researchers of a diverse affiliation and background, and in a variety of forms and ways (Sarantakos, 1998).

Human service practitioners often engage in casual experimentation, in working with clients with particular problems, try out new intervention strategies to see if they will prove beneficial to the client. Casual experiments fail because they are casual and not carefully planned. The wrong variables may have been selected for manipulation so that no matter how they were changed, the desired result could not be obtained (Monette,1998). Casual experiments prove incorrect because intervention strategy may not be the real source of change or it may be short-term improvements. Many things influence people's behaviour, and casual experimentation is not organized to sort out these influences.

Quasi-Experiments in Human Services

Often testing a hypothesis with a true experimental design is not feasible with the desired subjects and in the desired setting. Such a test may be too costly or too long to carry out, it may be inappropriate for the particular research problem or it may presume ability to manipulate an intervention that already has occurred. Usually, the best alternative to an experimental design is a quasi-experimental design in which subjects are not randomly assigned to the comparison and experimental groups. There are two major types of quasi-experimental designs – non-equivalent control group designs and before and after designs. It is this freedom of selection of respondents in research that enables many to opt for quasi-experimental research in human services.

Excerpts from Quasi-Experimental Research

Topic : Impact of Child Mental Health Orientation on School Teachers in Kerala

The Problem

Kerala compared to the other states of our country, has successful statistics with regard to the physical health of children, but the state has not fully exploited the resources of teachers in the promotion of child mental health. As a result, hardly any significant effort in training of school teachers in Kerala has been reported. The study was undertaken with the assumption that the government school teachers capability in the promotion of child mental health could be improved through training.

Research Design

In order to ascertain the impact of the orientation of school teachers on child mental health (intervention) on promotion of child mental health, this study was conducted using Pre-Post Two Groups Quasi-Experimental Research Design. In this design subjects are divided into two groups, viz., the experimental (intervention) group (E) and no intervention comparison group (C). The research design can be diagrammatically presented as follows:

E ⟶ Y_1 ⟶ X ⟶ Y_2

C ⟶ Y'_1 ⟶ Non-X ⟶ Y'_2

E ⟶ Experimental Group

C ⟶ Comparison Group

X ⟶ Orientation of School Teachers on Child Mental Health

Y_1 ⟶ Pre-Test Measurement on Child Mental Health for Experimental Group

Y_2 ⟶ Post-Test Measurement on Child Mental Health for Experimental Group

Y'_1 ⟶ Pre-Test Measurement on Child Mental Health for Comparison Group

Y'_2 ⟶ Post-Test Measurement on Child Mental Health for Comparison Group

The study was conceived of incorporating the characteristics of a pre-test post-test one Comparison Group Design and hence the primary task was to ensure the pre-test equality of the groups of teachers with regard to their background characteristics. The background variables selected for the study were the socio-economic, professional and personality characteristics of the teachers. Care was taken to equate the two groups at the time of their composition to include only comparable units into each of the groups. The comparability was established statistically using chi-square test and t-test for significance of difference between the two groups. However, it was not possible to find a no significant difference between the two comparable groups in all the identified variables. The experimental group was exposed to the orientation programme and the control group was used merely for the purpose of comparison of the pre- and post-measurements.

Universe and Sample

The universe included government school teachers both males and females teaching at the lower and upper primary sections of the four government high schools. The unit of the study was the school teacher working in government schools under the Ernakulam education district.

The four schools were similar in many respects in terms of management, facilities provided in the school, educational level of the teachers, strength of the students, and geographical location of the school. In addition, the teachers from both the groups were compared in a pre-test to make sure that they were average matched on the dependent variable at its pre-test measurement.

Planned Phases of the Experiment

The study was conducted in four phases: preparation of mental health package, pre-measurement on the dependent variables on the two groups so as to ensure the equivalence of the two groups, organizing mental health orientation, and post-test with the same set of previously used tools.

Intervention

For the purpose of orientation of school teachers, a package was devised by the researcher (which served as the independent variable for the study) identifying the three significant components of child mental health wherein the teachers play a greater role. They are:

1. the developmental needs of children,
2. the mental health problems in children, and
3. the healthy disciplining practices of children.

After having finalized the components of the package, this was delivered in the form of an orientation programme to the experimental group of school teachers. The effectiveness (impact) of this orientation programme, in relation to the three components of child mental health, was measured at the knowledge, attitude and perception of the practice levels. These were considered as the dependent variables for the study. In assessing the effectiveness of the orientation programme on the school teachers, the researcher also attempted to find out which of the identified components of the package had greater impact on all selected teachers.

Internal Validity

It is generally less important that a group of experimental subjects be representative of some large population than that experimental and control groups be similar to one another. Though it was not possible for the researcher to assign the subjects (teachers) to the experimental and control groups randomly, every effort was made to select the schools ensuring similarity in many respects.

History: The respondents were government school teachers where extra-curricular events in the form of the training programmes, workshops and any other input of information do not occur frequently. The researcher could thus ascertain that no other factors would have intervened during the period of study.

Maturation or passage of time: The study was completed within a maximum period of two months, hence, the researcher guarded against the threat of maturation of the respondents.

Instrumentation: The same set of tools was used for both the groups during pre-testing and post-testing.

Experimental mortality: The respondents dropping out during the experiment were guarded by keeping the programme in a concise manner.

Findings

The study concludes that the Child Mental Health Orientation Programme has brought about significant improvements in the teachers' knowledge of mental health of their pupils, leading to positive attitude and also perception of healthy and constructive practices in dealing with their pupils. Besides, it is also proved that the impact of the package was experienced by all the teachers who were exposed to it.

Ethical Issues Considered

After the whole experiment was complete, the researcher delivered the same orientation package to the teachers of the control group, thus taking care of the selective distribution of benefits:

- study participants were briefed regarding the study before taking consent,
- written and oral consent was sought,
- confidentiality was ensured with institution identities protected,

- feedback of the study results were given,
- training programmes for the control group members were conducted after the final assessment, and
- data was used only for research purposes.

Utility of Research Findings

As an outcome of the experiment, the researcher proceeded to follow up with the school mental health programme by addressing the mothers of the school children on the important components of child mental health. She also identified a few children who had difficulty in pursuing their education due to financial reasons in the scheme of educational sponsorship project of the School of Social Work where she is a faculty member. A Training Module on Child Mental Health for school teachers was developed and was made use of in teachers' training programmes. A book titled *Mental Health in Class Room* was published in English, and is serving as a teaching material for MSW students and for trainers in the field of child mental health.

Future Directions for Research on Family: Major Areas for Family Intervention

A family practitioner's role comprises planning and implementing a combination of interventions ranging from development to remedial, and using individual, group, as well as community methods to strengthen the family's coping mechanisms and to rehabilitate them. Besides planning and implementing the services, the practitioner needs to monitor and evaluate them and raise public awareness about the services. Family interventions may be planned through primary (family courts, family service centres) or secondary settings (schools, hospitals, industries, police stations, etc.).

The field of family should have theory, research and practice interlinked in a cyclical manner. The goal should be improvement in quality of family life and promoting family welfare.

There is paucity of applied family research in India. The few studies conducted may have little direct applicability for intervention and for influencing policy decisions. The reason being that these are not conceived as part of research design. By its very nature the field requires an interdisciplinary approach, development of linkages among the various social sciences disciplines.

There is thus need to develop national or regional level research centres in different areas to take up the task of documenting available research resources and disseminating information on ongoing research. Such centres should build up bibliographies, maintain reprints of relevant articles and research reports, collect standardized measurement tools, and collect statistics on various aspects of a problem. Depending on the nature of the problem and objectives of research, various methods may be adopted – field experiment, quasi-experiment, survey method, correlational method, evaluation method, etc. The outcome of family research should be visualized as knowledge building, evaluation and monitoring, providing consultation, policy analysis and implementation.

References

Aronson, Elliot and Judson Mills, 1959. "The Effect of Severity of Initiation Liking for a Group," *Journal of Abnormal and Social Psychology*, 59 (September): 177-181.

Barlow, D.H., S.C. Hayes and R.O. Nelson, 1992. *The Scientist Researcher: Research and Accountability in Clinical and Educational Settings.* Boston: Allyn and Bacon.

Bharat, Shalini, 1994. "Research on Families with Problems: Utility, Limitations and Future Directions" in *Enhancing the Role of the Family as an Agency for Social and Economic Development.*

Cook, Thomas D. and Donald T. Campbell, 1979. *Quasi-Experimentation: Design and Analysis Issues for Field Settings.* Chicago: Rand McNally.

Campbell, Richard T. and Julian C. Stanley. 1966. *Experimental and Quasi-Experimental Designs for Research.* Chicago: Rand McNally.

Drake, Robert E., Gregory. J. Mchugo, Deborah R. Becker, William A. Anthony, and Robin E. Clark, 1996. "The New Hampshire Study of Supported Employment for People with Severe Mental Illness". *Journal of Consulting and Clinical Psychology,* 64: 391-399.

Eichler, M. 1988. *Nonsexist Research Methods: A Practical Guide.* Boston: Allen and Unwin.

Elliott, D.S. and D. Huizinga. "Social Class and Delinquent Behaviour in a National Youth Panel: 1976-1980", *Criminology,* 21 (1983), pp. 149-177.

Goleman, Daniel. 1993. "Placebo Effect Is shown to be Twice as Powerful as Expected". *The New York Times,* August 17, p. C3.

Goldfinger, Stephen M., Russel K. Schutt, George S. Tolomicenko, Winston M. Turner, Norma Ware, Walter E Penk, et. al. 1997. "Housing Persons who are Homeless and Mentally Ill: Independent Living or Evolving Consumer Households?" pp. 29-49 in *Mentally Ill and Homeless: Special Programmes for Special Needs,* edited by William R. Breakey and James W.Thompson, Amsterdam, The Netherlands: Harwood Academic Publisher.

Hunt, Morton, 1985. *Profiles of Social Research: The Scientific Study of Human Interactions.* New York: Russel Sage Foundation.

Ivanoff A., B.J. Blythe and S. Briar. "The Empirical Clinical Practice Debate", *Social Casework: The Journal of Contemporary Social Work,* 68 (1987), pp. 290-298.

Joseph Mary Venus, 2003. *Mental Health in Class Room,* Kochi: Rajagiri College of Social Sciences.

Liang, Diane Wei, Richard Moreland, and Linda Argote. 1995. "Group Versus Individual Training and Group Performance: The Mediating Role of Transactive Memory". *Personality and Social Psychology Bulletin,* 21: 384-393.

Monette Duane R., Sullivan Thomas J., DeJong Cornell R., (1998) *Applied Social Research: Tool for the Human Services.* Fourth Edition Orlando: Harcourt College Publishers.

Milgram, Stanley.1965. "Some Conditions of Obedience and Disobedience to Authority" *Human Relations,*18: 57-75.

O'Hare, T. "Integrating Research and Practice: A Framework for Implementation". *Social Work,* 36 (May 1991): 220-223.

Price, Richard H., Michelle Van Ryn, and Amiram D. Vinokur, 1992. "Impact of a Preventive Job Search Intervention on the Likelihood Depression Among the Unemployed", *Journal of Health and Social Behavior*, 33 (June): 158-167.

Polyska, Maciej, Radeij and Joanna (1987). "The Attempt to Change the Attitude Towards Mentally Disturbed Persons Through Education: Experiment in the Group of Teacher". *Psychiatria – Polska;* Sept-Oct. Vol. 21 (5), pp. 401-106.

Reid, W. "The Social Agency as a Research Machine". *Journal of Social Service Research*, 2 (1978), 11-23.

Reinharz, S. (1983), 'Experiential Analysis: A Contribution to Feminist Research', in G. Bowles and R. Duelli-Klien (eds). *Theories of Women's Studies,* Boston: Routledge and Kegan Paul, pp. 162-91.

Rossi,peter H. and Howard E. Freeman.1989, *Evaluation: A Systematic Approach*, 4th ed. Newbury Park, CA: Sage.

Schutt, Russell k. 1999: *Investigating the Social World*, Pine Forge Press

Sherman, Lawrence W. and Richard A. Berk.1984. "The Specific Deterrent Effects of Arrest for Domestic Assault." *American Sociological Review*, 49: 261- 272.

Sarantakos, Sotirios,1988. *Social Research.* London: MacMillan Press Ltd.

Tata Institute of Social Sciences, Unit of Family Studies, Mumbai.1994. *Enhancing the Role of the Family as an Agency for Social and Economic Development.*

Venus Mary (1988) Impact of Mental Health Orientation on School Teachers, Unpublished PhD Thesis.

7

Social Work Research Ethics

Select Perspectives

J.S. Gunavathy

In India, professional social work is of recent origin and is unfortunately a term that is misunderstood and loosely used. It is often treated on par with social service or charity. Professional social work is a fast emerging profession. Social work is the profession committed to the pursuit of social justice, to the enhancement of the quality of life, and to the development of the full potential of each individual, group and community in society (http://www.aasw.asn.au/). Social work's approach is unique among the helping professions because it focuses on people's problems in the context of their social environment.

The three objectives of social work are caring, curing and changing. At the heart of social work value system is a concern for the well-being of all people. Social work practice also seeks to treat people experiencing problems in social functioning. Social change has also been an integral part of social work (Morales and Sheafor, 1989). Social work practice consists of the professional application of social work values, principles and techniques to one or more of the following needs: helping people obtain tangible services; counselling and psychotherapy with individuals, families and groups; helping communities or groups provide or improve social and health services; and participating in legislative processes, (NASW, 1973).

Social work educationists and professionals are called to engage themselves in continuous research so that they can contribute to the body of knowledge, to be abreast with the evolving circumstances in the field of practice and also to experiment with the existing body of knowledge. Quality in research cannot be ensured by merely following a set of prescribed procedures or methodology, especially in a field that is closely associated with human beings. Proper ethical standards need to be adopted and maintained in any social science research and more so in social work research. Social work research as a distinct field of knowledge, is an emerging field. This paper seeks to present select insights into social work research ethics – the what, why and how aspects of the same. An attempt has also been made to present some of the structures and mechanism prevailing in institutions abroad.

Evolution of the Concept of Research Ethics

Two major events – one in Europe and the other in the United States – served as major catalysts for efforts to codify a set of ethical standards for research.

After World War II, Nazi physicians conducted cruel and harmful experiments on human subjects (involuntary prisoners). Their experiments included those to (a) determine how long it was possible for human beings to live in ice water; (b) other prisoners were injected with diseases such as malaria, and epidemic jaundice in order to test vaccines; (c) to test antibiotics, human beings were wounded and had limbs amputated; and (d) other prisoners were given intravenous injections of gasoline or various forms of poison to study how long it would take them to die.

The 'Syphilis Experiment' was conducted by the U.S. Public Health Service (PHS) with black males from Tuskegee, Alabama, in 1932. Four hundred and twenty five with syphilis and 200 without syphilis, all poor and semi-illiterate, were studied. None were told they had syphilis. The intent was to observe them over a span of years to learn how the disease progressed. Although there was no cure for syphilis when the study began, fifteen years later, penicillin was discovered to be an effective cure for the disease but the study was continued for an additional 25 years by the PHS and treatment withheld. The participants were allowed to spread the disease to their wives and lovers with untold consequences. The study ended only when it received public notoriety.

These two episodes brought home to people the need to codify standards for ethical conduct to enable researchers to have guidelines available.

The first effort along these lines was the Nuremberg Code, developed in 1946, in direct response to the atrocities committed during the World War II. It was a set of ethical standards by which research with human subjects was to be judged. The Code demanded that every research subject be told (a) the nature, duration and purpose of the experiment; (b) the method and means by which it is to be conducted; (c) all inconveniences and hazards reasonably to be expected; and (d) the effects upon his health or person which may possibly come.

The Nuremberg Code was limited to issues of ethics in medical research. A number of international organizations developed their own codes of ethics for distinguishing ethical from unethical clinical research. Later, the 1964 Declaration of Helsinki (ethical principles for medical research involving human subjects) further expanded the rights of human subjects.

Following these two interventions, many measures were taken at the national levels. For instance, in 1966, the U.S. Public Health Service established ethical standards for medical research that emphasized the following: (a) full disclosure of relevant information to be made to participants; (b) the decision to participate must be completely voluntary; and (c) researchers must obtain documented, informed consent from participants.

In addition, the U.S. Congress passed the National Research Act (Public Law 93-348), which required any organization involved in the conduct of biomedical or behavioural research involving human subjects to establish an Institutional Review Board (IRB) to review the research to be conducted or sponsored. This Act also created the National Commission for the Protection of Human Subjects of Biomedical and Behavioural Research. They produced recommendations for public comments in 1978. The Department of Health, Education and Welfare (now, the Department of Health and Human Services) refined the recommendations and, in 1981, issued them as regulations for research being conducted with its funds. In 1983, specific regulations protecting children were incorporated. This led many universities to establish IRBs (sometimes called Human Subjects Committees). (http://www.uic.edu/classes/socw/socw560/Ethics1.htm)

Thus, the concept of ethics for research involving human subjects has branched out into that applicable to social work.

Conceptual Clarification: The 'What' of Social Work Research Ethics

Before we dwell on the concept of 'social work research ethics', it is but appropriate to present the meaning of social work research.

Social work research addresses psychosocial problems, preventive interventions, treatment of acute and chronic conditions, and community, organizational, policy and administrative issues. Covering the lifespan, social work research may address clinical, services and policy issues. It benefits consumers, practitioners, policy makers, educators, and the general public by:

- examining prevention and intervention strategies for health and mental health, child welfare, aging, substance abuse, community development, managed care, housing, economic self-sufficiency, family well-being, etc.;

- studying the strengths, needs, and interrelationships of individuals, families, groups, neighbourhoods, and social institutions; and
- providing evidence for improved service delivery and public policies (http://www.socialworkers.org/research/researchMore.asp).

Thus, social work research refers to the application of scientific methods of analysis to social work problems. Topics for theoretical and applied research in the field cover a broad range of areas including social work theory and practice, social and public policy and practice, human services management, social philosophy, social welfare policy/history and international social development. Topics may also be related to a specific social problem or issue, or a particular field of practice.

The 'Why' of Social Work Research Ethics

Social workers must not only involve themselves in independent research, but also keep current with emerging research by other professionals, and should collaborate in multidisciplinary research with other interested professions, such as medicine, nursing, genetic counselling, psychology and law. Social work research must be guided by basic ethical and cultural principles.

Sources of ethical dilemmas in social work research include those arising from: (a) the research problem being studied; (b) the methods or procedures used to obtain valid and reliable data; (c) the kinds of persons serving as research participants; (d) the type of data collected – sensitive information etc.

Adherence to ethical standards in social work research is essential to uphold the quality of data of evidence-based studies. Incorporating the same will help the social workers to contribute to, support, and be aware of the development of research-based and practice-relevant knowledge of the psychosocial, cultural, economic, and ethical implications of social issues/problems on individuals, families and society. This will enhance social work practice. Promotion of the well-being of the individual will be ensured. Similarly, it will help manoeuver research weighing the benefits and the risks involved. Thus, informed consent, the equitable selection of subjects, privacy and confidentiality, the right to withdraw from studies, and avoidance of harm are among the standards that are essential for ethical research studies.

The 'How' of Social Work Research Ethics

A University of Illinois publication presents the following important ethical issues to consider:

Informed Consent

Informed consent refers to telling potential research participants about all aspects of the research that might reasonably influence their decision to participate. Participants must be aware that they are participating in a study, must be informed of all the consequences of the study, and must consent to participate in the study. Very often people are asked to sign a consent form, which describes the elements of the research that might influence a person's decision to participate.

Anonymity

A response is considered anonymous when the researcher cannot identify a given response with a given respondent.

Confidentiality

The researcher is able to identify a given person's response but essentially promises not to share the information publicly.

Privacy

Privacy refers to the ability to control when and under what conditions others will have access to your beliefs, values, or behaviour.

Physical or Mental Distress/No Harm to the Participants

Potential research subjects should be given sufficient information about the study to determine any possible risks or discomforts as well as benefits.

Sponsored Research

In case of funded research, the following issues emanate:

1. *Conditional publication of results:* Conditional publication of results refers to the publication of results only if they turn out in a certain way (i.e., a preferred way). Such conditional publication violates the integrity of the research process and the autonomy of the researcher.
2. *The nature of the research project itself:* Ethical questions arise if the researcher heavily modifies the study to cover matters not in the agreement.
3. *Issue of informed consent and sponsorship:* Information about sponsorship can influence the decision of whether to participate. To deceive people regarding the sponsorship of a study in order to gain their participation is unethical.

Fraud and Scientific Misconduct

Fraud refers to the deliberate falsification, misrepresentation, or plagiarizing of data, findings, or the ideas of others (Monette and Sullivan). This may include things such as reporting research that has not been conducted, or manipulating data in a deceptive way. Misconduct is a broader concept that includes fraud and carelessness or bias in recording and reporting data, mishandling data, and incomplete reporting of results.

This comes in during dissemination of research results, which may be made through sources such as a report to a sponsoring agency, publication in a professional journal, or a news release to the media. Researchers should ensure that consumers of the research are not adversely affected. Deception or fraudulent disclosures of research results can cause human service practitioners to design useless or dangerous interventions based on faulty studies. Peer review and study replication are two ways used to detect fraud. Others are supervision of novice researchers, and guiding against prolific researchers (http://www.uic.edu/classes/socw/socw560/Ethics1.htm).

Structures and Mechanisms Prevailing in Educational Institutions Abroad

Illustration 1: The National University of Singapore

The National University of Singapore requires that all research proposals, including student third year projects, honours theses and post-graduate research projects must be reviewed by the Departmental Research Ethics Committee (DREC) The ethical principles prescribed are:

1. Participants should give informed consent.
2. Participants should not be given hurtful or unduly stressful procedures.
3. Deception of participants is to be avoided and is allowed only when the deception is minor and clearly justified by the value of the knowledge obtained in the research.
4. Use of psychological tests should observe the relevant guidelines.
5. Participants should be debriefed as appropriate.
6. Confidentiality in respect of all results, bio data or other information relating to participants must be observed.
7. Investigators must not misrepresent their skills or allow an assumption of professional expertise to stand uncorrected.
8. Permission is to be obtained through proper channels where outside institutions or organizations are involved.
9. The University, the Department and the discipline should not be brought into disrepute by discourteous or irresponsible actions.
10. Supervisors must not put pressure on students to undertake projects about which the student has ethical objections.

11. Illegal activities will automatically be deemed unethical (http://www.fas.nus.edu.sg/swk/research4_1.htm).

There are also prescribed procedures for considering ethical issues.

Illustration 2: Dundee University, United Kingdom

'The Research Ethics – Code of Practice' of the Dundee University, UK applies to all staff, students, contract researchers and others engaged in research for which the Faculty has or shares any responsibility. It aims to help researchers uphold scientific standards, comply with the law and avoid social and personal harm. The Code of Practice has been drawn from the ethical guidelines of the UK professional associations relevant to the Faculty: The British Educational Research Association, the Scottish Educational Research Association, the British Association of Social Workers, the British Sociological Association and the British Psychological Society. The principles covered include (i) general ones (with respect to criminal records disclosure, protection of participant, colleagues, safety of the researcher, and relationship with host institution) and those relating to (ii) recruitment and consents (with respect to competence and representation, personal conduct, and consent), (iii) confidentiality and data protection (with respect to confidentiality and data protection act), (iv) debriefing (with respect to Debriefing and advice to participants), and (v) dissemination (with respect to relationship with commissioning or funding agencies, responsibility to the research profession and the public, intellectual ownership and property rights, and publication and dissemination). Every study has to undergo a research ethics formative assessment before being commissioned at the institutional level (http://www.dundee.ac.uk/fedsoc/research/researchethics/).

Illustration 3: Canterbury Christ Church University, United Kingdom

Research governance describes the mechanisms through which the quality and ethical standards of the research carried out by any member of the University and the Faculty are ensured and is enshrined within both University and Faculty procedures. Although originally intended for research in health and social care the University has adopted research governance principles to cover all research involving human participants.

In essence, research governance sets standards for the conduct of research.

- Defines mechanism through which standards are delivered.
- Improves research quality and safeguards the public by:
  - enhancing ethical and scientific quality,
  - promoting good practice,
  - reducing adverse incidents and ensuring that lessons are learned,
  - preventing poor performance and misconduct, and
  - monitoring compliance with research standards.

Adherence to the research governance principles implies that the Faculty is committed to:

- Ensuring all research undertaken is supported by an appropriate research sponsor.
- Ensuring that all proposals for research involving human participants undergo appropriate independent peer review, with scrutiny of the suitability of protocols and researchers or research teams whether the work is to be undertaken in the University or elsewhere.
- Ensuring that all research involving human participants, their data or, rarely, their organs or tissues, is referred for appropriate ethical review to safeguard the dignity, rights, safety and well-being of the participants.

- Ensuring that no research is undertaken by members of the Faculty (staff or students) in the absence of peer review and satisfactory ethical approval from either one of the internal committees or an appropriate NHS (National Health Service) or Social Care Committee.
- Ensuring that all approved work is declared to the University Research Ethics and Governance Committee.
- Promoting a high standard of health and safety in laboratory work (where relevant).
- Where appropriate, ensuring that there is close collaboration with partner organizations in NHS and Social Care Environments and that care is taken to ensure both the quality and relevance of joint working and avoidance of unnecessary duplication of functions.
- Ensuring that systems are in place to monitor compliance with standards, investigate complaints and deal with irregular or inappropriate behaviours in the conduct of research.
- Ensuring that, wherever possible, research is pursued with the active involvement of service users and/or carers including, where relevant, those from hard to reach groups such as the homeless or drug abusers.
- Making information available on all health and social care research being undertaken in the Faculty.
- Ensuring that those agreeing to be involved in research (or their relatives) are informed of the findings at the end of the study.
- Making relevant and up-to-date regulatory and advisory documentation and procedural guidance available to staff.
- Ensuring that the findings of research are appropriately disseminated using, where appropriate, different media and writing styles for different audiences (http://www.canterbury.ac.uk/health/health-social-care-research/research-g-and-e.asp).

Illustration 4: NASW Code of Ethics

A portion of the Code directly pertains to the profession's concern for ethical research.

1. Social workers should monitor and evaluate policies, the implementation of programmes, and practice interventions.
2. Social workers should promote and facilitate evaluation and research to contribute to the development of knowledge.
3. Social workers should critically examine and keep current with emerging knowledge relevant to social work and fully use evaluation and research evidence in their professional practice.
4. Social workers engaged in evaluation or research should carefully consider possible consequences and should follow guidelines developed for the protection of evaluation and research participants. Appropriate institutional review boards should be consulted.
5. Social workers engaged in evaluation or research should obtain voluntary and written informed consent from participants, when appropriate, without any implied or actual deprivation or penalty for refusal to participate; without undue inducement to participate; and with due regard for participants' well-being, privacy, and dignity. Informed consent should include information about the nature, extent, and duration of the participation requested and disclosure of the risks and benefits of participation in the research.
6. When evaluation or research participants are incapable of giving informed consent, social workers should provide an appropriate explanation to the participants, obtain the participants' assent to the extent they are able, and obtain written consent from an appropriate proxy.
7. Social workers should never design or conduct evaluation or research that does not use consent procedures, such as

certain forms of naturalistic observation and archival research, unless rigorous and responsible review of the research has found it to be justified because of its prospective scientific, educational, or applied value and unless equally effective alternative procedures that do not involve waiver of consent are not feasible.

8. Social workers should inform participants of their right to withdraw from evaluation and research at any time without penalty.
   (i) Social workers should take appropriate steps to ensure that participants in evaluation and research have access to appropriate supportive services.
   (ii) Social workers engaged in evaluation or research should protect participants from unwarranted physical or mental distress, harm, danger, or deprivation.
   (iii) Social workers engaged in the evaluation of services should discuss collected information only for professional purposes and only with people professionally concerned with this information.
9. Social workers engaged in evaluation or research should ensure the anonymity or confidentiality of participants and of the data obtained from them. Social workers should inform participants of any limits of confidentiality, the measures that will be taken to ensure confidentiality, and when any records containing research data will be destroyed.
10. Social workers who report evaluation and research results should protect participants' confidentiality by omitting identifying information unless proper consent has been obtained authorizing disclosure.
11. Social workers should report evaluation and research findings accurately. They should not fabricate or falsify results and should take steps to correct any errors later found in published data using standard publication methods.

12. Social workers engaged in evaluation or research should be alert to and avoid conflicts of interest and dual relationships with participants, should inform participants when a real or potential conflict of interest arises, and should take steps to resolve the issue in a manner that makes participants' interests primary.
13. Social workers should educate themselves, their students, and their colleagues about responsible research practices (http://www.socialworkers.org/pubs/code/code.asp).

Limitations

- In India, the concept is still in the nascent stage – rather unheard of.
- The research ethics are common to all disciplines dealing with human participants. They are not exclusive to social work.
- The concept seems more pronounced only in health settings.
- When weighed against the personnel, money and time factors, especially in a developing country like ours, ethics takes a back seat.

It might be premature to talk about social work research ethics leave alone social work research, especially when the social work profession is in the nascent stage in a country like India.

Concluding Remarks

It might even be premature to talk about social work research ethics as the field is yet to be fully developed. Social work research ethics may be adhered to in the research activities either in the said form or otherwise. But, there may be instances known only to the researcher where 'compromises' have been made. It is not the intention of the author to point fingers at anybody but to institutionalize the same in the framework of social work research so that it will add to the professionalism of the discipline in the long run.

References

Australian Association of Social Workers (AASW) (2002). *About Social Work*. AASW. Retrieved from http://www.aasw.asn.au/on 15th January, 2006.

Canterbury Christ Church University (2006). *Research Governance and Ethics.* Retrieved from http://www.canterbury.ac.uk/health/health-social-care-research/research-g-and-e.asp on 15th June, 2006.

Faculty of education and Social Work, Dundee University (n.d.). *Research Ethics - Codes of Practice.* Retrieved from http://www.dundee.ac.uk/ fedsoc/research/researchethics/on June 15th, 2006.

Morales, Armando and Sheafor W. Bradford (1989). *Social Work: A Profession of Many Faces.* Boston: Allyn and Bacon, pp. 13-14.

National Association of Social Workers (NASW) (1973) as cited in Morales, Armando and Sheafor W. Bradford (1989). *Social Work: A Profession of Many Faces.* Boston: Allyn and Bacon, p. 17

— (2006). *Code of Ethics of the National Association of Social Workers.* Retrieved from http://www.socialworkers.org/pubs/code/code.asp on June 15th, 2006.

— (2006). *What is Social Work Research?* Retrieved from http://www.socialworkers.org/research/researchMore.asp on June 15th, 2006.

National University of Singapore (2005). *Research Ethics Guidelines.* Retrieved from http://www.fas.nus.edu.sg/swk/research4_1.htm on June 15, 2006.

University of Illinois at Chicago (n.d). *Social Work Research.* Retrieved from http://www.uic.edu/classes/socw/socw560/Ethics1.htm on June 25th, 2006.

8

Social Work Research Curriculum in Select American Universities

A Review

Sudershan Pasupuleti

Social work research is the nucleus for social work practice that integrates social work curriculum and builds the knowledge base in terms of theories, conceptual and practice models and its continuous refinement making amenable for practice. The litmus test for the success of social work research is whether specific social work interventions in social work profession achieve the intended purposes and outcomes leading to client satisfaction (CSWE, 2003). The purpose of social work research is to update the theories, improve practice, develop practice models, improve outcomes for the clients, and evaluate social work interventions for effectiveness and accountability. Continuous development and adaptation of new models for practice and continuous refinement of practice are the overriding goals of social work research. From this perspective, social work research focus could range from pure research to applied research.

Social work education and training draws knowledge from different disciplines such as biology, medicine and social sciences. But knowledge and models of practice borrowed from other disciplines are tested and adapted to social work practice to achieve social work goals, which are different from the goals of other professions or disciplines. The social work research curriculum, therefore, tend to be interdisciplinary in the procedures and techniques of conducting research in the United States. The research methods and techniques used in social work context are described as social work research. Such a trend exists in many other disciplines including the newer disciplines as well. But, the goals and purposes of these methods and techniques in social work context are to enhance the knowledge base and promote effective practice leading to client satisfaction.

There is a new trend for combining quantitative and qualitative methods in a unique way to undertake trendsetting research in the United States. The combination of quantitative and qualitative methods is known as 'mixed methods' in social and behavioural science research (Greenberg, 2000). Such research projects are innovations in research methods that intend to capture comprehensive picture of social and behavioural phenomena by overcoming the limitations of quantitative and qualitative approaches. These trends are beyond the interdisciplinary and problem-focused. For example, the National Institute of Health, a premier public research-funding agency in the United States, recognizes the trend and fund the projects that tried unique combination of research methods to undertake cutting-edge research that could have impact on many disciplines.

In the recent past, there has been a growing interest among a section of social work educators in the United States in raising the standards for teaching entry-level research skills to undergraduate social work students (BSWs). This is viewed as an imperative to strengthen social work education and practice. These BSWs are expected to undertake research as part of their roles in the employing organizations and serving the clients with professional accountability. With under-prepared skills they would not be able to undertake research to meet job expectations. The Association of Baccalaureate Program Directors (BPD) constituted a national level committee to identify the areas of improvement for strengthening research component in the undergraduate social work curriculum. The committee is currently studying the situation to make recommendations.

Scope of Social Work Research

The scope of social work research is large in view of different areas of practice. However, social work research aims to build social work theory and practice by testing and validating knowledge that social workers use in their practice, which could range from needs assessment (survey research) to programme/intervention evaluation, and involve quasi-experimental to experimental research designs (intervention-based research) where new interventions or models are tried in a social work practice area. Further, social workers also use a new practice model – evidence-based practice – which is a recent phenomenon in social work and allied disciplines signifying systematic data (of current clients) collection before (pre-test) and after (post-test) intervention to demonstrate the impact of social work interventions. The evidence-based practice uses the single-subject design research or group design research where it is assumed as an integral part of social work practice. Social work research also embarks upon community-based and participatory research approaches to assess needs and undertake interventions to improve the conditions of clients and assess interventions.

Role of IASWR

The Institute for the Advancement of Social Work Research (IASWR) addresses why social work research is needed stating that social work research informs professional practice. Through social work research, the profession can assess the needs and resources of people in their environments. It also allows for the evaluation of the effectiveness of social work services and intervention in meeting people's needs. It can demonstrate relative costs and benefits of social work services and also advances professional education in the light of changing contexts for practice. Social work research also helps professionals understand the impact of legislation and social policy on the clients and communities we serve (IASWR, 2006).

As regards the doctoral education in the U.S., the guidelines for Quality in Social Work Doctoral Programs (2003) stated that well-educated doctoral students should be able to conceive and conduct scientifically-based research aimed at developing in-depth knowledge of a particular subject, problem, process, or phenomena, as well as to define the connection and contribution of that knowledge to the requirements of professional intervention with client. "Doctoral students should learn not just about research methodologies but also about the epistemological and ontological basis of these methodologies as well as other historical, philosophical, theoretical, empirical, and analytical material. Their education should foster their ability to think and write critically not only about their own and others' scholarly and professional contributions to social work but also about the place, role, contribution, and practice of social work in society" (GADE, 2003: 3).

Federal Regulations Relating to Research

Institutional Review Boards (IRBs) are mandated to regulate research that involves human subjects. They determine whether proposed research meets ethical standards/guidelines as outlined in the National Research Act, 1974 (Royse, 2003). Every institution that engages in research and involves human subjects should form IRBs based on the federal guidelines, regulate research conducted by investigators affiliated with their organizations and maintain the records relating to research. These boards (sometimes called human subjects committees) are constituted with seasoned researchers who understand various procedures and protocols needed for conducting research in social and behavioural, biological, medical sciences that involve human subjects. All research activity on human subjects is required to be reviewed and authorized by the IRBs. They have the mandate to approve, disapprove, and or modify research activities covered by the regulations. If the guidelines are not followed or violated, no federal grants will be awarded to such individuals and institutions.

Social Work Education and Curriculum in the United States

The purposes of social work education are to prepare competent, ethical and effective professionals, to develop social work knowledge, and to provide leadership in the development of service delivery systems. Individual social work programme at a college or university level tends to have its own strengths, missions, resources and specific goals that a programme intends to achieve. However, the programme needs to adhere to the standards and core content areas of social work education as described in the self-study submitted to CSWE for accreditation. Every programme's curriculum covers foundation contents that includes values and ethics, diversity, human behaviour in the social environment, social welfare policy and services, social work practice, research, field education as well as advanced or concentration content relative to family and child welfare, ageing, health and mental health, disability, and at-risk populations.

Research is one of the foundation courses taught in the BSW and in the foundation year of MSW programmes. In senior year of MSW programme and doctoral programmes advanced research courses are taught to deepen the abilities and understanding of the research process among the social work students to conduct independent research and actively contribute to the body of knowledge. The overall expectation is that students/practitioners will move from a position of only consumers to the producers of knowledge for social work practice.

Accreditation, Standards and Ethical Obligations

The Council on Social Work Education states in their policy and accreditation standards that research is to consist of "qualitative and quantitative research content (that) provides understanding of a scientific, analytic, and ethical approach to building knowledge for practice" (CSWE, 2003: 36). The goals of research courses are to prepare students to develop, use, and communicate empirical knowledge and promote evidence-based interventions. Social work practitioners are expected not only to provide high quality services to clients but also to initiate change and improve policy and social service delivery. Further, social workers are expected to evaluate their own practice.

Methodology

This paper is based on the data that came from participant observations and personal experience. The researcher himself was involved in the development of the self-study leading to a new MSW programme. The analyses were also based on the content analysis of syllabi collected from 60 social work educators teaching research courses at different colleges and universities across the United States. Further, CSWE accreditation standards and policy documents were reviewed besides self-study reports (detailed proposal for new programme is called self-study) of a few social work programmes. An e-mail request was sent out through list serve of BPD and CSWE for copies of the syllabi that they prepared to teach research methods' courses in social work programmes. Preparing a syllabus is the requirement for teaching a course. Various instructional activities, course expectations, grading criteria, and methodologies are listed in the syllabus, which becomes blueprint and contract between the educator and students of the class. The syllabi are rated by programme description and course objectives keeping the standards laid down for accreditation.

Salient Features of Social Work Research in United States

The salient features of the social work research courses in the United States are described here in the section.

Integration of Research with the Courses

Social work curriculum is meticulously designed to meet all the standards specified in EPAS. Linkages between different courses are delineated and clearly connected with programme goals. The course objectives are connected with programme goals. Hence, social work research component of curriculum is well integrated with the rest of the curriculum. The fitness between various courses and components of programme is thoroughly reviewed in the accreditation review process and the inconsistencies in the programme design are addressed before accreditation is accorded to a programme, to that effect the self-study is revised to meet the specified standards. The programme goals versus course objectives are demonstrated through a matrix that clearly shows convergence of different courses are related to social work graduate or undergraduate programme (Table 1).

Table 1

Analysis of Social Work Research

Criteria	*Programme*	*Rating*	*No. of syllabi*	*Percentage*
Course description versus standards	BSW	5	6	
		4	16	
		3	11	
	MSW	5	5	
		4	19	
		3	3	
Course objectives versus standards	BSW	5	9	
		4	21	
		3	3	
	MSW	5	5	
		4	19	
		3	4	

Rating on course description and objectives fitness rating	BSW	5	13	
		4	16	
		3	4	
	MSW	5	16	
		4	11	
		3	0	
Requirements of the courses	*BSW Programmes (N=60)*		*MSW Programmes (N=27)*	
	Requirements	*Number and Percentage*	*Requirements*	*Number and Percentage*
	Attendance and participation	61	Attendance and participation	78
	Assignments	94	Assignments	86
	Readings	30	Readings	50
	Using resources	25	Exams	85
	Exams	67	Preparation	75
	Preparation	65		
	Understanding the material			
Areas of assessment	Attendance and participation	70	Attendance and participation	68
	Assignments	82	Assignments	87
	Exams	82	Exams	50
	Readings	60	Readings	78
	Projects	37	Projects	68
	Quizzes	56	Quizzes	25
Primary methods of delivery	Lecture	82	Lecture	78
	Practical class experience	42	Practical class experiences	80
	Experiential	45	Experiential	65

Integration with Field Education

Social work students are expected to practice their research skills in the field. Field integrates various course objectives and expectations of the programme. Every student signs a contract of field education before starting it. The contract clearly depicts the expectations relating to different courses and their applications in the field including research knowledge. Although BSW students are expected to apply the foundation knowledge in social work research while MSWs are expected to use their advanced knowledge and skills in the field. Advanced knowledge involves specific application of research skills to evaluate social work interventions (at micro and macro levels) and talk about policy and programme implications of their research. They are prepared to approach social work practice based on the evidence/outcomes of interventions.

Research Course Objectives

Research course objectives are apparently linked to programme goals and integrated with course objectives of other courses being taken as part of the programme. The objectives clearly aim at teaching skills to social work students in a variety of research methods and tools that are used in the social work practice settings. And, these objectives correspond with professional expectations and ethical standards established by the National Association of Social Workers (NASW). However, there is some variability in the skill levels of graduate and undergraduate students. New methods are tried continuously to research into new problems and in new ways. Such methods are gradually integrated into social work curriculum and they are included in the required readings for the students.

Content Areas

Research objectives relate to foundation course contents such as purpose of research, ethics in research, research questions and hypotheses, conceptualization and variables, design of research (experimental, quasi-experimental and non-experimental), measurement, data collection methods and tools, analysis of data (covers the whole range of statistical techniques, namely, descriptive statistics to inferential statistics including regression) and an overview of advanced research methods including advanced statistical procedures such as structural equation modelling, multi-modelling, path analysis and factor analysis (exploratory and confirmatory). Further, there are trends of combining qualitative and quantitative methods of research in the name of 'mixed methods'. These new approaches are geared to heighten the rigour of research in social work, which are ideally suited for social work situations.

Prior to taking research foundation course students are expected to have completed a statistics class. All students of social work, both BSW and MSW, should take a foundation course in research methodology. The undergraduate course(s) focus on foundation knowledge and skills in social work research. The students learn about the context and settings of research, purposes of research, research process and steps of research which include selection of problem, literature search, preparing hypotheses, designing the study, preparing sample design, and development or preparation of tools for data collection. Students should also have basic knowledge and skills of data analysis and interpretation of results besides skills of writing research reports.

Teaching Methodologies

Wide-ranging methodologies are employed to teach research at graduate and undergraduate levels (see Table 1). There is greater focus on building the skills besides transmitting knowledge about the research process and techniques among graduate students (Ph. D and Master's students). The majority of educators use practical and experiential teaching methods to deliver social work research courses. However, there are a substantial number of educators who still use the methods that are lecture-based. Many educators have taught research courses involving students in real research projects to provide hands-on experience in research process to them.

Teaching Resources and Textbooks

There are wide-ranging social work research textbooks available for both graduate and undergraduate students in the United States. Although the content and methods are interdisciplinary, they are adapted to social work context and developed as resource books. The books are good sources of current knowledge and reflect social work language and illustrations. The illustrative material in the social work research textbooks is drawn from social work practice areas and developed as resources. Such resources provide a great deal of information to students besides citing a context for application of social work research skills. Use of textbooks to teach social work courses is helpful to students learning social work skills including social work research.

Evaluation of Outcomes of the Courses

Outcome assessment is a part of teaching and learning process. Students assess educators' performance in terms of instructional style, knowledge, clarity in course expectations, fairness, and explaining the concepts. Some educators use pre- and post-course assessments to demonstrate students' learning outcomes. Application of research skills is assessed as part of assessing students performance in field education.

There are assessments before graduation, after graduation for all courses and programme effectiveness. The instruments developed by BPD are used in assessing knowledge and competences acquired by the students through the programme. Students' performance in licensure examination is another indicator of their learning.

Curriculum committee in the department of social work reviews the curriculum based on the issues and concerns raised by faculty and field instructors to address them. Finally, renewal of accreditation requires thorough review of the courses and issues and concerns that were experienced during previous period and explanation about how those issues are/will be addressed in the self-study.

Conclusion

Social work research curriculum in the universities of the United States is effectively designed and integrated with the rest of the social work curriculum. More resources and textbooks on social work research are available to teach the courses. The primary focus of teaching social work research is on building skills among social workers to undertake independent studies although expectations vary from graduate to undergraduate levels. Despite well-designed and integrated curriculum, there are issues and concerns relating to the research skills among the undergraduates and graduates that still need to be addressed in the United States.

References

Council on Social Work Education (2003). *Handbook of Accreditation Standards and Procedures* (fifth edition). Alexandria, VA: CSWE.

Gambrill, E. and Epstein, L. (1985). Behavioral social work: Past, present, and future. *Research on Social Work Practice*, 5: 460-84.

Institute for the Advancement of Social Work Research (2006). About IASWR. Retrieved July 7, 2006, from the Institute for the Advancement of Social Work. http://www.charityadvantage.com/iaswr/ABOUTIASWR.asp

Myers, L.L. and Thyer, B.A. (1997). Should social work clients have the right to effective treatment? *Social Work*, 42: 288-98.

NASW (2006). What is social work research? Retrieved July 10, 20006, from website: http://www.naswdc.org/research/researchmore.asp

Anastas, J.W., Bronson, D., Crook, W., Doueck, H.J. and Harold, R.D. (2003). Guidelines for quality in social work doctoral programs (revised). Group for the Advancement of Doctoral Education (GADE), Retrieved 7/12/06, from http://web.uconn.edu/gadegidelines.pdf.

Royse, D. (2004). *Research Methods in Social Work* (fourth edition). The United States: Brooks/Cole.

9

Developing Research Interest Among Social Work Trainees

Problems and Challenges

Nagmani Rao

Social work is largely perceived as a practice profession with a strong interdisciplinary approach. There are three levels of training for developing personnel for the field of practice. Some institutes, apart from the regular degree programme, offer certificate courses of durations varying from six months to one year to prepare a cadre of paraprofessionals. There are a number of colleges that offer undergraduate courses involving theory and field practicum. Amongst postgraduate courses we find a range of approaches from the integrated to specialization-oriented courses. According to the 3rd UGC-CDC Report in Social Work Education (UGC,1990), there were 45 recognized institutions in India imparting professional social work training as deemed university, university affiliated colleges or as university or college departments. Many more would have been added to this since then, though not all are government aided. Of late, some universities have also started experimenting with the distant mode of education for social work.

The specific focus of this paper is on the social work professional training, which is imparted at the postgraduate level at the Karve Institute of Social Service (hereinafter 'Institute'), Pune, (Maharashtra). The first part of the paper would give an overview of the course with a somewhat elaborate discussion on the research component. Thereafter, the concerns about training for research in the field of social work would be discussed. The third part would discuss in detail how the Institute has tried to develop this process of research orientation amongst the trainees and efforts to bring about reasonable standards of research competence. The last part would discuss the kinds of challenges that have emerged regarding the compulsion as well as quality of research that one should aspire for when including research into social work curricula at the postgraduate level.

MSW Training

The UGC-CDC Report in Social Work Education has identified three major 'domains' and a fourth 'elective content' as the curriculum frames for professional social work education. The word 'domain' is understood "as a sphere of knowledge be it cognitive, affective, psychomotor/behavioural or that to support attitudinal change, all this singly, in combinations or altogether" (UGC, 2001: 10). The first of these domains, the 'core domain', refers to the courses which draw on the professional philosophy, ideology, values and ethics of practice and explicate the theory and concepts. The second, the 'supportive domain', gives training to develop knowledge and skills that assist the core domain and cover courses related to human growth, development, family and socio-political aspects related to development and environment and approaches to development. The third domain, called the 'interdisciplinary domain', comprises the theory, concepts and perspectives from other sciences to help understand and work with social phenomena necessitating change (UGC, 2001: 10). The 'optional content' refers to a set of optional or defined courses that enable a concentration in specific areas of interest or specialization.

The University of Pune (hereinafter 'University') syllabus for the MSW course here broadly follows the framework as defined by the UGC-CDC. At the Institute, the theory base of the two-year postgraduate degree course includes a mix of generic courses common to all specializations and papers related to each specialization. The practicum component includes concurrent field work (generic in the first year and specialized in the second year) and exposure visits at each level of training – orientation visits (during the first month of training), advanced orientation visits (at the end of the first term), study tour (at the end of the third term) and block placement (at the end of the fourth term). Supportive components to the practical aspects are the regularly conducted skill laboratory sessions and research laboratory sessions that seek to enhance trainees' learning for field work and research work respectively and the individual and group conferences which also enhance peer learning facilitated by the faculty. Whenever projects taken up by the Institute or other associations provide the opportunity, students are given hands on experiences through rural camps, field studies, disaster relief, etc. Apart from this, some of the specialization departments have also incorporated field based (social work) research by assigning students the task of identifying and conducting a micro study as part of their second year field work tasks.

Postgraduate trainees in social work come to the course from a wide range of subjects at the undergraduate level, from the social sciences, to pure sciences, commerce, social work (BSW), computer science, humanities, home science, etc. Occasionally, we have also had students who have opted to switch to social work after completing their engineering, medicine (BAMS), or postgraduation in other subjects. The diversity of students is also characterized by regional differences, language and rural-urban differences.

Given such a mix of disciplines and backgrounds, a challenge before the educators is to find common grounds to bring the trainees into a defined framework of learning. In this web of challenges is bringing in a process for a standardized way of learning research application as an essential part of the course requirement. Each student is expected to submit a full-length dissertation, called a project report in the University syllabus, in the second year. However, here, the process begins in the first term itself.

The Research Training Process

Mid-way through the first term (August end/early September) the Project Report Coordinator orients the students about the nature and process of research work. This is reinforced by a detailed discussion of each step in the process by the Research Lab Coordinator, who is usually also the teacher in Research Methodology. The trainees are given the project report manual at this stage, which gives step-by-step guidelines on how they should carry out their research work and the standardized formats for structuring their analysis and presenting the output in the form of the research report. After the orientation to project report work the students have brainstorming sessions with the faculty on potential areas of interest in research. During these discussions, the focus is on the motivating factors in selection of topics, the feasibility of a study and the student's capacity to handle the study.

Students then submit two to three topics for consideration by their specialization faculty and the approved topics at this level are then brought before the faculty meeting for a wider discussion and inputs, as also handling overlaps in topics between departments. Once the topics have been thus approved and research guides assigned, the list is put up for the students, usually by November/December. Students then meet with their respective guides, field experts and others to plan the background reading and some basic literature review to serve as a base for preparing the research proposal.

The proposals go through several revisions prior to final approval by the guide. The research component of the viva-voce at the end of the first year is based on this research proposal (see Annexure I for 'Outline of Project Report Proposal'). Following this, the trainees prepare, refine and pre-test the research tool(s) and finalize the population to be sampled. Students are normally expected to complete their data collection by June/July although this schedule is not strictly adhered to due to a host of reasons. During the third term, the trainees scrutinize and fill in data gaps, edit and process the data and plan out the report writing. At this stage, some more literature is looked at to supplement the content of the earlier phase of reading done during the proposal preparation stage. The report preparation work takes concrete shape only by the fourth term. The submission of the project report prior to appearing for the final exams is mandatory. The assessment of the project report is done by the panel of examiners appointed by the University and the focus of assessment is more on understanding and application of research methodology reflected through the study (see Annexure II for 'University Assessment Criteria for Project Reports').

Concern for Research in Social Work Training

The nature of social work intervention is marked by a variety of approaches and levels of work. The focus of practice being problem intervention, much greater emphasis across institutes of training is on developing skills and attitudes for individual, family, group or community level intervention rather than policy advocacy and macro-level intervention, although, theoretically speaking, professional social workers are also expected to be 'change agents'. (I believe this involves not only bringing about micro-level situational change but also macro-level structural and systemic changes). In fact, at a number of fora and at personal meetings with professional educators, P.D. Kulkarni, the eminent social development and social policy expert, has bemoaned the extremely limited impacts made by social work professionals in India in bringing about macro policy changes. Another major lacuna observed by a number of educators is the absence of sufficient indigenous teaching material in the schools of social work in India. At the risk of sounding controversial, this author believes that part of the explanation for this lies in the lack of a research orientation amongst social work professionals who seem to lay greater emphasis on 'practitioner' roles and the gulf between academic research and field needs. "In spite of efforts to integrate applied and scientific orientation, the role of research in social work education is not clearly defined and in many programmes remains peripheral... social work practitioners do not sufficiently rely on research to inform their practice... social work agencies do not engage in or encourage research endeavours as a regular part of their programme activity" (Rosenblatt, 1968; Kirk et al., 1976 as cited in Wechsler, 1981: 22).

Lal Das (2000) has also critiqued the lack of practice research linkages when he states that the lack of fit between research and practice is such a greatest drawback in social work education that practice courses draw more from 'practice wisdom' and research courses lack a practice orientation. The resulting parallel tracks between research and practice during training is later reflected in professional work. He has expressed serious concern about this widening gap between research and practice whereby it is assumed that one can be a good researcher or a practitioner but not both. Such attitudes are frequently reflected in presentations as, for example, witnessed in a Ph.D wherein the scholar explained the lack of academic rigour in her study to the fact that she is a 'practitioner' and not an 'academic' intellectual. To my mind, this artificial separation of field level 'practitioner' roles and 'intellectual' researcher/educator/theoretician roles is unnecessary and limits the impact of the profession.

Advantages of Developing Research-Practice Linkage in Academics

Despite an appreciation of the value of research in making need assessment and for monitoring and evaluation tasks, the number of practitioners (or even, for that matter, educators) involved in serious research work to build the theoretical body of social work, as a discipline, is far from sufficient. This results in a dearth of documentation by social work professionals of valuable field experiences and writings on social work research as well as their near absence from policy making processes. Educators are therefore compelled to borrow and adapt from writings by foreign (read Western) authors and works from other social science disciplines. Such borrowing and adaptation is bound to be selective and subjective affecting any efforts at standardization of training modules for social work research and training.

Much of the syllabus of research in social work training also reflects a major component of social research rather than social work research. Many students therefore find research learning rather abstract and theoretical and are unable to grasp the application components of research for their own field. Many entrants to this field are more inclined towards the 'practitioner' component and therefore wonder at the utility of research, which they think may be more relevant to the more academic theorizing fields like Sociology or Psychology and that the emphasis in professional social work training should be more on developing the 'helping skills'.

As mentioned earlier, the multidisciplinary background of entrants into the postgraduate course, as also the lack of conviction about the value of research in social work both amongst trainees as well as a section of educators and practitioners, create obstructions in developing a strong research orientation during training. In many universities and institutions, the choice of doing a research project is kept optional. It is believed that not all trainees would use research in their future careers and many may not have the required ability and interest for research. Under these circumstances, it seems logical and efficient to give inputs more thoroughly to the select few who show an interest and inclination for developing research abilities. Some colleges substitute a full-fledged research dissertation with doing a defined number of 'term papers', having small basic research components.

Despite the practical difficulties involved, I would argue in favour of all students receiving a reasonably good grounding in research at the postgraduate level on three counts. The first is that it is increasingly realized that research is a useful tool for planning, impact analyses, advocacy, lobbying and public opinion building during mobilization processes and, therefore, equipping trainees with research skills would widen the scope of their employable abilities. The second is that stimulating research interests among budding professionals paves the way for at least some of them developing extensive case material from the field and these would create the base for the much needed indigenous material and knowledge building for training in future. Last, but not the least, is that research would develop the needed analytical and writing abilities of future professionals and thus address the criticism that most trained social workers have the necessary interactive communication skills but not the kind of abilities and confidence that would make impacts at 'higher' levels of communication.

"For social work research to develop, integration of research and practice efforts must proceed on all levels involving practitioners and administrators of social agencies as well as social work researchers" (Wechsler, 1981: 23). It is with this kind of a vision that we have made small beginnings at the Institute with respect to training students in research.

Developing Research Orientation

The University of Pune used to give the option to the colleges of social work to decide whether students should submit two term papers (of 50 marks each) over two years or one project report (assessed for 100 marks). Until some years ago, the Institute did not expect the students to carry out a full-fledged research project, but one term paper each in the first and second years, which involved a small (non-sampled) process of primary data collection and its presentation in the form of a term paper.

Practically speaking, the students learnt how to gather information and present basic percentage analyses with neither any research rigour nor a real understanding of the entire process of research.

At a practical level, each faculty would simultaneously guide 12 to 15 students, most of whom were very raw in their understanding of research methodology. Time was therefore a major constraint in giving sufficient inputs. Apart from this, there were no standard guidelines or common understandings on what were the learning competencies to be achieved through this process. Therefore, when some of the faculty insisted on some basic standards of competencies from their students, they faced resistance from the latter who complained that "it was too much effort for just 50 marks". Some of us felt that these half-baked efforts were ineffective in developing a research orientation in our trainees and therefore initiated discussions on the matter with colleagues.

Initial resistances to switch from term paper to project report were based on reservations about students' abilities and interest in research. Many of our students come from rural, poor backgrounds and may be first generation learners. Some faculty felt that the compulsion to carry out the work of a project report would create too much stress on the students which would lead to a compromise on quality. However, eventually, considering the requirement in the field, a consensus was reached to try out a more systematic method of training the learners in research by stretching the research process over the span of one and a half years, the process beginning towards the end of the first half of the first year.

This switch over from term paper to project report work started with the batch of 2000. Given the lack of previous research exposure of a majority of our students, just doing a theory course in Research Methodology at the first year level was insufficient to prepare them to apply research in their own work. Although research laboratory sessions had been conducted with earlier batches, these were in a compressed form and not always consistently carried out. It was therefore felt that conducting regular research laboratory sessions would better equip trainees to apply research to their own studies with reinforcement from their faculty guides. As such, we are still experimenting and evolving what could be considered an effective process of developing research orientation and capacities in our trainees. The following paragraphs would share the efforts and critical learning that we have gained through this process thus far.

Efforts at Standardization Guidance to Students

At the end of the first batch, which worked on project reports, we realized that the hurried decision for a switch over had prepared neither us, as guides, nor the students, to carry out the research work at an enhanced level. We went through a workshop, facilitated by an external practitioner, who had also taught and guided social work students at the postgraduate level, to discuss these difficulties. This workshop helped us to look critically at the fact that we need to plan our trainees' research process much more systematically and that the lab sessions should also be less intimidating and reach out more effectively by enhancing students' participation. Another important fact that emerged was that our own orientations towards and experiences in research were far from uniform and we needed to come to a common framework of understanding about research and the competencies we expect our students to build through training. We therefore subsequently took two major decisions. One, we would bring the methodological aspects of our students' study proposals for discussion in a series of faculty meetings called for this purpose by the Project Report Coordinator. The second was that we would conduct the research laboratory sessions more regularly and extensively so that students are put through a step-by-step experience of the important stages of research work.

During the next two years, we followed this pattern of a common discussion of the proposals very consistently and periodically reviewed these efforts. The major problems confronted here were that the common discussion of sixty odd students' proposals was turning out to be an extremely time-consuming process and not all were willing to invest so much time for this when there were so many other work pressures. In one of the subsequent batches, a group of faculty decided to experiment by meeting as a group of faculty guides along with their respective students after regular lecture hours with each of their students presenting the methodological aspects of the proposal. In this way, suggestions were collectively given by a group of faculty as well as students who participated in the discussion. This process, though found very useful by faculty guides and students alike, could however not be sustained because of constraints of the time-table when the revised curriculum of the University enhanced the number of subjects.

The faculty conducting the research laboratory sessions also expressed the concern that a single faculty could not effectively reach out to all students within the limited time slot assigned per week for these sessions because of the sheer variation and size of the group. Students' feedback also indicated that there was a lack of synchronization of inputs about research between what was taught by the methodology teacher, what was learnt through research lab and the inputs received from guides, leading to a lot of confusion in the students' minds.

An outcome of these discussions was that for the next two years we had a group of four interested faculty members who come together to jointly conduct the lab sessions. One of us was the Research Methodology teacher; the other, who was the Project Report Coordinator, planned and coordinated the sessions and each faculty conducted sessions by turn, with the remaining team members pitching in to sit with the small groups for the group exercises. A tentative session-wise time-table was also displayed and circulated and the core team met periodically to take reviews and give each other feedback to help for better planning and conducting of the sessions. Other faculty colleagues were also invited to sit as observers in any session they desired so that they could give critical feedback and reinforce lab learning through guidance.

With a view to converge efforts at developing research ability of students, we also made efforts for self-learning at the level of faculty to enhance our guiding skills. This involved two kinds of processes: conducting research-related training workshops wherein external experts were invited; and reporting about the progress and problems related to the research lab during faculty meetings and inviting suggestions from faculty colleagues.

Apart from this, a project report manual was prepared by the Project Report Coordinator, a copy of which was given to each faculty member and also students from each batch during the orientation to project report work. It is expected that the faculty guides would monitor the use of this manual by the students during the entire course of their research work. The manual itself has also been pre-tested on three batches of students. It has also been carefully reviewed by internal faculty and a few external experts and is now in the process of being prepared for publication, incorporating the suggestions received over the years through students and there peers' feedback.

With further efforts at standardizing guidance and students' outputs, feedback to faculty about students' research work was carried out with respect to two batches. In one batch, the research lab core group randomly selected two to three project reports guided by each faculty and gave critical review and suggestions, which were discussed in the faculty meeting. It was later felt that external peer review would perhaps be more acceptable and one of the resource persons who had facilitated at one of the faculty development workshops for research was invited to carry this out. Each faculty was asked to select what they considered as one 'best' and one 'worst' project report amongst the students from the outgoing batch and these were given over to the external reviewer for comments. Subsequently, these comments were given in writing to the concerned faculty and personally discussed with them by the external reviewer, in the presence of the then Director.

During the last few years, a policy decision has been taken that the Research Methodology teacher would take the primary responsibility to plan and conduct the research lab so that there is practical reinforcement of the theoretical inputs and part of the confusion due to multiple inputs could be minimized. Other faculty members have pitched in whatever ways they can and whenever they can to conduct the group exercises. Many faculty guides also consult with/refer students to the Research Methodology teacher whenever there is a felt need to discuss aspects related to research methodology.

Current Modules in Research Laboratory

The research laboratory sessions are conducted two hours per week with a more intense focus during the second year of the postgraduate course. However, to keep pace in advance of the research work calendar, during the past few years, we have started the process towards the end of the first term in the first year itself. The broad sequence of sessions is as presented in Table 1.

The first five components are covered at the first year level and if time permits even the sixth component is begun or guidelines for tool construction are given with demonstration and sample tools kept for students' reference. The remaining components are attempted to be covered during the second year. The schedule is however kept flexible according to the pace of the group. As a result, sometimes, we are compelled to compress some of the latter components within the limits of the time-table.

Table 1

S.No.	*Module*	*No. of Sessions*	*Methodology*
1.	Orientation to research laboratory relevance of lab sessions to project report work; what project report process entails; importance of topic related reading and clarity of research concepts and process for preparing proposal, guidelines for topic selection and preparation of proposal.	1	Lecture and discussion
2.	Group formation and brainstorming for topic selection: deciding on basis for group formation (random mixed groups/specialization-wise/languagewise) and forming groups; consensus on topic.	1	Small group discussion and open group sharing
3.	Background reading and literature review: purpose of reading and process and sources for selecting readings; methods for notes taking for easy retrieval; standard format for preparing bibliographies.	2-3	Lecture, discussion, exercise
4.	Defining scope, objectives, research questions, hypotheses (if relevant).	2-3	Small group discussion and open group sharing
5.	Operationalising concepts, defining variables, listing items of information.	2	Discussion and exercise
6.	Tool construction	2-3	Discussion and exercise
7.	Sampling, pre-testing and refining tool	2	—" —
8.	Data collection and scrutiny	2-3	—" —
9.	Preparing the codebook, coding	3	—" —
10.	Entering codes on master-sheet	2-3	—" —
11.	Tabulation and interpretation	2-3	—" —
12.	Diagrammatic presentation	2	Demonstration and exercise
13.	Guidelines for preparing the report, and the abstract	2	Discussion and illustration

Critically looking at the learning impacts of our efforts, we can certainly not claim that we have been uniformly able to develop high levels of research capabilities in our trainees. Much of the impact depends on the extent to which students' interest and participation can be sustained throughout the process. There are often fluctuations and these ebbs and flows do affect the pace as well as impact. Another critical factor in concretizing application of learning is the extent of regular reinforcement from research guides. We have no systems in place to monitor this. At a general level, we can certainly say that the feedback from students and the quality of many reports indicate that the efforts are showing some results and that the students do find the lab sessions useful to enhance their understanding about research application. However, we need to continue improvising and innovating to reach our goal of developing the research mindset and diminishing the stress factor in research so that the entire process becomes more enjoyable and meaningful while the students are going through the process rather than in retrospect.

Questions and Challenges

Research, as an important part of the curriculum, today, has become more acceptable within the Institute. Yet, certain questions continue to be debated or still need to be addressed: Is it really desirable to make a full-fledged project report compulsory for all students? Can we develop alternate research exposure for the students who seem less inclined to carry out academically sound research? How ambitious should we be in pitching the level of research competence to be achieved? What should be the benchmark criteria to decide the levels of complexity/simplicity that guide the direction of student' research work? How can we offset the limitations of our students with the field requirement for research competencies without creating a learning environment, which would make them feel intimidated by research? How can we enhance our own capacities as research guides who can cater to the heterogeneity of background and levels of our trainees? In what ways can we use our students' researches to cater more effectively to the needs of field practitioners? Although we have tried to develop standardized criteria for assessment of project reports, we do find lacunae in their utilization at the time of assessment at the University. Given the fact that we are just one of the colleges within the University, what would be an effective way of standardizing assessment across the colleges? How should we address the issue of ethical concerns in research in student level research studies? These are but few of the questions where a consensus still needs to emerge.

In seeking answers to these questions, it is not enough for us to only look back at our own experiences as educators. We need to learn from the experiences of other professional training institutes. We also need to study the kinds of competencies and work profiles our past students reflect in the field. It would be useful to keep a continuous channel of communication open with field practitioners to see in what ways our own as well as our students' research endeavours can contribute to develop and strengthen field practice. In addition, most importantly, we eventually need to go beyond the formal classrooms to contribute to building the orientation and capacities of the field personnel to make research an important component of their field interventions.

References

Gokarn, N.A. (1990). *Report* of the Curriculum Development Centre in Social Work Education, New Delhi: University Grants Commission.

—. (2001). *UGC Model Curriculum*, New Delhi: UGC.

Lal Das, D.K. (2000). *Practice of Social Research*, Jaipur: Rawat Publications.

Rao, Nagmani (2001). *Project Report Manual* (unpublished), Pune: Karve Institute of Social Service.

Rubin, Allen and Babbie, Earl (2001). *Research Method for Social Work* (4th ed.), USA: Wadsworth Thomas Learning.

Wechsler, Henry (1981). *Social Work Research in the Human Services* (2nd ed.), New York.

Annexure I

Outline for Project Report Proposal

1. Title of the study
2. Statement of the problem
3. Significance of the study
4. Review of related literature
5. Scope of the study
6. Objectives of the study
7. Assumptions underlying the study
8. Hypotheses/research questions
9. Significant variables in the study
10. Operational definition of concepts
11. Listing items of information
12. Research methodology
    - research design
13. Sampling design
    - universe
    - sample size
    - methods and techniques to draw sample
14. Sources of data
    - primary source(s)
    - secondary source(s)
15. Tools for data collection
16. Time calendar for research process
17. Budget

Annexure II

University Criteria for Assessment of Project Reports (MSW)

Headings	*Marks allotted out of 100*	*Criteria*
1. Title	5	Clarity and precision in relation to scope and objectives:
2. Methodology	24	a. The various sections of the methodology chapter should indicate the methodology as it has been used by the researcher in the particular study. There should be no theoretical presentation of research methodology in general.
		b. Framing of objectives, hypotheses, research questions must be clear, feasible, practicable and consistent with objectives and scope of study and properly worded.
		c. Hypotheses must also properly indicate variables used for relation or association.
		d. Sampling – reflecting correctness and clarity about sampling method used, justifiable by the study (rationale).
		e. Research design – clarity, correctness, rationale.
		f. Tool – consistent with title, objectives and scope.
		g. Operational definitions – if concepts used in objectives and hypotheses are operationally defined.
3. Data collected	40	a. Data collected should be reflecting the questions framed in the tool.
		b. Analysis of findings – presentation should be scientific and factual without reflecting researcher's biases.
		c. Use of statistical analysis of data.
4. Presentation	10	a. Neatness and clarity of presentation.
		b. Correctness of sequencing and presentation of chapters, appendices.
		c. Bibliography as per defined standard formats.

Part II

Data Analysis and Interpretation

10

Content Analysis

A Method in Social Science Research

B. Devi Prasad

Content analysis is described as the scientific study of content of communication. It is the study of the content with reference to the meanings, references and intentions contained in the messages. The term 'content analysis' is more than 50 years old.

In 1952, Bernard Berelson published *Content Analysis in Communication Research*, which heralded recognition for the technique as a versatile tool for social science and media researchers. Some scholars adopted it for historical and political research as well (Holsti, 1968). However, the method achieved greater popularity among social science scholars as well as a method of communication research (Wimmer and Dominick, 1994:163). The development of content analysis, as a full-fledged scientific method, took place during World War II when the US government sponsored a project under the directorship of Harold Lasswell to evaluate enemy propaganda. The resources made available for research and the methodological advances made in the context of the problems studied under the project contributed significantly to the emergence of the methodology in content analysis. One of the outcomes of the project — the book entitled *Language of Politics* published in 1940s (Lasswell et al. 1965) — still remains a classic in the field of content analysis. Later on, the method spread to other disciplines too (Woodrum, 1984).

Definition and Purpose of Content Analysis

Content denotes what is contained and content analysis is the analysis of what is contained in a message. Broadly, content analysis may be seen as a method where the content of the message forms the basis for drawing inferences and conclusions about the content (Nachmias and Nachmias, 1976). Further, content analysis falls in the interface of observation and document analysis. It is defined as a method of observation in the sense that instead of asking people to respond to questions, it "takes the communications that people have produced and asks questions of communications" (Kerlinger, 1973). Therefore, it is also considered as an unobtrusive or non-reactive method of social research.

A number of definitions of content analysis are available. According to Berelson (1952), content analysis is a research technique for the objective, systematic and quantitative description of the manifest content of communication. Holsti (1968) says that it is a technique for making inferences by systematically and objectively identifying specified characteristics of messages. Kerlinger (1986) defined content analysis as a method of studying and analyzing communication in a systematic, objective and quantitative manner for the purpose of measuring variables.

Krippendorff (1980) defined content analysis as a research technique for making replicable and valid inferences from data to their context. As for Weber (1985) it is a research methodology that utilizes a set of procedures to make valid inferences from text. These inferences are about sender(s) of message, the message itself, or the audience of message. According to Stone (1966), content analysis refers to any procedure for assessing the relative extent to which specified references, attitudes, or themes permeate a given message or document.

A careful examination of the above definitions of the content analysis method shows emphasis placed on aspects such as system, objectivity, quantification, context and validity – with reference to the inferences drawn from the communication content. As Weber (1985) pointed out, these inferences are drawn about the sender, the message or the receiver of the message. Thus, content analysis is all about making valid, replicable and objective inferences about the message on the basis of explicit rules. The material for the content analysis can be letters, diaries, newspaper content, folk songs, short stories, messages of radio, television, documents, texts or any symbols.

Further, like any other research method, content analysis conforms to three basic principles of scientific method. They are:

1. *Objectivity:* It means that the analysis is pursued on the basis of explicit rules, which enable different researchers to obtain the same results from the same documents or messages.
2. *Systematic:* The inclusion or exclusion of content is done according to some consistently applied rules whereby the possibility of including only materials which support the researcher's ideas is eliminated.
3. *Generalizability:* The results obtained by the researcher can be applied to other similar situations.

Figure 1

Where does Content Analyst Find Himself/Herself?

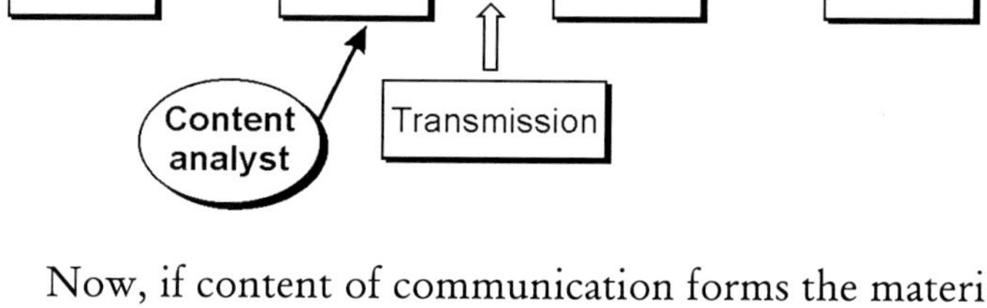

Now, if content of communication forms the material for content analysis, where does a content analyst find himself/herself in the communication process? Figure 1 shows the communication process and where the analyst figures.

As can be seen, the analyst figures at the point of the message, and as Holsti (1968:601) points out, draws inferences about sender(s) of message, characteristics of message itself, or the effects of the communication on the audience – that is, the researcher interprets the content so as to reveal something about the nature of the audience or of its effects. Lasswell (1965) incorporated these components in his classical formulation:

"Who says What to Whom with What Effect?"

Table 1, adopted from Berelson (1952), gives a comprehensive picture of the different uses/applications of the method of content analysis.

Table 1

Purposes of Content Analysis

Purpose	*Questions*	*Research Problems*
To describe the characteristics of content	What?	• To describe trends in communication content. • To relate known characteristics of sources to the messages they produce. • To check communication content against standards.
	How?	• To analyze techniques of persuasion. • To analyze style.
	To whom?	• To relate known characteristics of the audience to messages produced for them. • To describe patterns of communication.
To make inferences about the causes of content	Why?	• To secure political and military intelligence. • To analyze psychological traits of individuals. • To infer aspects of culture and cultural change. • To provide legal evidence.
	Who?	• To answer questions of disputed authorship.
To make inferences about the effect of content	With what effect?	• To measure readability. • To analyze the flow of information. • To assess responses to Communication.

Uses of Content Analysis

Now, an attempt is made in this section, using some studies as examples, to explain about the applications of content analysis.

Though scholars from various disciplines such as social sciences, communications, psychology, political science, history and language studies use content analysis, it is most widely used in social science and mass communication research. It has been used broadly to understand a wide range of themes such as social change, cultural symbols, changing trends in the theoretical content of different disciplines, verification of authorship, changes in the mass media content, nature of news coverage of social issues or social problems such as atrocities against women, dowry harassment, social movements, ascertaining trends in propaganda, election issues as reflected in the mass media content, and so on.

One of its most important applications has been to study social phenomenon such as prejudice, discrimination or changing cultural symbols in the communication content. For example, Berelson and Salter (1948), in their classic content analysis study, highlighted the media under-representation of minority groups. They studied prejudice – a consistent discrimination against minority groups of Americans – in popular magazine fiction. They content analyzed 198 short stories published in eight of the popular magazines during the period 1937-1943 and discussed their findings under the broad categories such as the distribution of characters, their role, appearance, status and their goals which the authors further classified as 'head' goals and 'heart' goals.

To understand the changing cultural symbols, Taviss (1969) content analyzed popular fiction in the 1900s and the 1950s to test the hypothesis that social alienation had been decreasing in middle class American society, while self-alienation had been increasing. The results indicated, for instance, an overall rise in the appearance of alienation themes, a slight decrease in social alienation and a large increase in self-alienation. Similarly, Lowenthall (1944), in his famous article "Biographies in Popular Magazines", examined the changing definitions of heroes in popular magazines in the US, and observed a still ongoing drift away from working professionals and businessmen to entertainers. In another interesting study, Chai (1978) studied the political conflict in Red China following the death of Mao Tse-Tung in 1976, by analyzing the content of 40 obituary notices, received by the central committee of the Communist Party of China, as it was impossible for American scholars to survey or to observe first hand Chinese reaction to Mao's death.

One of the most frequent uses of the content analysis method is to study the changing trends in the theoretical content and methodological approaches by content analyzing the journal articles of the discipline (Loy, 1979). Using this approach, Vijayalakshmi et. al. (1996) analyzed 194 research articles published in the *Indian Journal of Social Work* from 1971 to 1990 to identify characteristics of authors, and document the trends in empirical content, subject areas, and methodological characteristics such as source of data, research design, sampling, and statistical techniques used in the articles. Similarly, public attitudes towards important issues such as civic amenities, unemployment and so on were assessed by analyzing the content of editorials or letters to the editor in newspapers (Inkeles et al., 1952, 1953; Devi Prasad et al., 1992).

One significant area of its use has been the analysis of newspaper content of the election coverage and editorial treatment to mould the opinion of voters. For example, Devi Prasad et al. (1991), analyzed the editorials and letters to the editor published in four dailies in India before the 1991 elections to find out the prominent election-related themes, which figured in the news and direction of their coverage in the respective newspapers.

As a known unobtrusive research method, content analysis is sometimes used to study sensitive topics to corroborate the findings arrived at by other methods. Devi Prasad (1994) analyzed the dowry-related news items published in three English and six regional language daily newspapers during the period from 1981 to 1988. The news items were analyzed to understand the background of the dowry victim, persons involved in the conflict, possible causes of conflict, nature of victim's abuse and death, and nature of reporting.

Content analysis has also been used to ascertain trends in the communication content of dailies, weeklies, cartoons, and coverage of development news, political news and crime news. Murty (2001) analyzed the news items, letters to the editor, and editorials of four selected dailies in India published during the calendar year of 1995, to make a comparative study of the coverage of development news. Political science researchers have used this method to analyze the propaganda devices used by the warring groups (George, 1959; Lasswell et al., 1965).

Other important applications of the content analysis method were systematic analyses of advertisements in newspapers and magazines to draw useful inferences on national culture, as well as media preferences of advertisers (Auter and Moore, 1993; Wang, 1996). Similarly, television, radio and movies offer rich sources of material for content analysis. Many scholars have explored changes in women's roles, sexual behaviour and health, and violence by analyzing the content in television and movie messages (Head, 1952; Lowry, 1989; Olson, 1994).

The above examples throw light on the range and diversity of studies, which made use of the method of content analysis. They also show the variety of messages used to draw inferences about the source, content of the message etc. Though a versatile method, content analysis has its strengths and limitations. An understanding of these will help us use the method effectively.

What content analysis can do?

1. It goes beyond the impressionistic observations about the phenomena and can help us make a quantitative expression about the phenomenon, i.e., express it in numbers, in percentages, which will be more specific and objective.

2. It is an unobtrusive research technique useful to study sensitive research topics.
3. It is context sensitive and therefore can process symbolic meanings of data. Though predominantly seen as a quantitative method, it can effectively capture qualitative content as well (Stempel, 1989:121). The context sensitivity of the method will be useful in articulating the qualitative dimensions such as for example, the direction of coverage of news items as favourable or unfavourable.
4. It is a safe method in the sense that if the researcher found that a portion of the necessary information was missing or incorrectly coded, it is possible to return to the text and supplement the missing data. This is not always possible in experimental or survey research (Woodrum, 1984).
5. It can deal with large volumes of data. Processing may be laborious but of late computers made the job fairly easy.
6. It is a shoestring methodology, which is typically labour-intensive and requires minimum capital investment.

What it cannot do?

1. Its inferences are limited to the content of the text only. Similarly, symbols are processed and coded according to the attribution given by the researcher or coder. There is no guarantee that the sender or receiver shares the same attributed meaning.
2. When it deals with semantic differences or differences in regard to the meanings of words, the findings can be less valid and reliable.
3. It is argued that content analysis which confines itself to counting the individual units and their frequency of occurrence such as for example the number of times the word 'globalization' appeared, may fail to capture the meaning or significance with which these symbols are used in the texts analyzed.

4. The reliability and validity issues in content analysis still remain unresolved (Krippendorff, 1980).
5. The method cannot be used to test casual relationships between variables (Chadwick et al., 1984).

Doing Content Analysis

Content analysis begins with a specific statement of the objectives or research questions to be studied. The researcher asks the question, what do I want to find out from this communication content and frames the questions for study. The researcher must therefore locate a source of communication relevant to the research question and ask questions that can be solved by content analysis.

The objective of content analysis is to convert recorded 'raw' phenomena into data, which can be treated in essentially a scientific manner so that a body of knowledge may be built up. In fact, the researcher who wishes to undertake a study using content analysis must deal with four methodological issues: selection of units of analysis, developing categories, sampling appropriate content, and checking reliability of coding (Stempel, 1989).

More specifically, studies using content analysis usually involve the following six steps:

1. Formulation of the research question or objectives
2. Selection of communication content and sample
3. Developing content categories
4. Finalizing units of analysis
5. Preparing a coding schedule, pilot testing and checking inter-coder reliabilities
6. Analyzing the collected data

In the following pages, we shall explain each step in brief and use an article as an example to relate steps involved in taking up a content analysis study. However, we wish to add a caution that as content analysis is a versatile method, the sample article may reflect only a limited number of the wide range of options practised in the method at each step.

Formulation of the Research Question or Objective

As mentioned earlier, by making a clear statement of the research question or objective, the researcher can ensure that the analysis focuses on those aspects of content, which are relevant for the research. Content analysis is a method for analyzing textual content. Therefore, the selection of topic should be one that can be answered by analyzing the appropriate communication content.

In other words, what is it that we would hope to be able to say about something by analyzing the communication content or a body of texts? For example, a research question in one study (Devi Prasad and Sampath Kumar, 1991) asked, "which election issues had figured prominently during 1991 elections in the editorials and letters to the editor of selected dailies and how these dailies differed in terms of the frequency of appearance and the direction of treatment (favourable unfavourable, or neutral) of these issues". Thus, as with other methods of social research, well-formulated research question or objective can give focus to a study using this method. In the name of frequency of appearance of items or symbols, content analysis should not however fall into the 'counting for the sake of counting' syndrome. For simply counting for the purpose of counting will not yield any meaningful results.

Selection of Communication Content and Sample

The next step would be to locate relevant communication content to answer the research question and to determine the time period to be covered. If the body of content is excessive, then a sample needs to be worked out. Though sampling in content analysis is not so much different from sampling in surveys, because of the unique nature of the source material used in this method, there developed some special sampling techniques for content analysis. Thus, depending upon the nature of the communication content – whether it is a new item, editorial, short story or a TV serial – the sampling techniques differ. The use of constructed week and consecutive day sampling to control the bias of cyclical trends in news coverage (Riffe et al., 1993; Budd and Donohue, 1967), and of basic space unit approach (Danielson and Mullen, 1965:108-10) to take a sample from large volumes of newspaper content – are some of the examples. Useful advice on some of these sampling techniques in content analysis is discussed in Budd and Donohue (1967). Murty (2001) used in his study the constructed week and consecutive day sampling and gave a detailed description of the steps involved. A typical description of samples in content analysis specifies a topic area and time period. Thus, the description of the sample for the study on dowry-related violence is given in the following Box 1:

Box 1

In his study on dowry-related violence, Devi Prasad (1994) used content analysis to examine the characteristics of dowry-related news:

- To examine the frequency and uniformity of the occurrence of certain characteristics of dowry-related death or abuse.
- To draw inferences of a comparative nature to help understand the nature and variety of dowry cases reported in the newspapers.

Developing Content (Subject) Categories

Content categories can be defined as compartments or 'pigeonholes' with explicitly defined boundaries into which the units of content are coded for analysis. They in fact flow from the research question and should be anchored in a review of relevant literature and related studies. Content categories are constructed in response to the query: What classification would most efficiently yield the data needed to answer the research questions raised?

Box 2
Method and Sample

The newspapers, when reporting dowry-related news, present a variety of facts about the incident: the background of the victim, persons involved in the conflict, possible causes of conflict, and the nature of victim's abuse or death.

A purposive sample consisting of three English daily newspapers (*Indian Express, The Hindu,* and *Deccan Chronicle*), and six regional languages (Telugu) daily newspapers (*Eenadu, Andhra Prabha, Andhra Jyoti, Andhra Bhoomi, Udayam* and *Visalandhra*) were selected. The prime consideration in the selection of the newspapers was prominence, as reflected in their circulation and regional representation.

The daily newspapers were surveyed from January 1981 to December 1988. The leading English language daily, *Indian Express*, and the leading regional language (Telugu) daily, *Eenadu*, were taken as the 'base' daily newspapers and all dowry-related news items that appeared during the period were taken from these two daily newspapers.

In order to eliminate duplication, news items from the other dailies were included in the sample only when the *Indian Express* or *Eenadu* did not report these items or did not detail full information about them.

One hundred and twenty-five dowry-related news items were collected and formed the data for analysis. The sample, however, does not indicate the incidence of dowry-related cases either in the various states or in the country as a whole for the period surveyed because it is possible that cases of dowry-related abuse or death might not have been reported in the print media.

The first step in category construction is preliminary examination of the communications by the researcher on a small scale or as a pilot study so that such examination will result in the identification of possible content categories into which material can be coded. Usually, one experiments with several categories before finalizing a set of categories that can be used for the study. Sometimes, category systems already developed by other researchers may also prove useful for your study.

Developing the category system to classify the body of text is the heart of content analysis. Berelson (1952:147) rightly points out: "Content analysis stands or falls by its categories. Particular studies have been productive to the extent that the categories were clearly formulated and well adapted to the problem and the content."

To be useful, every content category must be completely and thoroughly defined, indicating what type of material is and is not to be included. Such definitions, in most of the cases, should be written down before coding begins. These form the operational definitions of categories. According to Chadwick et al., (1984), categories must be mutually exclusive so that a word, a paragraph or a theme belongs to one and only one category. Also, the categories must be exhaustive so that all units examined fit in an appropriate category. Sometimes, a 'miscellaneous or residual category' is added for units that occur rarely or are uncodable for other reasons. The content categories developed for the dowry-related violence are shown in the Box 3.

Box 3

Content Categories Developed for the Study on Dowry-related Violence

- Victim's background – age, education and occupation
- Background of the victim's husband
- Nature and patterns of dowry giving
- Duration of marriage at the time of incident
- Location where the incident took place
- Type of abuse/nature of death
- Nature of demands leading to the conflict
- Persons participating in the abuse of the woman
- Types of endings/outcomes
- Reporting the endings/outcomes

Finalizing Units of Analysis

At this stage, that is, once the categories are identified and defined in terms of the research objectives, the content analyst asks two interrelated questions. They are:

1. What unit of content is to be selected for classification under the categories?
2. What system of enumeration will be used?

Let us begin with the first question. The unit of analysis is the smallest unit of content that is coded into the content category. The units of analysis vary with the nature of data and the purpose of research. Thus, the unit of analysis might be a single word, a letter, a symbol, a theme (a single assertion about one subject), a news story, a short story, a character, an entire article, or an entire film or a piece of programme.

There are two kinds of units of analysis: (1) recording units, and (2) context units. The *recording unit* is the specific segment of content in which the occurrence of a reference/fact is counted or the unit can be broken down so that reference/facts can be placed in different categories. For example, if it is a single word, say 'democracy', the number of times the word appears can be counted. Similarly, a sentence, or a paragraph, a news item or an article containing a symbol or a theme, or a group of facts, can also be a unit. Thus, a news item containing a group of facts can be coded in different categories. According to Nachmias and Nachmias (1976: 135), five major recording units have been used frequently in content analysis research: words or terms, themes, characters, paragraphs and items. The 'item' may be an entire book, an article, a speech or the like.

However, for instance, 'attitude toward democracy' cannot be inferred solely on the basis of the frequency with which the word 'democracy' appears in the communication. Here, the context unit becomes relevant. Thus, the *context unit* is the larger body of content that may be searched to characterize the recording unit (Berelson, 1952). For example, if the coding unit is the word, then, the context unit may be the sentence or the paragraph in which the word appears and characterizes the recording unit.

Coming to the second question, in content analysis, the counting or quantification of the units is performed by using three methods of enumeration: (a) space/time, (b) frequency, and (c) intensity or direction. A unit of analysis can be measured in terms of space (for example, number of column inches) or time (minutes devoted to a news item on the TV). In the case of frequency it is the number of times a given unit or theme is recorded. Intensity or direction implies the measurement of the symbolic meaning contained in the message. For example, the direction of treatment (favourable, unfavourable, or neutral) of the role of election commission in the 1991 elections by the editorials in the selected newspapers (Devi Prasad and Sampath Kumar, 1991).

Box 4

Units of Analysis

Four types of news items, *the News Story, the Human Interest Story, the Editorial and Other* (which includes a news photo or a letter to the editor, that may answer any of the six basic questions that a news story covers) were chose as units of analysis, as they cover the required information for this study and also deal with facts with the minimum degree of distortion.

Preparing a Coding Schedule, Pilot Testing and Checking Inter-Coder Reliabilities

Defining categories and preparing coding schedule for the analysis and coding of content are simultaneous steps. A coding schedule resembles a survey questionnaire and contains different dimensions of the communication content to be coded. Next, piloting the coding schedule is a crucial step before launching the full-scale content analysis. Test coding of a small sample of the material to be analyzed helps reveal inconsistencies and inadequacies in the category construction.

Coding the unit of analysis into a content category is called *coding*. Individuals who do coding are called *coders*. The coder may be the investigator himself/herself or employed by the investigator. Careful training of coders, which usually results in a more reliable coding, is an essential task in any content analysis. It is probably desirable, even in a small-scale study using content analysis, to have more than one coder to independently code the units and to check the inter-coder reliabilities. Chadwick et al., (1984:249) suggested a method of computing inter-coder reliability by calculating a coefficient of reliability. It is calculated by dividing the number of units placed in the same category by the number of units coded:

$$\text{Coefficient of reliability} = \frac{\text{Number of units in the same category}}{\text{Total number of unit coded}}$$

Holsti (in North et al., 1963) suggested a formula[1] to arrive at inter-coder reliabilities:

$$R = \frac{2(C_{1,2})}{(C_1 + C_2)}$$

Analyzing the Collected Data

How should the data be analyzed? The definition of the research problem gives direction to data analysis, the patterns to be examined, and the relationships to be explored. As in the case of analysis of survey data, the starting point can be the description of the profile of the main categories such as for example characteristics and types of content by period, actors, and so on. Later, the analysis can move to conduct more complex analyses comparing two or more dimensions, periods or data sets. Tables – univariate and bivariate – can be prepared and cross-tabulations can be arrived at. Depending on the nature of data, the statistical principles that apply to other areas of survey research will also apply to content studies with a few differences (Stemple, 1989:132). The findings can be presented forcefully even with simple percentages and cross-tables. Tables 2 and 3 from the sample article on dowry-related violence are shown here. In one case, in Table 3, the death occurred in a place close to the couple's residence where the husband, a police constable, murdered his wife and threw her body into the river.

Table 2
Distribution of Various Means and Methods Adopted for Committing Murder of the Woman

Method	*Percentage*
Pouring kerosene and setting fire to her	46.3
Poisoning	14.6
Beating to death	9.8
Strangling	7.2
Beheading	2.5
Drowning	2.5
Not mentioned	17.1
N = 41	100.0

Table 3
Distribution Showing the Types of Ending by Where it Occurred
(in percentage)

Location	*Suicide*	*Murder*	*Death under suspicious circumstances*	*Abuse*
In-laws' place	25.6	27.2	9.6	20.0
Couple's place	4.8	4.0	0.8	3.2
Parent's place	1.6	-	0.8	-
Elsewhere	-	1.62	-	0.8
N = 125	32.0	32.8	11.2	24.0

One important development in content analysis is the use of computers in data analysis. Computer programmes like the "General Inquirer" can identify within a body of text, those words and phrases that belong to specified categories (Stone et al., 1996). However, when text must be searched for ideas or themes, or when coding 'contexts units' with an eye for, let us say, ascertaining direction of treatment – then human coders are more sensitive than computers. Other more popular programmes such as SPSS, Atlas *ti*, QSR NUDIST, Minitab etc., are useful in assisting analysis of both quantitative as well as qualitative data generated through the method.

To sum up, content analysis is a useful research technique for analyzing large bodies of text. It offers objective guidelines in the coding of the text and to draw inferences from the data. It helps in the coding of the text according to systematic and objective rules and in drawing inferences from the data. A successful content analysis study is the outcome of a series of good decisions. The process starts from the point of deciding whether the method is suitable to study the research topic under question. After clearly setting out the objectives of the study, the researcher proceeds to make decisions relating to units of analysis, developing content categories, sample and the sampling period. Orienting coders, checking inter-coder reliabilities and selecting appropriate statistical designs for presenting results are some of the essential tasks, which add rigour to the study.

Content analysis has its limitations. What it does not tell us is about causal connections between variables under study. For example, it is good at capturing the changing trends in the subject content of professional articles published in a journal (Loy, 1979). But it cannot answer why there were changes in the subject content. Further, though a popular research method both in the social sciences and mass communications, it is still used as a technique to supplement the findings of mainstream research designs such as survey research. Woodrum (1984) rightly argues that "content analysis remains an underutilized research method with great potential for studying beliefs, organizations, attitudes and human relations. The limited application and development of content analysis is due more to unfamiliarity with the method and to its historic isolation from mainstream social science than to its inherent limitations".

References

Auter, P.J. and Moore, R.L. (1993). Buying from a friend: A content analysis of two teleshopping programmes, *Journalism Quarterly*, 70(2): 425-436.

Bailey, Margaret (1969). The women's magazine short story heroine in 1957 and 1967, *Journalism Quarterly*, summer, 364-366.

Berelson, B. (1952). *Content Analysis in Communication Research*, New York: The Free Press.

Berelson, B. and Salter, P.J. (1946). Majority and minority Americans: An analysis of magazine fiction, *The Public Opinion Quarterly*, 10: 168-190.

Budd, R.W., Thorp, R.K. and Donohue, L. (1967). *Content Analysis of Communications*, New York: The Macmillan Co.

Cartwright, D.P. (1953). Analysis of qualitative material. In L. Festinger and D. Katz (eds.), *Research Methods in the Behavioural Sciences* (pp. 421-470), New Delhi: Amerind Publishing Company.

Chai, R.T. (1978). A content analysis of the obituary notices on Mao Tse-Tung, *Public Opinion Quarterly*, 41:475-487.

Chadwick, B.A., Bahar, H.M. and Albrecht, S.L. (1984). Content analysis. In *Social Science Research Methods*, pp. 239-257, New Jersey: Prentice-Hall.

Danielson, W.A. and Mullen, J.J. (1965). A basic space unit for newspaper content analysis, *Journalism Quarterly*, pp. 108-110.

Devi Prasad, B. (1994). Dowry-related violence: A content analysis of news in selected papers, *The Journal of Comparative Family Studies*, 25(1): 71-89

Devi Prasad, B. and Sampath Kumar, R.D. (1991) Opinion moulding by the press: An analysis of the election related content of editorials and letters to the editors, *Media Asia*, 18 (1): 24-29.

Devi Prasad, B., Visweswara Rao, K., and Sampat Kumar, R.D. (1992). Civic concerns in an emerging city and its adjoining regions: A content analytic study of critical letters to the "Action Please" column in *Indian Express*, *NAGARLOK*, 24(2): 32-42.

Geiber, W. (1964). News is what newspapers make it. In L.A. Dexter and D.N. White (eds.), *People, Society, and Mass Communications* (pp. 173-182), New York: Free Press.

George, A.L. (1959). *Propaganda Analysis*, Illinois: Row, Pereson and Co.

Hansen, A., Cottle, S., Negrine, R. and Newbold, C. (1998). *Mass Communication Research Methods*, New York: Palgrave.

Head, S.W. (1952). Content analysis of television drama programmes, *Quarterly of Film, Radio, T.V.*, 9 (2): 175-192.

Hirsch, W. (1962). The images of the scientist fiction: A content analysis. In Barber, B. and Hirsch (eds.), *The Sociology of Science*, New York: The Free Press.

Holsti, O.R. (1968). Content Analysis. In G.Lindzey and E.Aronson (eds.), *The Handbook of Social Psychology* (2nd ed.) pp. 596-692, Vol. II, New Delhi: Amerind Publishing Co.

Inkeles, A. and Geiger, K. (1952). Critical letters to the editors of the Soviet Press: Areas and modes of complaint, *American Sociological Review*, 17(1): 694-705.

— (1953). Critical letters to the editors of the Soviet Press: Social characteristics and interrelations of critics and the criticised, *American Sociological Review*, 18(1): 12-22.

Jacobs, Jerry (1976). A phenomenological study of suicide notes, *Social Problems*, 15(1): 60-72.

Kerlinger, F.N. (1986). *Foundations of Behavioural Research* (3rd ed.), New York: Holt, Rinehart and Winston.

Krippendorff, K. (1980). *Content Analysis: An Introduction to its Methodology*, London: Sage.

Lal Das, D.K. (2000). *Practice of Social Research: Social Work Perspective*, Jaipur: Rawat Publications.

Lasswell, H.D., Leites, N. and associates (eds.). (1965). *Language of Politics*, Cambridge: MIT Press.

Loy, Pamela. (1979). Content analysis of journal articles as a technique for historical research, *Journal of the History of Sociology*, 1, 2, Spring: 93-101.

Lowenthal, L. (1994). Biographies in popular magazines. In P.F. Lazarsfled, and F.N. Stenton, (eds.), *Radio Research*, pp. 507-548, New York: Duell, Sloan and Pearle.

Lowry, D.T. and Davis, E.T. (1989). Part-time TV portrayals of sex, contraception and venereal diseases, *Journalism Quarterly*, 66(2): 347-352.

Markoff, J., Shapiro, G., and Weitman, S.R. (1975). Toward the integration of content analysis and general methodology. In D.R. Heise, *Sociological Methodology-1975*, pp. 1-58, London: Jossey-Bass.

Murty, D.V.R. (2001). *Developmental Journalism*, New Delhi: Dominant Publishers.

Nachmias, D. and Nachmias, C. (1976). Content analysis. In *Research Methods in the Social Sciences*, pp. 132-139, UK: Edward Arnold.

North, R.C., Holsti, O., Zaninovich, M.G. and Zinnes, D.A. (1963). *Content Analysis: A Handbook with Applications for the Study of International Crisis*, Evanston: North-Western University Press.

Olson, B. (1994). Sex and the soaps: A comparative content analysis of health issues, *Journalism Quarterly*, 71(4): 840-850.

Riffe, D., Aust, C.F. and Lacy, S.R. (1993) The effectiveness of random, consecutive day and constructed week sampling in newspaper content analysis, *Journalism Quarterly*, 70(1): 133-139.

Stempel, G.H. (1989). Content analysis. In G.H. Stempel and B.H.Westley (eds.), *Research Methods in Mass Communications*, Englewood Cliffs N.J.: Prentice-Hall.

Stone, P.J., Dunphy, D.C., Smith, M.S. and Ogilvie, D.M. (1966). *The General Inquirer: A Computer Approach to Content Analysis*, Cambridge, Mass: MIT Press.

Taviss, I. (1969). Changes in the form of alienation: The 1900's vs. the 1950's, *American Sociological Review*, 34 (February): 45-57.

Vijayalakshmi, B., Devi Prasad, B. and Visweswara Rao, K. (1996). Trends in social work literature: A content analysis of the Indian Journal of Social Work, 1971-90, *Indian Journal of Social Work*, 57(3): 442-460.

Wang, J. (1996). The siren songs of consumption: and analysis of foreign advertisements in two Mainland Chinese newspapers 1985-1993, *Gazette*, 56(3): 201-219.

Weber, R.P. (1985). *Basic Content Analysis*, New Delhi: Sage.

Wimmer, R.D. and Dominick, J.R. (1994) *Mass Media Research: An Introduction* (4th ed.), California: Wadsworth.

Woodrum, E. (1984). Mainstreaming content analysis in social science: Methodological advantage-obstacles and solutions, *Social Science Research*, 13(2): 1-9.

11

Computer-Assisted Quantitative Data Analysis and Interpretation

T. Saraswati and D.K. Lal Das

In a research project, there are various scientific activities in which researchers engage in order to produce knowledge. Although each research project is unique in some ways, all research projects, regardless of the phenomenon being studied, have to undertake data analysis and interpretation.

Once data collection is over, the researcher turns his/her focus of attention on its processing and analysis. There are now some technological advances in data processing and analysis which not only reduce the time considerably, but also increase accuracy to a great extent. Today, most quantitative data analyses use computer programmes. There are a number of computer programmes (software) available for the analysis of social data. One of such computer softwares most frequently used in social science research is the SPSS (Statistical Package for Social Sciences). The SPSS software is able to manage, analyse, and display data. The main feature of the software is that it provides a powerful statistical analysis and data management system in a graphical environment.

Once the data are collected, they must be processed. A codebook has to be prepared where numbers are given for the responses. This is very much essential if we wish to process our data through computer.

Data Analysis

Data analysis involves re-categorization of variables, tabulation, explanation and casual inferences. The purpose of data analysis is to prepare data as a model where relationships between the variables can be studied. Analysis of data is made with reference to the objectives of the study, hypotheses and research designs. This analysis is made with a view to draw meaningful inferences and generalizations.

We need to plan how we will analyze the data. It is advisable to prepare a plan of analysis of data spelling out the various applications of statistical tests carefully while the study is being designed. It is better to have a planned strategy that can be adapted than to end up with piles of data with no organized plan.

It is also essential to explain how we are planning to compare or contrast different variables. In addition, it is necessary to consider which statistical tests we are planning to apply to evaluate the associations/differences between the variables.

A researcher has to make his/her plan for each and every stage of the data analysis. As such, a good researcher makes a perfect plan of data analysis. For this the researcher has to take into consideration the research design of the study. It is the design of research which helps to develop the framework of his/her plan of data analysis.

To some researchers data analysis is not a very serious activity. They feel many a time that data analysis is a job of computer assistants. As a consequence, they have to be contended with the results given by them which may not help to achieve their objectives. To avoid such situations, it is essential that data analysis must be planned in advance and instructed to computer assistants accordingly.

Setting up of Analytic Models

The first step in data analysis is to set up the analytic model of data analysis. These models are diagrammatic presentation of variables and their interrelationships.

To illustrate the process of making analytical model we will consider a study on the life satisfaction of elderly persons. The major objectives of the study are:

1. to assess the extent of life satisfaction among older adults, and
2. to identify the causative factors that determines life satisfaction among older adults.

Hypothesis

"There may be a direct association between physical and psychological health, loneliness, social supports, and spiritual well-being and life satisfaction of older adults."

From the proposed hypothesis it is very clear that the life satisfaction among older adults is the dependent variable in the study. Further, the researcher wishes to examine the association between independent variables – physical and psychological health, loneliness, social supports, and spiritual well-being – and the dependent variable – life satisfaction.

Univariate Analysis

Univariate analysis refers to tables, which present data relating to one variable. Univariate tables, which are more commonly known as frequency distribution tables, show how frequently an item repeats. Usually, frequency distribution tables are prepared to examine each of the independent and dependent variables. Tables 1 and 2 present one independent variable and one dependent variable respectively. These are frequency tables. The distribution may be symmetrical or asymmetrical.

The characteristics of the sample, while examining the percentages, further properties of a distribution, can be found out by various measures of central tendencies. However, the researcher is required to decide which is most suited for a particular analysis. To know how much is the variation, the researcher has to calculate measures of dispersion.

Computer software Statistical Package for Social Sciences (SPSS) was used to process and analyze the data. The SPSS outputs are presented below:

Table 1
Physical and Psychological Health of Respondents (Independent Variable)

Physical and Psychological Health	*Distribution of Respondents*	
	Frequencies	*Percentages*
High	110	38.6
Medium	107	37.5
Low	68	23.9
Total	285	100.0

Table 2
Life Satisfaction Among Respondents (Dependent Variable)

Life Satisfaction	*Distribution of Respondents*	
	Frequencies	*Percentages*
Low	83	29.1
Medium	142	49.8
High	60	21.1
Total	285	100.0

The frequency distribution of a single variable is the frequency of observation in each category of a variable. For example, an examination of the pattern of response to variable 'physical and psychological health of the respondents' in Table 1 would provide a description of the number of respondents who have high, medium and low level of physical and psychological health. To analyze the data it is necessary to convert the frequencies into figures that can be interpreted meaningfully. Frequencies expressed in comparable numbers are called proportions or percentages. Proportions and percentages permit the comparison of two or more frequency distributions. For instance, while the distribution of respondents by 'physical and psychological health' displayed in Table 1 clearly shows the predominance of respondents from 'high' (poor health). Whereas a reversed trend is observed in the case 'life satisfaction' in the distribution of respondents in Table 2, which indicates that the proportions of respondents with 'low' scores is considerably higher than the respondents with 'high' scores.

Bivariate Analysis

Once we describe the independent and dependent variables we look for bivariate associations/relationships among the variables. We know that many a time two variables go together. For example, it is observed that as children grow, their weight increases; and that the crime rate is higher in urban areas than in rural areas. These observations are statements of relationships/associations: age and weight between living conditions and crime. Or, when we say that people who live in slums are usually unskilled is to describe a relationship between living conditions and occupation. This statement can be made only if it is known that people who have better living conditions are also trained for skilled work. In other words, to state a relationship between X and Y is to say that certain categories of variable X go with certain categories of the variable Y. This is known as the principle of co-variation. The principle of co-variation is basic to the idea of relationships/associations and it refers to the notion that observations can be represented by cross-tables.

Bivariate Analytic Model

The bivariate associations among dependent and independent variables can be diagrammatically presented as follows:

Bivariate Analytic Model

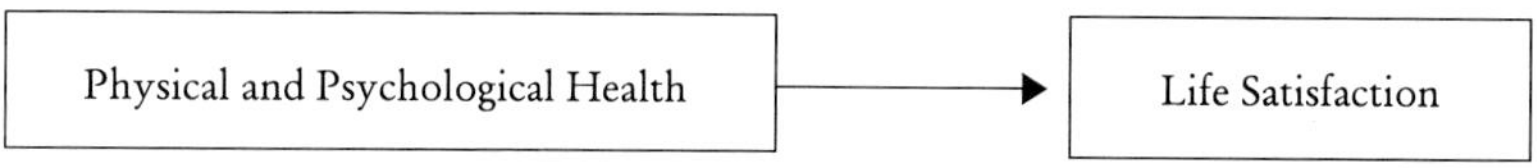

Percentaging Bivariate Tables

To analyze a bivariate table, generally, we transform the frequencies into percentages. The basic purpose of percentaging is to summarize a bivariate table and compare its univariate distribution to assess relationship between the variables.

To know the association between independent variable – physical and psychological health – and the dependent variable – life satisfaction, the data pertaining to these variables are cross-tabulated. A bivariate table presents data of two variables with row or column percentages. Such a table with row percentages is shown below (Table 3):

Table 3

Physical and Psychological Health and Life Satisfaction

Physical and Psychological Health	*Life Satisfaction*			*Total*
	High	*Medium*	*Low*	
High	37(33.6)	63 (57.3)	10 (9.1)	110 (100.0)
Medium	22(20.6)	56 (52.3)	29 (27.1)	107 (100.0)
Low	1 (1.5)	23 (33.8)	44 (64.7)	68 (100.0)
Total	60(21.1)	142 (49.8)	83 (29.1)	285 (100.0)

Figures in parentheses show row percentage.

$\chi^2 = 70.397 df = 4 p = {}^{\cdot}000$ *significant* $C = 0.445$

The next step is a comparison of the univariate distribution to determine the extent of co-variation between extents of physical and psychological health and the life satisfaction of older adults.

Principle of Table Reading

Comparing the percentage differences in the table is a quick method for assessing the extent of a relationship between the variables. Comparisons are always made in a direction opposite to the one in which the percentages have been computed. If the percentages have been computed across the rows as in Table 3, then, we compare percentages down the column.

As such, first, we have to compare the percentages of the first column, which presents the sub-category of respondents who have perceived 'high' life satisfaction. It is evident that larger proportions of respondents who have perceived high physical and psychological health (33.6), have also perceived higher level of life satisfaction than those who discerned low physical and psychological health (1.5). Similarly, we can also examine the sub-category of respondents who have perceived 'low' life satisfaction. In this category we find a larger proportion of respondents who have perceived low physical and psychological health (64.7) have also perceived lower level of life satisfaction than those who discerned high physical and psychological health (9.1). We may therefore infer that older adults with higher level of physical and psychological health are likely to have higher life satisfaction.

The association between the variables can also be examined by various statistical techniques depending upon the level of measurement of the data. Since the data are in nominal levels of measurement, the Chi-square test would be more appropriate in this case. Apparently, association among independent variables – physical and psychological health – and the dependent variable – life satisfaction – is statistically significant and hence the variables are associated. Therefore, it may be inferred that older adults with higher physical and psychological health have higher level of life satisfaction.

In bivariate analysis the researcher also explains the nature and the degree of association. That is, whether the relationship is positive or negative and it also indicates the degree of association in terms of high, moderate or low. Analysis of the nature of association clearly shows that independent variable is positively associated with the dependent variable 'life satisfaction'. The Coefficients of Contingency (C) show the degree or strength of correlations between the variables. Results show that correlation among physical and psychological health and life satisfaction is 'moderate'.

Results of the bivariate analysis show that the variables are associated. In other words, we may say that life satisfaction of older adults depends on physical and psychological health. That means the results are in line with the analytic models presented in the beginning of this paper.

The examination of a bivariate association is the first step in data analysis. Next, the substantive implications of the findings are evaluated. And, in the last, causal inferences are drawn.

The bivariate measure of a relation is limited to the establishment of co-variation and its direction. To interpret the findings and to assess the causal priorities of the investigated variables, one introduces other variables into the analysis.

Suppose, one finds a relationship between parent's age and child-rearing practices; that is, older parents tend to be more restrictive with their children than younger parents. One may claim that the variables are causally related and that increasing age of parents is associated with a shift from permissive toward restrictive attitudes. However, alternatively, it is a possibility that a difference in child-rearing practices is due, not to a difference in age, but rather to a difference in orientation. Older parents were exposed to an orientation stressing restriction, whereas younger parents behave according to a more liberal orientation advocating more permissive practices. In other words, relationship between parent's age and child-rearing practices is due to a fact that the variables 'age' and 'child-rearing practices' are both associated with a third variable, i.e., 'orientation'.

An observed correlation between two or more variables does not, of itself, permit the researcher to make causal interpretations. A bivariate relationship may be the product of chance, or it may exist because the variables are related to a third, unrevealed variable.

Furthermore, the phenomenon under study can often be explained by more than a single variable. In either case, the introduction of additional variables serves the purpose of clarifying and elaborating the original relationship. The analysis of more than two variables serves three major functions in empirical research: control, elaboration and prediction. The first function substitutes for the mechanism of experimental control when such is lacking.

Bivariate analysis of data is followed by trivariate analysis for cause-effect analysis. The purpose of trivariate analysis is to substantiate the findings of bivariate analysis. The bivariate analysis establishes co-variation and its direction. To draw the causal inference, one has to re-examine the bivariate relations by controlling the effect of other variables into the analysis. Suppose, one finds a relationship between 'smoking habits' and 'academic performance of students', that is, those students who smoke frequently have bad academic performance. If we wish to interpret the result at this juncture, we would say that there is a cause-effect relationship between the variables and that increasing/decreasing the frequency of smoking will increase/decrease the academic performance. However, it is also possible that decrease in the academic performance is not due to increase in the frequency of smoking but rather to mental depression. That is, students with high level of depression generally smoke more frequently just to get some relief and also mental depression acts adversely on academic performance. In other words, the relationship between 'smoking habits' and 'academic performance' is due to the fact that both the variables are associated with a third variable, i.e., 'mental depression'.

Bivariate relationship may be observed because of two reasons: either just due to chance, or due to a third variable which is yet to be revealed. Above all, the change in the dependent variable may be explained by more than one single independent variable. In both the cases, re-examination of the bivariate relationship by controlling the effect of third variable serves the purpose of clarifying and elaborating the original relationship.

Trivariate Analysis

Trivariate and multivariate analyses serve three important functions in social research, viz., control, elaboration and prediction. Firstly, whenever the experimental control is not possible, trivariate analysis is used to examine the bivariate relationship to see if the relationship is due to a third variable. Secondly, bivariate relationship is clarified by introducing a third variable. Finally, trivariate analysis helps to identify more independent variables to account for the variation in the dependent variable.

Variable as a Control

If the two variables are associated, it is not necessary that there is cause and effect relationship between them. It is essential that the effects of other variables are ruled out as alternative explanation of the relationship. For example, a relationship between 'knee joint pain' and 'amount of rainfall' can probably be accounted for by the variable 'humidity'. Humidity is related to both knee joint pain and amount of rainfall and this joint relationship produces a statistical relationship that has no causal significance. The original bivariate relationship between 'knee joint pain' and 'amount of rainfall' is called spurious. It is mandatory for a researcher to reveal such variables and substantiate the bivariate relationship. It is the basic principle of all research designs and is achieved by a process called 'control'.

In experimental research designs the subjects are divided into two groups, viz., experimental group and control group, by using the process of randomization. This assures that all the extraneous variables are controlled and the groups differ only with regard to their exposure to the independent variable. However, it is rather difficult to manipulate groups before the study in quasi-experimental research designs. As such, statistical techniques are used as method of control in quasi-experimental and survey research designs. The statistical techniques are used during data analysis. There are two methods of statistical control: (1) cross-tabulation, and (2) partial correlation. In the first method data are cross-tabulated and sub-groups are compared. In the second method – partial correlation – a statistical procedure is used to nullify the effects of extraneous variables.

Cross-Tabulation as a Method of Control

In this method the sample is divided into sub-groups according to the categories of the controlled variable. The variables which show an association with independent and dependent variables are selected as control variables. The original bivariate association is re-examined within each sub-group. There are three possibilities: (1) the original bivariate association is not affected by the third variable, (2) the original bivariate association is effected by the third variable and the association is disappeared, and (3) the original bivariate association is partially affected. While, when a third variable completely accounts for the bivariate association between the independent and dependent variable, the association is referred as spurious whereas if a third variable does not account for the bivariate association between the independent and dependent variable, the association is referred as non-spurious.

Trivariate Analytic Models

Let us suppose that another independent variable 'spiritual well-being' has shown association with the independent variable 'physical and psychological health', and the dependent variable 'life satisfaction'. To substantiate the original association between 'physical and psychological health' and 'life satisfaction', we decide to re-examine the association taking 'spiritual well-being' a third variable as control variable.

The bivariate associations between dependent and independent variables with a third variable as control can be diagrammatically presented as follows:

Model

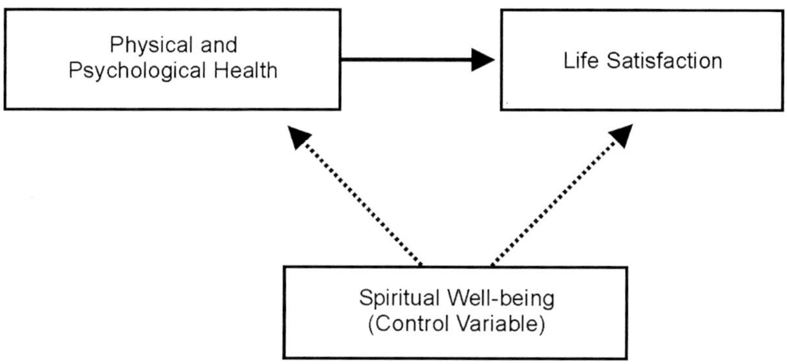

Let us re-examine the bivariate association between 'physical and psychological health' (independent variable) and 'life satisfaction' (dependent variable) controlling the effect of 'spiritual well-being' (a third variable as control variable). To do this we prepare partial tables using SPSS package by cross-tabulation of data pertaining to independent and dependent variable and control the effect of a third variable on the original bivariate association. The results of cross-tabulation of data are presented below in Table 4:

Table 4
Physical and Psychological Health and Life Satisfaction (Controlling for Spiritual Well-Being)

Spiritual Well-Being			*Life Satisfaction*			*Total*
			High	*Medium*	*Low*	
Low	Physical and Psychological Health	High	3 (75.0)	11 (32.4)	3 (8.3)	17 (23.0)
		Medium	1 (25.0)	13 (38.2)	8 (22.2)	22 (29.7)
		Low	0 (0.0)	10 (29.4)	25 (69.4)	35 (47.3)
		Total	4 (100.0)	34 (100)	36 (100)	74 (100.0)
P2=8.83	df =4	df=4	p = .001		c=.45	
Medium	Physical and Psychological Health	High	21 (58.3)	30 (42.3)	5 (12.5)	56 (38.1)
		Medium	14 (38.9)	30 (42.3)	19 (47.5)	63 (42.9)
		Low	1 (2.8)	11 (15.5)	16 (40.0)	28 (19.0)
		Total	36 (100.0)	71 (100)	40 (100)	147(100)
	χ^2=26.104		Df =4		p = .000 c=.38	
High	Physical and Psychological Health	High	13 (65.0)	22 (59.5)	2 (28.6)	37 (57.8)
		Medium	7 (35.0)	13 (35.1)	2 (28.6)	22 (34.4)
		Low	0 (0.0)	2 (5.4)	3 (42.9)	5 (7.8)
		Total	20 (100.0)	37 (100)	7 (100.0)	64 (100.0)
	χ^2=14.149		df =4		p =,007 c=.42	

In Table 4, it is observed that the original bivariate association remains unaffected by the third variable 'spiritual well-being'. In the total sample as well as in each sub-group of 'spiritual well-being' the proportion of 'life satisfaction' is unchanged. The result shows that the original bivariate association between the two variables is not accounted for by the control variable 'spiritual well-being'. Thus, it may be concluded that 'spiritual well-being' has no effect on the association between 'physical and psychological health' and 'life satisfaction'. In other words, we can infer that the association between 'physical and psychological health' (independent variable) and 'life satisfaction' (dependent variable) is non-spurious. The results of the analysis can be diagrammatically shown as below:

Non-Spurious Association between Independent and Dependent Variable

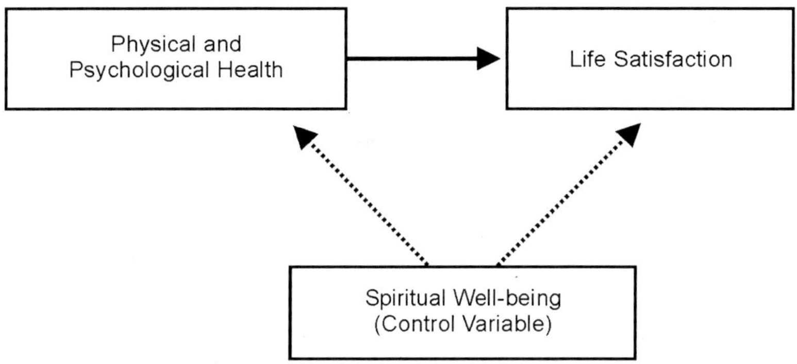

Multivariable Analytic Model (Simultaneous Effect)

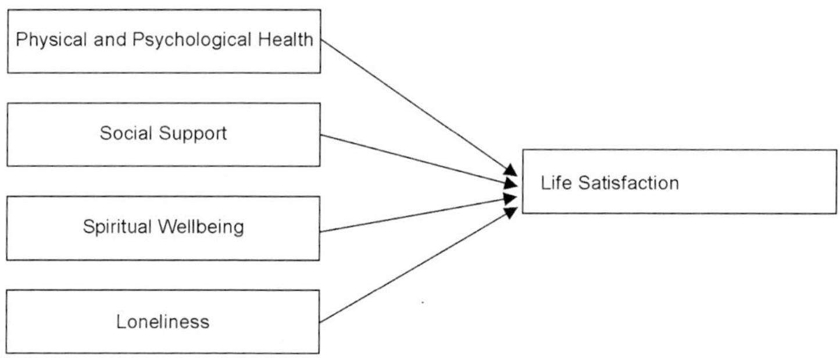

Multivariate Analysis

So far, we have discussed the relations between three variables where one independent variable is to determine the dependent variable for controlling the effect of a third variable. In rarity, particularly in social sciences, however, there is hardly any situation where one independent variable determines the dependent variable. Often, we have situations where a set of independent variables is associated with dependent variable. In other words, more often, several independent variables contribute to the prediction of the dependent variable. Multiple

Regressions is commonly used to estimate the effect of multiple independent variables.

References

Bailey, Kenneth D., 1978, *Methods of Social Research*, London: The Free Press.

Baker, L. Therese, 1988, *Doing Social Research,* New York: McGraw Hill.

Blalock, Hubert M., 1972, *Social Statistics*, New York: McGraw Hill.

Doby, J.T. et. al., 1953, *An Introduction to Social Research,* London, Harrisburg: Tackpole Co.

Kerlinger, Fred R., 1964, *Foundations of Behavioural Research,* Delhi: Surjeet Publications.

Lal Das, D.K., 2000, *Practice of Social Research: Social Work Perspective*, Jaipur: Rawat Publications.

Monete, Duane R. et. al., 1986, *Applied Social Research: Tool for the Human Services,* Chicago: Holt.

Nachmias, D. and Nachmias, C., 1981, *Research Methods in the Social Sciences*, New York: St. Martins Press.

Sellitz, G. et al., 1973, *Research Methods in Social Relations,* New York: Holt, Rinehart and Winston (3rd edition).

Wilkinson, T.S. and Bhandarkar, P.L., 1977, *Methodology and Techniques of Social Research*, Bombay: Himalaya.

Part III

Research in Fields of Social Work

12

Research in Correctional Social Work with Social Work Intervention

V.V. Devasia

Research in correctional social work includes the totality of research design in organizing a scientific study of social work intervention in correctional settings in order to have diagnosis, treatment and rehabilitation of inmates or persons undergoing corrections or the systematic study of the correctional setting itself (Rubin and Babbie, 2004). Social work is a helping profession. Its focus is on the interactions between individuals and systems in the social situation. Individuals are dependent on systems for help in obtaining material or emotional resources and services and opportunities they require to actualize their aspirations and to help them cope with their life tasks. Hence, the goal of research in correctional social work is social work intervention.

What is the nature of a scientific design that is applicable in correctional setting and whether such a design can envelope the different methods of social work, like casework and group work and probation and parole. There are restrictions that the correctional settings impose upon the delinquent or criminal.

Yet, if the correctional experience is to be useful one and social work researchers work a genuine helping, these limitations must be easily dealt with through correctional research. Therefore, social work research, based upon the understanding of the dynamics of the helping process, hold great promise for useful service in correctional settings.

Social Work Research in Corrections

According to the Social Work Curriculum Study (Boehm, 1959: 54), "Social work seeks to enhance to social functioning of individuals, singly and in groups, by activities focused upon their social relationship which constitute the interaction between man and his environment. The activities can be grouped into three functions: restoration of impaired capacity, provision of individual and social resources and prevention of social dysfunction." Hence, social work research tries to evolve remedial action on problems in several areas of society by doing empirical studies. Research in correctional social work highlights three functions of social work, understanding the different dimensions of restoration of impaired capacity, provision of individual and social resources and prevention of social dysfunction, and all the three are intertwined and inter-dependent.

For Thyer (2005) research in correctional social work helps the restoration that can be curative or rehabilitative. Its curative aspects are to eliminate factors that have caused breakdown of functioning, and its rehabilitative aspects to organize and rebuild interactions. Provision of resources can be developmental and educational. The developmental aspects are designed to further the effectiveness of existing social resources or to bring to full use of personal abilities for more effective social interaction. The educational aspects are structured to make familiar the public with specific conditions and needs for new or changing social resources. Prevention of social dysfunction involves early discovery, control and elimination of conditions and situations that potentially could hamper effective social functioning. The two main divisions of prevention of social dysfunction are prevention of problems in the area of interaction between individuals and groups, and the prevention of social ills.

The underlying assumptions of research in correctional social work are:

1. Research in correctional social work has problem-solving functions.
2. Research in correctional social work is scientific in nature with a value foundation.
3. Research in correctional social work came into being and continues to develop because it meets human needs and aspirations recognized by society in order to help the law-breakers and, hence, it assumes some of the socialization and control functions of society.
4. Research in correctional social work takes its values from those held by the society of which it is a part.
5. The scientific base of research in correctional social work consists of three types of knowledge:
   (i) Tested knowledge or verified knowledge;
   (ii) Hypothetical knowledge that requires transformation into tested knowledge; and
   (iii) Assumptive knowledge (or "practice wisdom") that requires transformation into hypothetical and thereafter into tested knowledge.

The correctional social work researcher uses all three types of knowledge, and carries a professional responsibility for knowing at any time which type of knowledge he is using and what degree of scientific certainty attaches to it.

6. The knowledge needed for research in correctional social work is determined by its goals and functions and the problems it seeks to solve.
7. The internalization of professional knowledge and values is vital in correctional social work research since it is an instrument of professional help.

8. Social work skill is expressed in the practice of research in correctional social work mainly with empathy, confidentiality and self-determination. It constitutes the scientific and artistic creation resulting from three internal processes of the researcher: first, conscious selection of knowledge pertinent to the research; second, fusion of this knowledge with social work values; and third, the expression of this synthesis in data collection, processing analysis and interpretation of data (Devasia, 1981).

Research in correctional social work constitutes commitment for the social worker. It also means that the functions assigned to correctional social work by society represent a two-fold responsibility. The first is to determine the social work intervention through which it seeks to reach socially approved goals and modify them as necessary in the light of changing social needs. The second is to exercise discipline and control over the nature and characteristics of correctional research that would keep its professional accountability. Research in correctional social work not only helps individuals and groups to overcome their conflicts with the society in relation to law, but also assists them to prevent from law breaking and enrich daily living. So, the main focus of research in correctional social work is to help law-breakers to improve their social functioning. Social work is an art because it requires great skills to understand people and to help them to help themselves (Morris, 2006). It is a science because of its problem-solving method and its attempt to be objective in determining facts and in developing principles and operational concepts. It is a profession entity because it encompasses the attributes of a profession. All these are true in relation to research in correctional social work.

Social work values are basically the values of democratic societies that are mainly the worth of the individual, the inherent dignity of the human person, society's responsibility for contributing to the common good, etc. For the National

Association of Social Workers (1958: 5-9) the following four values are listed basic to the practice of social work:

1. The individual is the primary concern of this society.
2. There is interdependence between individual in this society.
3. They have social responsibility for one another.
4. There are human needs common to each person, yet each person is essentially unique and different from others.

In providing correctional help, the dignity and individuality of the law-breaker should be respected. All other values in social work originate from these primary values and contribute to the achievements of goals based on the primary values. The values dictate ways in which the correctional researcher should interact with others in carrying out his professional activities so as to actualize the primary values.

Knowledge of research in correctional social work may be enhanced by consideration of some of its distinguishing characteristics. It stresses the total person in the total environment (see Shekar, 1982: 56-58) in a correctional setting. Its emphasis is on the importance of the family in molding and influencing behaviour. Utilization of community resources in helping the law-breaker to overcome law-breaking behaviour is another important dimension.

Correctional Research as a Social Work Process

Correction is a social process by which modern society deals with officially identified law-breakers. So, correction is a part of social control. The correctional agency tries to rehabilitate or neutralize delinquent or criminal behaviour of adolescents or adults through corrections. Corrections function with social and legal authority after the criminal court has held an adult to be guilty of violation of law, or when the juvenile court acts in a youngster's interests after a referral has been made alleging a delinquent act. As delinquents and criminals are sentenced to institutions and are placed on probation and parole, various professional agencies become interested in making these efforts as effective as possible and social work research is one of these.

Correctional system emerged from social work, in the 19th century, as the result of major modifications in the penalty system. Death, mutilation and banishment were the primary penalties for law-breaking before 19th century. The administration of these punishments needed only the hangman and the warden of the prison as personnel where criminals and delinquents were held for trial and execution. In the beginning of last century, due to correctional research, human life received more dignity and respect and substitution of varying periods of restricted supervised status in the penalty system gradually emerged. At the same time, social work as a profession was growing fast and an important area of focus involved was the delinquent and the criminal. The modification of the penalty system did more than require a different kind of administrative structure and personnel. It made possible the idea of treatment.

With the increasing knowledge, about the dynamics of human behaviour and how it is modified, it became possible to give attention to the rehabilitation of the offender. Hence, correctional research as a social work process has been understood as the scientific study of the administration of the penalty in such a way that the offender is "corrected". It means the criminal's or delinquent's present behaviour controlled and his general life adjustment modified (Mark, 1996). So, the correctional research requires both control over the behaviour of the delinquent or criminal during the period of his penalty, and services designed help him achieve socially acceptable mode of participation in the community.

Research in Correctional Social Work and Task of the Researcher

To rehabilitate officially identified delinquents and criminals, every democratic society has created a system of correctional agencies. These agencies have been given the task of administering the penalties assigned to delinquents and criminals.

These agencies are expected to protect the community during the offender's period of supervised status by controlling his behaviour. Furthermore, they are expected to help the offender so that he can return to normal status better able to be a constructive member of the community. Correctional institutions and community corrections that are probation and parole are the main agencies in the correctional system. The different kinds of institutions under corrections are as follows: 1. Prisons; 2. Borstal Schools; 3. Certified, Special Approved School; 4. Remand/Observation Homes; 5. Beggar Homes; 6. Reception Centres, Protective Homes; 7. State Homes; and 8. Probation Hostels.

The nature of the penalties that these agencies administer is essentially that of a handicapped personal and social status. This period of downgraded status is spent under supervision either in an institution or in the community under the guidance of correctional personnel. The handicaps inherent in this status include: loss of certain civil rights such as voting; right to enter into certain contracts; loss of liberty; restrictions on mobility; and restrictions on privacy, i.e., the offender must keep in contact with the supervising officer and must discuss most aspects of his basic social adjustment.

Research in correctional social work directly or indirectly helps the offender to change his offending behaviour, therefore, he can relate constructively to others and become socially acceptable. This is done through working with the individual to help him to change through better understanding of himself and by tapping his own strengths and resources; and through modification of his environment to bring about healthy social climate in which he has to live (Bentz and Shapiro, 2006). The social work researcher encourages the offenders to talk about his problems, to feel about them, and to come to an insightful understanding of himself accompanied by socially constructive behaviour. The tasks of the social work researcher in corrections include four particular aspects such as investigation for the purpose of securing information about the client's failure or success in meeting the obligations of his legal status; the use of controls to modify client behaviour; acting as a legal authority in the client's life with responsibility for value change; and correctional decision-making.

Doing research on and with the offenders, all the above tasks are important especially helping them to adjust better to society. The correctional social work researchers most important task is to change the values and behaviour of the offenders so that they become agreeing in action with the values of the particular community (Schutt and Engel, 2005). Therefore, social worker's aim is to help the offender, not to punish him. The goal is to utilize the knowledge and skills of the profession in a corrective manner, to rehabilitate the offender, to help him to help himself, so that he can return to and become a part of his society and to lead a constructive life.

Research in correctional social work would be effective in working with delinquents and criminals because it creates knowledge of delinquent and criminal behaviour as one from of deviance and the psychological and social strains that in various constellations press individuals towards such behaviour (Padgett, 1998). It also helps to develop a body of techniques that is learned by the offender in order to commit offences and to protect himself in dealing with community authorities. The diagnostic approaches now in use and the problems inherent in applying them to the correctional caseload. Research in correctional social work develops skills in identifying the social as well as psychological strains effective in the causation of offending behaviour, besides modifying the offender's environment so that strains toward conformity are substituted for those that press toward criminal deviance. It develops attitudes of acceptance of delinquent and criminal deviants without condoning anti-social behaviour.

These knowledge, skills and attitudes help the correctional social work researcher to deal more effectively with the offender, i.e., for the reformation and rehabilitation of the offender that is the goal of research in correctional social work.

The researcher helps to strengthen motivation of delinquents and criminals. Through talking with them sympathetically and understandingly, the social work researcher aids them. The correctional social work researcher allows the offenders to ventilate their feelings. Most offenders need to share with someone, in confidence, their inner feelings, their fears and frustrations, as well as their hopes and aspirations. In correctional setting the social worker provides a safe emotional climate in which offenders can express and verbalize them. The researcher provides needed information to offenders in correctional settings (Potocky and Rodgers, 1998). By giving information, the social work researcher can help offenders to make decisions. The researcher does not make decisions for the offenders, but he helps them to consider rationally, their problems and the alternatives that face them.

By defining situations and problems the researcher helps the offender. He assists the offender not only in thinking about a problem, but also in feeling about the situation. The researcher also assists the offender in modifying his environment. With his knowledge of community resources, the social work researcher is able to help the offender and his family to tap different kinds of financial and social resources to meet their needs. Understanding the reorganizing behaviour patterns of the offender is an important function of the correctional social work researcher. This includes helps for sexual deviants, chronic alcoholic and drug addicts and those who have deep personality problems. Facilitating referral is another important function of the researcher. Referral may be made to a clinical psychologist, psychiatrist, school teacher, physician, or other professionals who may help the offender with a particular problem. The social work researcher's comprehensive knowledge of the community resources is used to advantage in making referrals.

Research in Social Work Methods in Corrections

The social work researcher in correctional setting make use of the methods of social work to achieve his goals. The mobilization of inner capacities and environmental resources is accomplished primarily through the relationship between the caseworker and the client. The relationship that is established during the period of treatment process enables the client to work toward a constructive solution of his problems. Social casework is an art in which knowledge of the science of human relations skill in relationship are used to mobilize capacities in the individual and resources in the community appropriate for better adjustment between the client and all or any part of his total environments. So casework is the process of dealing with the individual case. It is concerned with the individual in relation to his social environment and aims at his successful adjustment.

A professional casework relationship is one that enables the client to express facts, attitudes and feelings with a guarantee that the worker's response will be geared to the client's needs, not to the worker's need. The caseworker, as a social work researcher, is responsible for facilitating communication both verbal and non-verbal, without which no relationship can be established and developed (Armaity, 1978). The relationship is connected with the treatment process. The two types of casework treatment currently used in correctional settings are the supportive treatment method and curative treatment. The former requires the use of a number of techniques that help the client to improve his functioning within the framework of his established ego mechanisms of defence. The latter requires the use of different techniques that help the client to improve his functioning through modification of selected ego mechanisms of defence. The outward form of the client's behaviour and selected internal process are modified.

In correctional institutions caseworker as a social work researcher keeps the relationship a realistic one, using the possible elements in the relationship to motivate and influence the client toward a maximal solution of his problems. Thus, in the correctional settings, the caseworker's activity in respect to motivation is directed toward reducing the strength of factors inhibiting the client's use of help, and toward identifying and utilizing the constructive motivating forces that the client has already developed. This is for purpose of adaptation and mastery and toward offering opportunities that may induce constructive motivation where it does not exist.

The social work researcher attempts to establish a relationship that, over a period of time, frees the individual to express his feelings, muster his ego strength, change his anti social values and become a law-abiding citizen. Thus, relationship is the social caseworker's core contribution along with the use of community resources. It means the caseworker accepts the client, understands and respects him. The client gradually develops feelings toward the caseworker, and shares his ideas, emotions and worries. Then, through a bond of warmth and support, changes are effected. The social work researcher is non-judgmental, sensitive to the needs of the offender, and conveys a feeling of respect for the integrity and individuality of the offender regardless of his criminal conduct.

The helping process depends upon a relationship between social work researcher and client within which the client may, if he is able and willing to ask, receive, and use help in clarifying his own wants and purposes, in relation to the resources available to him, and in mustering his own powers to achieve his chosen ends. In many instances, the offender is likely to express his needs about concern situations such as the way he left things at home, or the job he left behind, or some detail of institutional life such as change of work assignments, or living quarters, or a suspected discrimination against him in privileges. The basis of the client's complaints may be real and may furnish a specific issue upon which the caseworker and the inmate can work together. But casework as a social work research with offenders is neither primarily concerned with the individual offender as a separate entity apart from his surroundings, nor with the social environment and its improvement.

Case work however, has a general interest in both the offender and the environment, since its goals is to find a means of adjustment and an equilibrium between the two. For the successful accomplishment of this task, the social work researcher must understand the offender, his capacities and abnormalities and also the social situation and its resources and dangers. Furthermore, his knowledge must be broad enough to go beyond the offender involved the embrace the scientific principles that lie at the back of personality development, behaviour and the social forces that govern family and community.

The basic assumptions underlying casework as social work research, which are applicable in helping the offender, are: (1) every individual must be seen as a person of dignity and worth; (2) behaviour, whether acceptable or unacceptable to the community, expresses a need of the individual; (3) an individual can and will change his behaviour if the right help is given time and in the right amount; (4) if the offer of help is given before the problem becomes seriously aggravated, the response is likely to be better; and (5) the family is the most influential force in the development of personality in the crucial early years (Alston and Bowles, 2005).

The emphasis in casework as social work research varies from case to case, since the cause of maladjustment may lie primarily with the individual, or with the environment, or in some combination of these personal and social factors. The casework as social work research may be directed at strengthening the personality, in order to increase the capacity and understanding the offender. This is true, for instance, in the case of those who suffer from nervous and emotional disorders, from frustrations and conflicts, which prevent successful adjustment in any situation. In other cases, the emphasis may be directed at a change or enrichment of the environment, to eliminate harmful conditions and make use of helpful resources. This is true for example in the case of children who live under conditions in delinquency area where is difficult for even the most normal type of personality.

In attaining both immediate and ultimate goals in social work research in this context, three fundamental processes are seen interplay at every point: the use of the resources; assisting the offender to understand his needs and possibilities; and helping him to develop the ability to work out his own social programme through the use of available resources. Therefore, casework is a joint action in which both the caseworker and the offender take part and in which they develop a definite relationship. In correctional settings casework as social work research has been in use over considerable period of time, especially in relation to probation. In other correctional settings, especially in institutions, not only is casework a later development nonetheless, it is very difficult to apply (Shekar, 1982). The prison or Borstal school programme is one of mass treatment and often casework is neglected.

Social Group Work as Social Work Research in Corrections

Group work with delinquents and criminals is often seen as a powerful technique for modifying behaviour and attitudes. Although demanding and sometimes complex, group work is based on some rather simple and well-supported observations about how people grow and interact. According to the Curriculum Study (Murphy, 1959: 78), "Social group work is a method of rendering service to persons, through providing experience in groups. Development of the person towards his individual potential, improvement of relationship and social functioning competencies, and social action are recognized as purposes of social group work. The worker functions within a framework of ethical and social values." In social group work in corrections the worker is also a researcher and helps members and group to use their abilities and strengths. The worker uses himself in different ways in relation with specific objectives. The group member and the group are inextricably interrelated and the condition of each is bound to affect the other. There can be three main reasons for the use of the group in treatment of the delinquent and criminal. First, the dynamics of the offender himself; secondly, the specific correctional setting in which he finds himself; and thirdly, the specific purpose for which society has put him into the correctional setting.

There is a phenomenon appearing in the delinquent that shows that one of his outstanding identification as well as support is the group. This phenomenon is certainly closely related to the age of the delinquents, since all adolescents seek their status far more in the group of contemporaries than though closeness with adults. The use of the group work method becomes, therefore, essential because the delinquent can often not be reached otherwise. He must be approached on his own group with the security of the surrounding other delinquents. The purpose and goals of the group related to this understanding are many.

Group work as social work research in correctional settings, the programme media is varied. The group members are allowed for outlet of hostility, and not reduce the group to unacceptable behaviour. Programme should allow, at times, for the individual need of withdrawal by letting a group member to something for himself without feeling guilty that he does not participate, but help him feel accepted by presence in the group. Besides the help with outlet of feelings, programme should include the opportunity for real achievement. It should strike a balance between more individual and more cooperative projects, according to the readiness of the group members. It must also allow for pure enjoyment and aesthetic satisfaction. In these days the use of the group as a tool in correctional work has been recognized more and more.

Social Work Research in Police Department and Courts

Social work research in police department and courts is in the infant stage in India. But, in certain European countries, United

States of America and Japan, professional social workers work with the police especially in their youth bureaus as researchers. They help police to understand properly the delinquents whom they apprehend. They also help the police to develop a rehabilitative attitude rather than a punitive one. Social work researchers play a major role with the police in trying to prevent delinquency and crime. The researchers work for preventive aspect of delinquency and crime (Sikka, 1980). The rationale behind this is that if more time and talent can be put into preventing anti-social behaviour in the first place, society as well as individuals and families will be much better off. With the help of the social worker, police work with delinquents in recreational activities and clubs to prevent delinquency and crime.

Often social work researchers are attached to juvenile courts, performing the role of probation officers. They have various functions in the juvenile court. Conducting investigations to find out various causes and facts in a violation of law is an important function. A social work researcher can generally be objective and can secure a picture of the total situation that is helpful to the court. In juvenile courts, the magistrate makes decisions based on the report submitted by the probation officer. Investigations are usually related to the delinquents but most often involve the family, close relatives and another key persons in the lives of the accused. Another important function of the social work researcher is to represent the court after the magistrate has made the decision. Probation involves regular interviews and contacts between the probation officer, who is the social worker, and the offender. The social worker tries to use his knowledge and skills to help bring about desired changes and modifications in the behaviour of the offender, who is in probation.

Social Work Research in Probation

Social work research with probationers includes not only casework and assistance in employment but also enforcement functions as well. It is a type of treatment supervision. The probation officer, who is also a social work researcher, uses the resources in the community skillfully to enhance his effectiveness in working with the probationers. Social work research with probationers is done on the basis of mutual trust, cooperation and responsibility between the social work researcher and the criminal. The researcher has to find the balance between control and corrections that the probationer can best use. There are four general principles that usually are the basis for attaining this balance:

1. Change comes from within the person; therefore, a probationer must be a participant in any correctional treatment programme designed to help him by the social work researcher.
2. The needs, problems, capacities and limitations of the individual criminal must be considered in planning the treatment programme with him by the social work researcher.
3. Legally binding conditions developed by the social work researcher of probation are essential and in the best interests of the criminal and the community.
4. The goal of correctional treatment, as developed by the social work researcher, is to help the criminal understand his own problems and enable him to deal adequately with them.

The most important aim of correctional treatment in probation is not to control the criminal but to help him understand himself and gain independent control over his own behaviour. On certain occasions, the criminal needs security or the implied presence of a supporting authority figure. The implied presence of the probation officer is sometimes more important than actual supervision. This implied supervision means that the probation officer could appear at any time, and thus provides control on deviant behaviour. The use of the family to help the correctional treatment of the probationer is necessary. An interested family provides the psycho-social ties that assist in providing the controls the criminal requires. There are various steps in a successful correctional treatment in probation.

The correctional programme that presently appears to hold the greatest promise based on the belief is that of rehabilitating the criminal and the social work research highlights this aspect in his/her study (Panakal, 1973). A basic method in this process is to deal with problems in their social context that means in the interaction of the criminal and the community. The aims of rehabilitation are furthered much more readily by giving correctional treatment to a criminal in the community than by imprisonment. Modern theories of corrections influence the training of probation officers and place greater emphasis on developing the criminal's effective participation in family, work and the religion that offer access to a successful normal life in community. Family has a major role in shaping the personality of an individual. It is a universal social institution that nurtures, protects and shapes the individual from childhood to maturity. There are two major approaches that mould the methods of family therapy. The first is the application of the family as a centre of correctional treatment on behalf of one or more of its members. The second approach visualizes the whole family as the target for correctional treatment. This is the essentially re-integrative type of family therapy. Its objectives are the rehabilitation of the entire family as a healthy functioning unit in the community.

Generally, there are three phases in a social work research process with probationers:

1. Social inquiry into the total situation of the probationer.
2. Social diagnosis, that is, inquiry into the relationships and attitude of the criminal.
3. Correction or reformation of the criminal's behaviour and personality.

In the last phase, there are again three categories, such as induce right notions of conduct in the criminal, induce motives that will assure loyalty to good norms of conduct, and develop the probationer's latent abilities. Hence, treatment of criminal behaviour is the core casework.

There are three principles of treatment in probation:

1. Treatment based on the consent of the probationer.
2. Treatment planned with the effective participation of the probationer.
3. Treatment planned to restructure the probationers thinking and emotions.

Social work research in probation implies that the probation officer, who is also a researcher, has a respect for individual differences and that he should have not only a natural desire to serve criminals but also an understanding of the process that develops criminal personalities and the consequences of criminal behaviour. The caseworker is sensitive to, understands, and appropriately responds to these needs and the client is somehow aware of the caseworker's sensitivity, understanding and response.

Probation is a suspended sentence to begin with, as a basis for providing correctional treatment and social work researcher tries to understand the need of the probationer and the society. It is an instrument of the court that is not leniency. Probation is using the material brought out by pre-sentence investigation the causes as well as the effects of anti-social or criminal behaviour of an individual brought to the court. Probation is casework. Hence, it is not only working with a criminal but also considering all the surrounding factors. Probation is helping a criminal fit into a community, fitting him into their standards. Only skilled and competent persons can effectively serve both as caseworkers and law-enforcement officers.

Through probation, a criminal is helped to be an enlightened citizen and a reformed individual of an interdependent community. It is the most meaningful method of re-educating a criminal. Hence, prison authorities should seriously consider the alternatives to imprisonment before starting the construction of more prisons in this country.

Social Work Research in Parole

According to the Manual of Correctional Standards (1954), every person released from a prison should be released under supervision. The prisoner does not have a right to parole, but for the good of the prisoner and the community, all should be given the opportunity of a period of supervision after having the regimentation and confines of the institution. Any method of release that does not include the process of careful selection of those to be released and of optimum time for their release in addition to the necessary degree of supervision after release is not an adequate approach to parole administration. Parole symbolizes the combination of punitive and correctional philosophy. So, supervision, i.e., casework is necessary for the offender to adjust with the new environment. It has humanitarian, correctional and penological aspects (Devasia, 1981). The arguments for placing parole supervision services under an independent parole can be summarized as follows.

The paroling authority is in the best position to promote parole and gain public acceptance for it. Since it is held responsible for parole failures, it should be responsible for supervision services. Among the arguments for including both parole supervision and institutions in a single department of corrections, with the parole authority having responsibility and authority only for case decisions, are these:

1. The correctional process is a continuum. All staff, institutional and parole, should be under a single administration rather than being divided, with resultant competition for government funds and conflict in policies.
2. A consolidated correctional department has the advantage of consistent administration, including staff selection, in service training and casework supervision.
3. Boards are ineffective in performing administrative functions. Their major focus should be on case decisions, not on day-by-day field operations.

4. The growing number of programmes part way between prison and parole can best be handled by a single centralized administration.

At least three different views of supervision, differently emphasizing punishment and treatment, are found among correctional social work researchers. The first one is based on the assumptions that parole is a system of leniency that permits the early release of many dangerous criminals from prison who should continue to suffer punishment. In parole work based on this view, emphasis is placed only supervision than guidance. A second conception is based on the assumption that reformation is a matter of individual self-determination to "make good" in free society. A supervisory system based on the view may be characterized as "watchful waiting". Here "supervision" is considered as "inspection".

Another conception is based on the belief that essential work of promoting adjustment has to be done after release from an institution, and that this requires assistance not to prevent the parole from exercising his own initiative, but to assist him in exercising it correctly, so that crime will not be repeated. While it is not assumed that all paroles are dangerous criminals, it is recognized that "reformation" in the form of self-resolution to "make good" is not always sufficient to prevent recidivism. Parole is viewed as a system of improving the welfare of the parole (often called a "client") by helping him in his individual, adjustment, within the limits of his capacity.

The word "treatment" is probably one of the most overlooked words in corrections. Whatever its semantic meaning, treatment and the treatment approach have come to suggest several connotations, that 'it' replaces an old system of dealing with offenders; 'it' considers the persons, his needs, strengths and limitations, as they differ from other individuals around him. Increasingly within the correctional field, we have come to accept the idea that the treatment approach to the offender is better than any other method. Hopefully, we can eventually demonstrate the greater effectiveness of this method over any other "non-treatment" oriented approach. In order to assist the individual to adjust to the community, the correctional social work researcher implements a three-stage treatment process: investigation, diagnosis and supervision.

In the investigation stage, the correctional social work researcher attempts to find out what is and what is within him and outside him that made offender the person with whom the social worker is dealing. With skillful questioning, he will find himself looking at aspects of the offender's life, so very necessary if he is to gain insight into the nature of his behaviour. From this framework of reference it is not too difficult to see the investigation as a very vital part of treatment process. The diagnosis is the codification of all that has been learned about the individual, organized in such a way as to provide a means for the establishment of future treatment goals and social work help.

The treatment supervision process entails the elaboration of knowledge about the individual through the process of communication, so that the individual will gain a more realistic appraisal of his own ability to function more acceptably in the community (Gauri Rani, 1972). The provision of certain material services may also be involved in the treatment process. One of the first major accomplishments of treatment comes about when the offender becomes aware both intellectually and emotionally that the social work researcher represents not only authority with the power to enforce certain restraints and restrictions, but that he is also able to offer material, social and psychological adjustment aids.

In the therapeutic, casework of the parole, crime prevention is incorporated in the treatment process (Devasia, 1988). The social work researcher's awareness of the fact that the person is having a problem in adjustment is seriously handicapped when interviews are held across a counter in a crowded office. The correctional social worker must be in a position to recognize that as a social worker in an authoritative setting, certain types of interrelationships are desirable and necessary. The interaction must be geared to dynamic of the offender's personality, and not to the exclusive satisfaction of the worker's own ego.

A person's feelings are mixed when he experiences a mutual incompatible combination of feelings. When feelings are mixed, anxiety arises and the greater the anxiety, the more the feelings are mixed and so on. Conflict is almost inevitable when feelings are mixed. The correctional social worker can sometimes provide a desired treatment effect by listening and feeding back what has been said with patience and acceptance. At other times, particularly with individuals whose response patterns reflect a primitive level of development, the officer may find it necessary to teach how to behave less disturbingly in confronting life situations. Treatment is a social work process involving both time and skill. The objective, regardless of the approach, is to create in an offender self-acceptance which did not exist before. The law usually states that any violation of the conditions imposed upon the person on parole constitute a violation of parole, and that for a violation of parole the person is to be returned to the institution. In practice, the supervising parole agent uses discretion and permits some technical violations without formally pronouncing them violations of parole. Many violations are not observed by the social work researcher as a parole officer, who is also a correctional social worker. When a parole violator is arrested, a court trial is not necessary in order to return him to prison and the decision of the supervising authority usually is final. However, if he has violated his parole by committing a new crime, he may be tried and sentenced for that crime. Since persons on parole are still being punished in violation hearings the usual rights to counsel and to other court procedures designed for protection of accused persons are not available.

A systematic and continuous programme for evaluation of parole programmes will require information in four areas. Outcome of parole must be defined in such a way that criteria of "favourable" and "unfavourable" parole performance are meaningful for programme evaluation and acceptable to leadership of a large number of social workers. Different types of offenders need to be studied, since differing parole outcome rates may be associated with differences in offenders rather than programmes. Information is needed on interactions between types of programmes and types of offenders that affect programme outcomes. Then, the apparently most fruitful programmes for each type of offender can be identified, further studied, and expanded, while programme that are harmful or not helpful can be eliminated by the social work researcher.

Social Work Research in Aftercare

Aftercare has become a relation on the basis of human equality, within which "authority" has no place. Practical experience indicated that it is possible to provide aftercare for paroles with important elements adopted from social casework by which the standards of aftercare have been raised considerably. The correctional researcher would be making a mistake if he assumed that the only way he can help is to be an instrument in bringing about some radical change in the individuals personality. The art of research lies in constantly focusing on the total personality of the individual. Different techniques used by the correctional social worker can be as follows:

Manipulative Techniques

Manipulative techniques are extremely important with the offender groups. Sometimes that manipulative service apparently peripheral is the first step in establishing a stable behaviour pattern, such as job finding, accommodation finding, betterment of community conditions and removal of discrimination. The subjective of intelligent manipulative work is not to take the problem away from the person seeking help. Rather it is to help him mobilize his own capacities to meet his environmental conditions only where he cannot do it. In case getting it done by the social worker will not dominate the client so that he will use the social worker as a crutch thereafter. The utilization of manipulative technique is not simple. It requires skill (Devasia, 1989).

Executive Techniques

Most correctional agencies are strictly service organizations. They may not have funds for direct administration, to persons under care. Hence, referral to appropriate agencies is an essential function of the social worker. Again, it must be intelligently done, at the proper time. Of important to the parole are such services by referral as these: job getting; education of children; medical care public grants housing loans; institutional placement; nursery care for children; legal aid; educational and vocational guidance recreation; social agency help, etc. Executive services, however, do not amount to a fragmentation of various aspects of a case, whereas each to be treated in itself (see Devasia, 1988: 144-153).

Guidance, Counselling and Leadership

Providing of guidance, counselling and leadership services implies certain things such as psychological, biological and sociological knowledge of human behaviour. An understanding of the individual and what he seeks in life helps him gain insight so that he may solve his problems. Casework is often able to help clients from disabilities then to help them live within their disabilities through social compensations. A correctional social worker may unable to help a person change at once so that he feels happy and comfortable in his family groups. But he might guide him into training himself for a better job. Guidance and leadership are not simply the giving of advice and expecting the individual to follow it. A person may need a crutch for a time, but he cannot grow if he uses the social worker as a crutch forever. He must be helped to make his own decisions, eventually to discard the help. The correctional social worker is not furnishing guidance and counsel when he tries to influence behaviour that must be determined entirely by the individual on a volitional basis.

Guidance and leadership do not mean moralizing. Guidance and leadership with parolees will probably be effective in direct ratio to the imagination and initiative powers of the social worker. The guidance technique may be useful, not alone in the immediate solution of present problems but in long-term planning to prevent the creation of problems in the future. The technique can be effective in the building and sustaining of morale. The approval and encouragement of the correctional social worker may keep up the courage and determination of a man struggling through a difficult situation. The warmth and objective judgement of the social worker can create the willingness on the part of the individual to ask him for help in any situation. Particularly with youthful offenders the support and encouragement of the social worker can play an important role.

The thinking of the parolee can be guided and influenced, so that he later becomes able to make his own decisions regarding a given situation, or generally thereafter in a similar type of situation. Developing an interest in a certain type of reading, for instance, can strengthen one's ethical sense, or increase his earning capacity. That there is at times a conflict between the interests of society and the drivers of the individuals is clear to all correctional workers. And therein lies a limitation that must be faced and evaluated both by correctional social worker and parolee. The social worker's behaviour has a dynamic base. The social workers must remember at all times, in field, that basically they will help people change only when they have aided them to eliminate certain compulsions, to resolve certain conflicts, so that they want to face reality in a stable, sensible, and satisfying way.

In most democratic countries prisoners are placed on parole for a specific period often equal to the period during which they still would have been detained if they had not received parole. In the case of prisoners serving long terms the parole period may amount to several years, especially in those countries where the granting of parole is made possible by law after one-third of the sentence has been served. The basic question is whether there should be a parole period at all. Although there appears to be merit in having a parole period fixed, at least tentatively, it has been demonstrated that certain individuals would benefit from having their period shortened in the course of parole whereas there is equally strong argument that certain individuals should have the parole period extended. If an individual is successful during his parole, the aftercare programmes must be terminated in due course.

While it is ordinary in the case that recidivism will result in parole termination, this is not necessarily true, nor advisable. If on the basis of the offence and the basis of the individual, there is adequate reason to believe that the parolee could achieve success if allowed to remain at liberty, the parole may be continued and the parolee's behaviour will determine the need of aftercare or its termination.

Conclusion

Social work research is effective in dealing with delinquency and crime in many countries. Juvenile delinquency and crime are major problems of modern society and social work research has an important role to play in the control correction and prevention and delinquency and crime. Social work attempts to help the individual, his family and the community to face and solve delinquency and crime through utilization of individual, family and community resources. Casework, group work and community organization are the basic processes utilized by the social worker in correctional settings. The correctional social worker is given authority in order to change the ways offenders (clients) express values in action. All social workers work with offenders in terms of values. More than any other function, the correctional social worker's task is defined in terms of changing values of the delinquent or criminal so that they become suitable in action with the values of the society. The social work researcher helps particularly with police department, courts, probation, institutions, parole and prevention. Therefore, professional social work research in correctional settings is a comprehensive constructive social attitude - therapeutic in some instances, restraining in some instance, but preventive in its total social impact.

References

Banerjee, Gauri Rani (1972) "Social Casework Services and the Juvenile Delinquent". *Papers on Social Work: An Indian Perspective*, Bombay: Tata Institute of Social Sciences.

Bentz, Valerie Malhotra (2006) *Research for Social Workers: An Introduction to Methods*, New York: Routledge.

Boehm, Werner W. (1959) *Objectives of Social Curriculum of the Future, Social Work Curriculum Study*, New York: Council of Social Work Education.

Desai, Armaity S. (1978) Review of Social Work Education in India: Retrospect and Prospect, Report of the Second Review Committee, New Delhi: University Grants Commission.

Devasia, V.V. (1988) "Prison as a Social System and Prisonization in Relation to Prison Administration" VI, XXXIV, No.1, pp. 144-151.

— (1989) *The Phenomenon of Murder*, Nagpur: Dattsons.

Devasia, Leelamma and V.V. Devasia (1989) *Female Criminals and Female Victims*, Nagpur: Dattsons.

Jones, Martyn (2005) *Social Work Research: Ethical and Political Contexts*, London: Sage Publications.

Mark, Raymond (1996) *Research Made Simple: A Handbook for Social Workers*, New Delhi: Sage Publications.

Morris, Teresa (2006) *Social Work Research Methods: Four Alternative Paradigms*, London: Sage Publications.

Murphy, E. (1959) *Social Group Work, Social Group Work Curriculum Study*, New York: Council for Social Work Education.

National Association of Social Workers (1958) "Working Definition of Social Work Practice" *Social Work*, No.3, April, pp. 5-9.

Panakal, J.J. (1973) "An Agenda for Criminology" *Indian Journal of Criminology*, 1 July, pp. 14-18.

Pitchandi, N. (1985) "Criminology Research, Training and Services," *Indian Journal of Criminology*, 13, 2, July, pp. 77-78.

Rubin, Allen and Earl R. Babbie (2004) *Research Methods for Social Work*, New York: Thomson Wadsworth.

Shekar, Sanober (1982) "Another Look at the Social Work Approach to Corrections" *Indian Journal of Criminology*, 10, 1, January, pp. 56-58.

Sikka, K.D. (1980) "Professional Social Work in Correctional Institutions" *Indian Journal of Criminology*, 8, 1, January, pp. 55-61.

Studt, Elliot (1959), *Education for Social Workers in Correctional Field*, New York: Council for Social Work Education.

Thyer, Bruce A. (2005) *Handbook of Social Work Research*, Thousand Oaks: Sage Publications.

13

Significance of Social Work Training to Human Resource Personnel

Ranjana Sehgal

The changing milieu presented by the post-industrial society has been rich with the possibilities of social work practice. Fast paced changes in the Indian society have unravelled immense potential for the growth of social work profession, which has today traversed into areas hitherto considered unconventional and outside its domain. Though, business and industry has been a non-traditional and unconventional setting for social work practice, many professional social workers have not only entered the corporate world but are making significant contributions to it and have come to be recognized as 'professionals with special skills' (McCarthy and Steck, 1990:20)

The Indian experience has been radically different from its western counterparts and we can proudly claim that India has been a forerunner in contributing to social work in industry, where it has gone through many vicissitudes unlike other countries. In the changed scenario of the levelling of the world, flattening and shrinking of the globe, there is no better time than now to make the presence of social work felt. This is the time to make its need and relevance more eloquent to the corporate world and take it to the doorsteps of the industry as also the communities and families of the workforce. In the race for survival, painfully defined by an all consuming desire to succeed and excel at any cost, human sensitivity, emotions and feelings have been put on the back burner, spiralling a breakdown of relationships within and without the world of work. A social worker through his/her sheer presence, backed by his/her specialized training and skills, can be the much needed soothing balm for the frayed nerves of industry's multitude and multitasking workforce. In the harried and brutally competitive business milieu of today, the need for social work is all-pervasive. In keeping with the needs of the modern corporate world, it has now become imperative that the delivery system of social work services should also change.

There is an imperative need to first undertake meaningful research, whereby we can show the industry the areas wherein social workers can make significant contribution as logical resource persons vis-à-vis their training, where none other can. Intervening in the corporate world without any sound database would be like adopting a trial and error approach and shooting in the dark. As things stand today, not only the area is poorly researched but also there is a serious dearth of meaningful literature on the subject. Hence, the role of research in industrial social work is not only relevant but is also badly needed in the scenario of impoverished literature on industrial social work. We need to do some basic research into the dimensions of partnership between social work and industry on which then the contents of social work training and practice can be founded enabling us to make our practice more effective and productive. There is a need to reorient our curricula and so design it, that it is responsive to the special needs of industry today, irrespective of the designations of the social workers appointed in industry.

Some of the areas that we need to look at for future research projects are the following:

- How the organizational structure, the corporate culture, values, etc., impact the relationships within an organization?
- Study the global, political and economic issues that impact the operations of an organization, especially in the areas of profits, marketing, management, production and finance and how these in turn affect the human resource issues such as hiring and firing, lay-offs, transfers, advancements, etc., and the role of social worker in helping the workforce cope with these.
- What leads to work pressures and how they impact the lives of individual workers and how an individual worker brings his personal characteristics to the workplace and conversely carries his work stress to his family and personal relationships?
- Making industry the base, how the social worker should reach out to the family and community of the worker?
- Study the range of intra-psychic and interpersonal issues including the personality factors or difficulties such as emotional problems, substance abuse, family issues and marital crisis and how they directly or indirectly affect the workplace and why strife and stress at workplace and in the family is on the increase and what role a social worker can play to reduce it.
- The business environment, its values, the nature of industry, profile of the employees, and how the industry perceives its people and their problems and steps it takes or wishes to take to deal with them.
- The number of social workers employed in industry today, their job profile and the nature of services provided by them to industry and its efficacy.
- The special skills particularly required of a social worker in an industrial setting and how the social workers have to apply their skills in response to this specific practice setting, retaining the professional objectives all the time. Social workers have to bring specialized skills to the world

of work and provide the much needed service to the industry. Gradually, they have to be recognized as specialized professionals in their own right.

However, it is suggested to the future researchers to empirically study these dimensions so that full-time industrial social workers are widely accepted into the industrial arena in India.

Excerpts from a Survey Research in the Field of Industrial Social Work:

Title: Social Work in Industry: Problems and Practices of Welfare Functionaries

Statement of the Problem

The appointment and functions of a social worker in industry in India has two dimensions to it. Though, the concept of industrial social work in itself is more than 80 years old, the appointment of full-time social workers in industry has only recently emerged in India and its significance has only begun to be realized by those enlightened industrial managements that are providing social work help to widen the scope of labour welfare to cover the all-round well-being of the employees and thereby giving a meaning and content to its basic welfare programmes. This is one dimension and the present study addresses itself to this dimension only to the extent of exploring the scope for the appointment of such full-time social workers in our Indian industries in future. One reason for not going into this aspect was that in the state of Madhya Pradesh where this study was undertaken this concept of appointing full-time social workers in industry had not taken roots and therefore their number was negligible.

The other dimension is that though industrial social work is a new field in India, the presence of social workers in industry is not a new phenomenon. The recommendations of the Royal Commission on Labour were instrumental for the appointment of labour officers in industry and subsequently the appointment of welfare officers was made mandatory under the Factories Act 1948. The welfare officers were primarily appointed to look after the health safety and welfare provisions of the Factories Act, 1948. The Sir Dorabji Tata Graduate School of Social Work, better known as Tata Institute of Social Sciences today, which was established in 1936, came to be recognized as the first postgraduate institution for the training of labour and welfare officers, with the consequence that there are a significant number of labour welfare and personnel officers in industry, who are also professionally trained social workers. Labour welfare and personnel management is a specialized field of professional social work and more than half of the students trained in the schools of social work till today have been trained for and actually working in industry. It is often alleged that the two major components in the industry, namely, the labour and the management, have not been able to use the social work skills and training to solve the social and emotional problems of employees in industry. The professionally trained social workers employed in the industrial field on the other hand are often heard complaining that they do not have at their disposal the requisite time and resources to put into effective use their social work training (Vishwanathan, 1963; Randeria, 1963; Vaid, 1963; Kudchedkar, 1979; Jacob, 1981).

With the fast growth of other training institutes, which impart degree/diploma in the field of personnel management/HRM, the question has sometimes been raised whether labour welfare and personnel management provides scope for social work practice or should social work withdraw itself from the field of labour.

Objectives

Few empirical studies, it appears, have examined the question, as to whether social work education is a suitable and adequate preparation for the personnel and welfare jobs in industry. Though trained social workers have been employed in industries for last so many years as personnel/welfare officers, hardly any empirical study has tried to find out, if the industrial settings provide them with enough opportunities to practise the social work methods and skills, and the obstacles that come in their way. The managements' views in this connection are also very significant, but hardly any data in this regard is available. The present study was a modest attempt to empirically explore these areas.

This was an exploratory study with various objectives. Apart from focusing on the problems and practices of the personnel/welfare functionaries in general, ascertaining the skills and abilities required and used by them, the primary aim of the study was to examine the relevance of social work training in the field of labour welfare and personnel management. This issue becomes pertinent due to the widely divergent views expressed about the justification of social work training for personnel/welfare officers. The study explored the extent to which the social work methods are practised by the personnel/welfare officers and the problems which come in the way of their practice. Broadly speaking, the study tried to examine the scope of social work within the limits of a personnel/welfare officer's job.

Variables under the Study

As one of the objectives of the study was to compare the personnel and welfare functionaries having different qualifications and particularly ascertain the merits of social work education as a suitable preparation for job in the personnel field, the qualification of these functionaries was selected as the key variable. However, some other variables such as designation, duration of service, size of the organization and location were also examined to understand the groups with the hope that the data may throw up some hypotheses which can become subjects for later research.

Coverage

The study was confined to industries of Indore, Dewas and Ujjain and Dhar districts of Madhya Pradesh. The rationale for their selection was that they are important industrial centres in the state where a significant number of small, medium and large-scale industries exist providing ample opportunities for the employment of personnel/human resource and welfare functionaries.

Out of the list of 170 industries operational in these four districts only those units were selected where a personnel/welfare functionary was appointed, irrespective of the nomenclature of their designation.

The study is the outcome of extensive survey of 70 such industrial units. All the personnel/welfare officers employed in these units were covered on a census basis and were the main source of data. Of the 155 personnel/welfare functionaries interviewed, 60 were trained social workers. To get the management's point of view, the heads of the organization and sometimes the owners themselves were interviewed. For adequate representation of the worker's point of view the best option was to take the views of the trade union officials. Adopting the purposive random sampling method one official from each of the unions functioning in each of the units was selected. A minimum of four workers were selected from each unit. The units where there were more than four unions the number was proportionately increased. Where there was only one union, four officials from the same union were selected. In 30 units there did not exist any union, hence, the worker's representatives on various committees were selected. Finally, a sample of 283 workers was drawn.

Methods and Tools of Data Collection

Interview, case study and observation were the main methods of data collection. The main source of information was the personal in-depth interview with the personnel functionaries, the top management and the trade union officials and interview schedule the main tool. Four structured schedules were mainly used, one each for the functionaries, management and workers and an additional interview schedule was constructed for the functionaries who were also trained social workers.

Eight case studies were also undertaken to give a qualitative dimension to the data and to verify the information collected through other tools. Four case studies each of functionaries with social work training and without training were undertaken The purpose was to take a closer look at the training/education received by them and how it equipped them for their job and to analyze the career graph of these officers against the absence or the presence of training.

Data Processing and Analysis

Four different sets of interview schedules after completion were scrutinized, verified and arranged serially. Four code books were prepared for the data collected from the functionaries managements workers and the social workers Thereafter, four master charts were prepared which were fed into and processed by the computer. The statistical analysis was obtained through computer after classifying and coding of the data. The single frequency tables and the cross-tables were obtained on the controlled variables mentioned earlier. A number of questions were priority questions for which tables had to be prepared manually to obtain the mean scores. Scoring techniques were extensively used. These techniques came into being because of a need felt by the social sciences to quantify data which are otherwise qualitative in nature The quantification of data affords objective measurement of the phenomena under study. The details of the scoring patterns were given at the relevant places in connection with the data analysis based on them. The technique of choice scoring was used for priority questions. This technique is used to ascertain the order of preference or in other words the degree of popularity. If a respondent ranks a particular specimen as number 1 at the top of a given specimen he evidently prefers it to other 9. If he ranks it 2 he prefers it to 8 and so on and so forth. Each priority/rank (R) can be converted into a choice score (C).

Major Findings

Profile

The functionaries had a mean age of 35 years; predominantly from the male sex having an average 11 years of service to their credit. They came from diverse academic disciplines. Broadly, they were divided into two broad categories of trained and non-trained functionaries with each category further comprising of two groups. The category of the non-trained functionaries on the one hand included graduates from different streams such as arts, commerce, science and law. They were the smallest group (7.7%). The other group comprised of post-graduates from different social sciences such as sociology, economics, psychology, etc. They were the second largest group (31%). In the category of trained functionaries one group consisted of professionally trained social workers. They were the largest group (38%). The other group in this category had either a degree or diploma in Personnel Management/HRD/Industrial Relations/Labour Welfare etc. It also included a few MBAs (22.6%). Nearly, 27 per cent of the functionaries had a degree in law.

Role Expectations

One of the objectives of the study was to find out the expectations of the managements and workers from the functionaries and the extent to which the functionaries covered under the present study had been able to fulfil the managements' expectations, on the one hand, and workers' expectations on the other. The data reveal that, first and foremost, the managements expected sincerity and honesty from functionaries. According to the functionaries, however, the managements mainly expected them to be multipurpose men.

Most of the managements were of the view that the functionaries employed in their organization had only partially fulfilled their expectations. It appears that the social work trained functionaries seem to be doing their job in a better way as the level of fulfilment of the managements' expectations was comparatively higher where only social work trained functionaries were employed.

As far as the expectations of the workers from the functionaries, and functionaries own expectations, are concerned, a near perfect matching of the perception of the two groups could be observed. According to both, the workers expected that, first and foremost, their problems be solved by the expectations were fully fulfilled belonged to small-size units whereas comparatively more workers from the large-size units stated that the functionaries had not at all fulfilled their expectations.

The highest percentage of those workers whose expectations were fully fulfilled belonged to small-size units whereas comparatively more workers from the large-size units stated that the functionaries had not at all fulfilled their expectations.

The functionaries were asked to introspect and tell as to how far they felt that they had fulfilled the workers' and managements expectations. An almost equal proportion of functionaries claimed to have either fully or partially fulfilled the managements' expectations. A comparison of the managements' and functionaries' opinion reveals a discrepancy as far as fulfilment of managements' expectations is concerned. While little less than half the functionaries felt that they had fully come up to the managements' expectations only one-third of the managements expressed this view, and an insignificant number of the functionaries accepted having not at all fulfilled their managements' expectations. Against this a comparatively larger proportion of the managements expressed this view.

Comparatively, more functionaries felt that they had been able to fulfil managements' expectations as against workers' expectations. More functionaries in the small organizations as against the large organizations felt that they had been fully able to fulfil the managements and the workers expectations. Thus, it appears that there seem to be more problems for the functionaries in the large organizations as against the small organizations as far as fulfilment of workers' and managements' expectations by them are concerned.

Importance of Training

The importance of training in the area of personnel management and labour welfare, referred to as human resource management today, is widely recognized and the managements of the large- and medium-sized organizations look for qualified candidates to fill these positions in their organizations. However, one finds untrained persons manning the personnel departments, a fact supported by the present study. As many as 60 out of the 155 functionaries were without any professional training in this area.

Views about Different Courses

A rating of the different courses by the functionaries revealed high rating for the post graduate social work course with specialization in labour welfare and personnel management. As against this the one without this specialization was considered inadequate by most. A generic social work course was thus rejected as an adequate preparation. The alignment of social work and personnel management was considered a good combination. A degree in pure social sciences was least appreciated. The managements too expressed the view that integration of social work with personnel management was the main reason for the appointment of social workers in industry in such large numbers.

Relevance of Social Work Training

One of the objectives of the present study was to find if the social work training was relevant to the needs of industry and if it adequately equipped the social workers for a job of this nature. In schools of social work, where labour welfare and personnel management is offered as one of the specializations, maximum number of students opt for it. They are sent to different industrial settings for their practical training. Here, they are not only exposed to the field of personnel management but are also expected to apply their social work knowledge and skills in finding solution to managements' and workers' problems. Despite the availability of candidates from other specialized courses in the field the social work graduates continue to be appointed in the personnel departments in large numbers. The functionaries with social work training were specifically asked to indicate the adequacy of the social work training vis-a-vis the demands of their job. It is encouraging to note that those who considered the training received by them as adequate were almost double than those who thought it was inadequate.

Differences between Social Work and Non-Social Work Trained Functionaries

Professional education and training in any field in the final analysis can be judged by the extent to which it equips the candidates to function efficiently in the field. The present study reveals that more managements found the social work trained functionaries effective on their job as against functionaries from other disciplines. A majority of 60 per cent managements found significant differences between social work trained and non-social work trained functionaries. On being asked to reflect on the differences more than half of them expressed that the social workers were proficient, and effective in solving workers' problems and could work effectively in crisis situations. "They rarely get ruffled by a crisis", observed one of them. A few, however, felt that those with an MBA degree made better managers and had more conceptual clarity. Nearly 19 per cent of the managers found no significant difference between the two groups.

The managements were of the view that that the social workers were more human in their approach and could effectively solve the problems of the workers. The social workers also expressed that their way of dealing with the workers and their approach to their problems were different from those adopted by other functionaries. Their social work training had made them more sensitive to human sufferings and human problems during the course of their training and they could bring this understanding to bear on the problems faced by the workers. It was observed from the behaviour of the functionaries with the workers and the views expressed by them that the social work trained functionaries did have an insight and understanding of the field of human relations. Their training helped them to bring certain attitudes towards their work which are desirable. In this context, it will be relevant to quote Dorothy Moses, "as I look back on my job as a welfare officer to the Indian Jute Association, I have often wished that I had the knowledge and understanding that I now have of professional social work concepts. I feel I could then have done a better job" (Moses, 1950).

Though the comparative analysis of the views of the functionaries from different disciplines did not reveal any significant difference but more of those with social work education had expressed the view that social work course had greatly helped them to acquire an open mind, an ability to understand human relations, develop positive attitude and a holistic approach and an ability to work against all odds.

Compatibility of the Values of Social Work and Industry

It is often alleged that social work has no place in industry as its values are in conflict with the goals of a business enterprise. As an employee of an industrial organization, social worker might find himself in a business which does not value the same concerns that social work stands for. The social workers are oriented to people and business to profit. As many as 40 per cent of the social workers confirmed the compatibility, 32 per cent were uncertain and 29 per cent felt that the values of industry and social work incompatible. The Chi square analysis did not reveal any significant variation in the opinion of the social workers working in the private and public sectors but comparatively larger proportion of those who found the values compatible belonged to the public sector.

Adequacy of Social Work Training

As many as 45 per cent of the social workers found the professional training received by them as adequate and 32 per cent found it inadequate. The data do not unravel any significant impact of duration of their service on their opinion.

Changes Suggested by Social Workers to Fill the Gaps in Social Work Training

Most of the social workers underlined the need to constantly revise and update the social work curriculum so as to make it more relevant to the needs of industry. They gave the following suggestions:

- Greater thrust to be given to the specialization papers incorporating the latest developments.
- The final year should be fully devoted to the specialization.
- More emphasis be given to conceptual understanding of human resource development, organizational behaviour, and human resource management so as to enable them to compete with the business schools.
- The field work training should be made more intensive under strict supervision of the faculty and industry staff.
- Field work should not become a formality. The training should be properly given and sincerely taken.
- Specialized knowledge made available should be assimilated to fundamental concepts which every social worker

must understand with regard to an individual in a given situation. For example, in resolving the problem of adjustment to work, the social worker has not only to identify the objective and the subjective difficulties that impact the worker's psycho-social adjustment to his work environment but also look for such organizational, technical and psychological forms that assist this process.

- Theory be made more relevant to the Indian conditions.
- There is a need to create greater awareness on the part of the managements about benefits of social work education and training.
- Compulsory block placement.

Conclusion

The study revealed that social work has ample scope in the field of labour welfare, personnel management and human resource management (HRM). With the emergence of the specialized field of HRM as a modern profession, the social work concepts may not be in the forefront as they were a few decades ago. The increasing emphasis on business management has also adversely affected the social work role in industry. Labour welfare is gradually being replaced by the concept of employee benefits and services. In the altered context, the question naturally arises of the relevance and adequacy of social work education to the current needs of industry and its suitability for those seeking jobs in this field. Many have recommended the need for social work training for effective work in the labour field and the opposite view that social work cannot be identified by personnel management has also been expressed by many experts (Vishwanathan, 1963; Randeria, 1963; Vaid, 1963; Kudchedkar, 1979; Jacob, 1981). Nevertheless, in spite of the conflicting claims and the controversy that prevails in this respect, the present study has revealed that despite various limitations, there are areas in the field of personnel management where social work techniques can be used with advantage. While trying to solve problems of the individual workers, the activities entered into by the functionaries are similar to those of social work. The social workers covered under the study found the methods of social work especially social casework useful in dealing with problems of absenteeism, indebtedness, indiscipline etc. This is why, in spite of all changes in the roles, status, functions, designations etc. of the officers, the healing touch and human approach of social work profession will continue to be in demand as long as our primary concern in industry is human being and his basic requirements, covering economic, social and psychological factors. Developments in the personnel field can only help, because these lay the greatest stress on human factor which will lead to better acceptance of social work role and functions (Jacob, 1981).

The study has revealed a gradual, if not sweeping, change in the attitude of the managements and owners of industry. Even in production-oriented industrial settings, there is an increasing recognition of the importance of the human factor, if not for its own sake, atleast for promoting organizational goals. Some industries have come forward to play their legitimate role in discharging their social responsibilities.

A social worker can help the employees to overcome their problems and can extend his/her services beyond the individual employee and the family and improve the community life of the employees. The job of the welfare and personnel functionaries primarily demands that they work with people and deal with their needs, whether they are their employers or workers in industry. Being in the possession of the body of knowledge and techniques that the profession of social work has developed is therefore an added accomplishment which will always stand these functionaries in good stead. Schools of social work should, therefore, resolutely pursue the path of preparing students with a certain social work bias and humanistic approach within the management function.

References

Jacob, K.K. (1981), "Social Work Practice in Industry", in Nair, T. Krishna (ed.) *Social Work Education and Social Work Practice in India*, Madras: Association of Schools of Social Work in India, pp. 194-203.

Kudchedkar, L.S. (1979), *Aspects of Personnel Management and Industrial Relations*, Tata Mc-Graw, New Delhi: Hill Publishing Company Ltd.

McCarthy, Dolores and Stech, Sarah B. (1990), "Social Work in Private Sector: Assessing the Corporate Culture" in *Occupational Social Work Today*, ed. by Shaumith Lala Ashenberg Straussner, New York: Haworth Press, Inc.

Moses, Dorothy (1953), "Training of Labour and Welfare Personnel", *Indian Journal of Social Work*, Vol. (1).

Randeria, K.N. (1963), "Personnel Management and Social Work", *Indian Journal of Social Work*, Vol. 24(2).

Vaid, P.N. (1963), "Personnel Management and Social Work", *Indian Journal of Social Work*, Vol. 24(2).

Vishwanathan, N. (1963), "Social Work in Industry", *Indian Journal of Social Work*, Vol. 24(2).

Part IV

Research Strategies

14

Qualitative Research in Social Work

An Overview

Surendra Singh

Social work, as a social profession, aims at bringing about desired changes in social system in order to reduce inequalities, guarantee freedom, ensure justice and promote brotherhood so that every member of society may be able to lead a decent and dignified life and may be empowered enough to deal with day-to-day problems, especially those which are social and psychological in nature. With advancements in social sciences, it has been accepted today that the life and problems faced by people should be viewed in totality by giving the required attention to their various dimensions through adoption of an interdisciplinary approach, and also that whatever people's life problems confronted by them are, their roots lie in the drawbacks in the system, and they or their individual inadequacies should not be held responsible for their creation. It is against this backdrop that social work is primarily concerned with bringing about planned and organized changes in the system to see that in future people do not become the victims of these problems. However, it does take cognizance of people's problems, especially psycho-social ones, and provides the required help to them in such a manner that they develop the capacity to face them on their own in future, particularly by making use of its knowledge base and repertoire of skills.

Knowledge is power in today's knowledge society in which the pace of knowledge development all over the world is too fast. In the present era of globalization in which the entire world has shrunk to the level of a 'global village', whatever new developments take place become known to people throughout the globe. Social work, as a system-changing and helping and healing profession, cannot afford not to engage in endeavours directed towards development of knowledge. This is precisely the reason why social work has in its armory one specific method known as 'social work research' which aims at converting assumptive knowledge into hypothetical knowledge, and again hypothetical knowledge into validated knowledge. This is done by undertaking a wide variety of researches in social work ranging from researches in social polity, planning and development to those in human development, human rights and psycho-social problems faced by individuals, groups and communities which hampers their effective functioning as a socially responsible member of society. It must be clarified here that social work as an auxiliary method of social work is employed for undertaking varied kinds of researches ranging from individual representing the lowest level to the highest level of social reality. Social work, like any other profession, has no option but to strengthen its knowledge base to the fullest possible level by promoting researches whose results may be instrumental in improving its effectiveness to enable it to justify its professional status which is being questioned from both within and without. Social work research also, under the influence of positivism, has generally been adopting deductive approach based on quantification through various types of methods and instruments of measurement, and in its this fascination for quantitative research, has relegated the field-based qualitative research to the background which not only helps in unravelling the inner and latent dimensions of social reality as experienced by people in their day-to-day life and living but also in formulating new concepts and grounded theories. In the present era in which lifestyles and social life of people are changing very fast, there is great need to understand the views of people who experience these changes by taking recourse to qualitative research. Flick, Kardoff and Steinke (2004:5) have rightly observed: "In an age when fixed social life worlds and lifestyles are disintegrating and social life is being restructured out of an ever-increasing number of new modes and forms of living, research strategies are required that can deliver, in the first instance, precise and substantial descriptions. They must also take into account the views of those involved, and the subjective and social constructs, Moreover, qualitative researches often provide such insights about people's life and their lifestyles as cannot be obtained with the help of quantitative research."

Qualitative research is a part of research which means the systematic enquiry to understand reality. It is a "firsthand involvement with the social world" (Filstead, 1990). It is primarily phenomenological directed towards "understanding the human experience from the individual's own frame of reference" (Bodgon and Taylor, 1975:2); and that is why it is also referred to as epistemology. In order to clearly understand qualitative research, a few definitions are being cited below:

> "Qualitative research is concerned with non-statistical methods of enquiry and analysis of social phenomena. It draws on the inductive process in which themes and categories emerge through analysis of data collected by such techniques as interviews, observations, videotapes, and case studies. Samples are usually small and often purposively selected. Qualitative research uses detailed descriptions from the perspective of the research participants themselves as a means of examining specific issues and problems under study" (McCoy, 1995; 2009).

"Qualitative research refers to systematic investigations that include inductive, in-depth, non-quantitative studies of individuals, groups, organizations or communities" (Barker, 1999: 393).

Thus, qualitative research refers to systematic exploration of people's experiences of their life worlds in which in-depth study of individuals, groups, organizations and communities is conducted with the help of non-quantitative methods by adopting inductive approach.

The difference between qualitative and quantitative social work research is being highlighted below with the help of a table prepared by Holosko, 2001:267):

Selected Differences Between Qualitative and Quantitative Social Work Research

Selected Criteria	*Qualitative*	*Quantitative*
Main purpose	To describe individuals and events in natural setting	To explore, describe test or assess phenomena
Philosophical perspective	Phenomenology	Positivism
Logical orientation	Inductive (G-S)	Hypothetic-deductive (S-G)
Dynamism	Process-oriented: Experiential and systemic	Deterministic: Linear and prescribed
Theory use and generation	Integrated throughout requisite grounded theory	To justify hypothesis questions and to validate
Researcher's role	Active (immersion)	Passive (immersion optional)
Problem specification	May emerge at the end	Early on
Method	Create as one evolves	Predetermined
Generalizability	Low	High

Source: Michael J. Holosco, "Overview of Qualitative Research Methods" in Bruce A. Thyer (ed.), *The Handbook of Social Work Research Methods*, Sage Publications, Inc., New Delhi, 2001, p. 267.

Both qualitative as well as quantitative methods should not be taken as contradictory but supplementary in that a researcher can have better and more comprehensive understanding of social reality by making appropriate use of both of them. It is noteworthy here that quantification of qualitative phenomena has become possible with development of methods and techniques and instruments of measurement. Now, what is qualitative can be transferred into qualitative and vice-versa. In this connection, an observation made by Carnap (1995:53) is quote worthy: "Quantitative determination can also be replaced by qualitative determination as is usual in science as well as in everyday life, for reasons of brevity and ease of understanding provided rules are set up for translating all such quantitative determinations so that the statement". It is rather cool here "might be translated into the statement the temperature here is between 5 and 10 degree Centigrade".

Which type of research – qualitative or quantitative – should be undertaken depends upon the nature of problem or issue that is to the investigated into. There may be situations in which both can be used together to have comprehensive understanding of the social world. In this connection, Kelle and Erzberger, 2004: 172) have also expressed the view that "as a rule qualitative and quantitative stages of data collection and analysis are carried out in parallel in a research project, each having their own data sets, and the resultant research outcomes are then related to one another". However, it should always be remembered that qualitative methods are used to venture into a new area about which we have very little knowledge, to understand the experiences and perspectives of clients, and the knowledge thus generated helps is formulation of hypotheses – tentative relationship between variables. Highlighting the relative merits and complementary nature of qualitative and quantitative methods, Kella and Erzberger (2004: 176) have observed: "The use of qualitative procedure is particularly indispensable when investigators have no a priori access to the typical meaning patterns and action orientations in the subject area being investigated. Depending on how much these action orientations and meaning patterns are influenced by social structure the linking of qualitative and quantitative methods may serve to illuminate different aspects of a social phenomena. Using quantitative methods the meaning of socio-cultural factors of context can then be investigated, and qualitative methods may be used to study the way in which these contextual factors are interpreted by the actors."

The process of qualitative research entails several steps beginning from identification of some important issue relating to the subjects of research and ending into development of some kind of "grounded theory", i.e., "theories grounded in empirical data of cultural description" (Glaser and Strauss, 1967: 11). Denzin (1989) has outlined 13 steps in conducting qualitative research. These are:

1. Learn to prepare oneself, read the literature and focus.
2. Select a field site and gain access to it. Get formal permission in writing.
3. Prepare for more time to do the study than one thinks is needed.
4. Adopt a social role, learn the ropes, and get along with members in the setting.
5. Watch, listen and collect quality data.
6. Take careful notes of all observations.
7. Focus on specific aspects of the setting and use theoretical sampling.
8. Begin to analyze data, generate working hypotheses and evaluate them.
9. Conduct field interviews with selected individuals.
10. Physically learn the field setting.
11. Complete the analysis.
12. Develop grounded theory to explain one's findings.
13. Write the final research report and disseminate one's findings.

Major steps in the qualitative research process are as under:

1. Selection of some issue relating to people's life world on the basis of whatever little knowledge is available.
2. Determination of purpose of research.
3. Decision about the sources of data – in case of field data decision about locale of the study and level of social reality to be explored.

4. Decision regarding the type of design to be used.
5. Decision regarding selection of relevant study unit(s) of the study.
6. Decision regarding methods and tools to be used for data collection.
7. Entry into field and collection of data – from field in case data are to be collected from human beings in a selected area, or from relevant documents in case of documentary sources.
8. Analysis of data (manual or computer-based) and interpretation.
9. Presentation of data.

Selection of Topic

The qualitative researcher has some rough idea about the topic. This preliminary understanding may be based on researcher's own experiences or his/her contacts with the subjects, discussion with some knowledgeable persons or study of some relevant documentary sources.

Determination of Purpose

Based on available knowledge relating to the topic of qualitative research, the investigator formulates main purpose of the enquiry which may provide direction for conducting qualitative research.

Decision about Locale and Level of Social Reality

At this stage the qualitative researcher takes decision regarding area in which study is to be conducted as also about the level of social reality – individual, group, community, organization, etc., to be explored in course of investigation.

Decision regarding the Type of Design

Contrary to the general impression among people that qualitative research does not have any research design, the fact is that "qualitative research designs do exist" (Flick, Kardorff and Steinke, 2004: 146). The research design in qualitative research depends upon the purpose, theoretical framework, research question, selection of empirical material, methodological procedures, degree of standardization and control, intention to generalize and available resources (Flick, Kadroff and Steinke, 2004: 146-47). The basic designs generally used in qualitative research are: case studies, comparative studies, retrospective studies, snapshots (analyses of state and process at the time of research), and longitudinal studies (Flick, Kadroff and Steinke, 2004: 147).

Selection of Relevant Unit(s) to be Covered in the Study

In qualitative research, selection of units of study is done purposively to ensure that unit(s) selected embodies/reflects the important characteristics in which the researcher is interested. While selecting study unit(s), it must be guaranteed that different facets are represented. While doing sampling, extreme cases, typical cases and critical cases (Patton,1990:169-74) should be covered.

As for the stage at which sample should be selected, Flick (2002:62) holds the view that decisions about selection in the research process are taken at three different levels during:

- data collection (case selection, case group selection),
- interpretation (selection of material and selection within material), and
- the presentation of results (presentation of material).

Sampling may be done deliberately in course of investigation. Such sampling has been given the name of 'selective sampling' by Schatzmann and Strauss (1973:81). It can also be done keeping in mind multiple perspective of time, place, individuals, events, activities which has been called ' theoretical sampling' by Strauss (1987: 16). This entails the process of picking the sources that can provide the vital information about the research problems (Mc Nabb, 2005:389); and involves selection of subjects and/or settings such that the emerging concepts and theories may be fully elaborated (Thyer, 2001: 348).

Decision regarding Method(s) and Tool(s)

Observation, particularly participant observation, in case of ethnographic studies and action research, interview, group discussion, transcription of conversation, tape recording, photography and videography are the methods generally used for collecting field data in qualitative research. Important tools which may be employed in the qualitative research are observation guide, interviewed guide, unstructured or semi-structured interview schedule, video camera, autobiographies, etc.

Entry into the Field and Collection of Data

Research field in qualitative research has a typical meaning. It refers to "naturally occurring social fields of action, as opposed to artificial situational arrangements deliberately engineered for research purposes" (Wolff, 2004: 195). Thus, field in qualitative research is comprised of people spontaneously interacting and acting in everyday life, and qualitative research is directed towards understanding how people themselves feel and experience the events that take place in their lives.

The qualitative researcher before entering the field must seriously think about the modus operandi of his/her entry in order that people in the field may accept him/her and continue to interact and act in the natural manner even in the presence of researcher (initially a stranger creating varied kinds of reservations in the minds of people; in other words, the researcher in due course must establish relationships based on mutual trust and confidence).

After success in gaining acceptance among people in the field, the real work of data collection should be done in such a manner that any kind of suspicion relating to researcher may not be caused in the minds of subjects. It must always be remembered that human memory is short, and documentation of relevant information should be done at earliest available opportunity.

Analysis and Interpretation of Data

Data collected from the field available in a written form are scanned thoroughly so that the researcher may be confident that the required material is actually available. After this, the process of coding begins so that various categories may be developed. Coding, in the word of Strauss and Carbin (1998:3), is "the analytical process though which data are fractured, conceptualized and integrated to form theory". In course of the process of coding some meaningful sets of identifiers are applied to various concepts and categories that emerge from data (Mc Nabb, 2004: 390). The coding done at the initial stage is known as open or substantive coding. It is done line by line to name the processes and situations which are discerned from data. It helps in identifying the core concepts instrumental in analysis. After open coding, axial coding is done to discover whether any identified characteristic can become a core concept. This is followed by selective coding focused on particular concept. Here, the researcher makes a deep probe into the data to identify such instances as are important but might have been overlooked. In the end, theoretical coding is done to regroup the categories, if necessary, to reinforce any important emerging finding. In the end, the researcher establishes relationship between various concepts and categories evolved in course of coding and builds up "grounded" or "middle range" theory.

Presentation

There are three main forms suggested by Mannel (1998) in which presentation of qualitative research may be made. These are: (1) realistic presentation, (2) confessional description, and (3) impressionistic description (Flick et al., 2004: 328). A presentation is realistic if it is factual, written in third person and dominated by a documentary style. Here, the researcher depicts the social world as impartially observed by him/her. In confessional description, the researcher describes in first person his/her personal feelings and experiences from the field. In case of impressionistic description the researcher highlights what he/she considers to be valuable among his/her activities in course of investigation. Since qualitative research primarily aims at exploring the experiences of subjects, the research report should be realistic, written in narrative style in third person.

All the above given steps can be condensed into four broad categories: (1) planning the study, (2) collecting the data, (3) analyzing the data, and (4) writing the report (Tutty et al., 1996).

Major Types of Qualitative Research Studies and their Relevance to Social Work

Qualitative research studies can be broadly classified into three major categories (McNabb, 2004: 343): (1) explanatory, (2) interpretive, and (3) critical. Explanatory research studies are directed towards developing a causal explanation of some social phenomenon. Those studies which are helpful in understanding actions of people in a socio-cultural contest are known as interpretive research studies. Critical studies are those which offer a social critique and highlight those social conditions which are harmful and alienate people. All the three types of studies, particularly those which are critical, are useful for social workers who, on the one hand, are concerned about introducing changes in egalitarian social system through modifications in social policies, laws, plans and programmes and are engaged in providing help to individuals, groups and communities as clients in dealing with their problems, especially those which are social and psychological. In a country like ours, where problems of unemployment, poverty, illiteracy, ill-health and insanitation are fairly widespread and society is divided on the basis of religion, caste, language, region etc., social work interventions are needed at both micro and macro levels.

Since social worker believes that the root cause of clients' problem lies in the social system and not in them, is based on democratic and humanitarian philosophy, is governed by principles of working with the clients by encouraging their participation in the helping process, and right of clients to make self-determination and make optimum use of people's own knowledge in solving their problems, all the three types of qualitative research studies, especially the critical ones, need to be undertaken.

The essence of social work lies in practice during professional training as also after that when trained social workers get employed either in government or in some non-governmental organization or set up their own organization in which they became self-employed, reasonably charging for their services. During their professional training, they are required to do field work, both concurrent and block, and in this process work with individuals, groups, communities, organizations, etc. to provide their services in solving their problems and improve their effectiveness, their qualitative research, orientation should start right from the time of placement for field work, particularly through discussion about their actual intervention with problem affected client, and interactions with personnel in the organization or people in the community, especially with formal as well as informal leaders, and with their field work supervisions who should be held responsible for developing knowledge and skills relating to qualitative research in social work of all the three types.

A note of caution in the end: social workers intending to engage themselves in qualitative research must have clear understanding of important theories taught to the students of Anthropology, Sociology and Psychology in the same manner as their counterparts involved in quantitative research should be fairly conversant with statistical methods and techniques.

References

Barker, R.L. (ed.) (1994). *The Social Work Dictionary*. Washington, D.C.: NASW Press.

Bogdan, R. and Taylor, S. (1975). *Introduction to Qualitative Research Methods*. New York: John Wiley.

Carnop, Rudolph (1995). *The Unity of Science*. Bristol, U.K.: Thoemmes Press.

Denzin, N.K. (1989). *The Research Act: A Theoretical Introduction to Sociological Methods*. Englewood Cliffs, NJ: Prentice Hall.

Filstead, W.J. (1970). *Qualitative Methodology: Firsthand Involvement with the Social World*. Chicago: Markhom.

Flick, Uwe, Kardoff, Ernst won and Steinke, Ines (eds.) (2004). *A Companion to Qualitative Research*. New Delhi: Sage Publications.

Flick, Uwe (2004). Design and Process in Qualitative Research. In Uwe Flick et al. (eds.).

— (2002). *An Introduction to Qualitative Research*. Thousand Oats, CA: Sage Publications.

Holosko, Michael J. (2001). Overview of Qualitative Research Methods, In Bruce A. Thyer (ed.), *The Handbook of Social Work Research Methods*. New Delhi: Sage Publications.

McCoy, R.G. (1995). Qualitative Research. In R.L. Edwards (ed.), *Encyclopedia of Social Work*. Washington, D.C.: NASW Press.

McNabb, David E. (2005). *Research Methods for Political Science: Quantitative and Qualitative Methods*. New Delhi: Prentice Hall of India Pvt. Ltd.

Patton, M.Q. (1990). *Qualitative Evaluation and Research Methods*. Newbury Park, C.A.: Sage Publications.

Schatzmann, L. and Strauss, A.L. (1973). *Field Research: Strategies for a Natural Sociology*. Englewood Cliffs, NJ: Prentice Hall.

Straurss, A.L. (1987). *Qualitative Analysis for Social Scientists*. Cambridge: Cambridge University Press.

Tutty, L., Rothery, M. and Grinvell, R. (1996). *Qualitative Research for Social Workers*. Needham Heights, M.A. Allyn and Bacon.

Wolff, Stephen (2004). Ways into the Field and their Variants. In Flick et al. (eds.).

15

Social Work and Qualitative Research

Natural Allies

S. Raja Samuel

The context for this paper comes from the overwhelming reliance on non-qualitative approaches in current social work research practice. Both academic and field-based practitioners of social work in India depend primarily on quantitative methods for accumulating and analyzing research data. This reliance on purely quantitative methods has ensured that the research carried out does not delve into the depths of the issues of concern. On account of this, a rich understanding of issues and subsequent action based on such an understanding has proved to be elusive. The other issue of concern is that non-social work professionals, working in the field of general social development and even science disciplines, have adopted qualitative social research approaches in a major way. It is high time that social work in India takes on board qualitative research approaches as the primary methodology of doing social work research. In this paper I look at some important features of the qualitative research paradigm and examine how they are closely aligned with social work, and narrate the advantages of using semi-structured interview method in my doctoral research.

Characteristics of Qualitative Research

Several writers have identified what they consider to be the prominent characteristics of qualitative research (Bogdan and Biklen, 1982; Lincoln and Guba, 1985; Patton, 1990; Eisner, 1991). The points mentioned below are some of the important ones.

Emphasis on Meaning

Qualitative research places a strong emphasis on the discovery of the meaning of the occurrence or the subject rather than the frequency of the occurrence. The meaning according to this paradigm is complex, multi-dimensional and dynamic.

For instance, if we study child labour, we focus on the process by which it occurs and seek explanation on why it occurs and what explain its various facets. We are not looking into merely the number of times a problem has occurred and the number affected. The emphasis on meaning is important for social work, as we search for solutions to the problem in collaboration with the client(s). The magnitude will only tell us that we need to act urgently, but the meaning will tell us how to act. Qualitative researchers pay attention to the peculiar as well as the pervasive, seeking the uniqueness of each case. By doing so the entire range of meanings gets captured in the process of data collection and interpretation. The outliers are not frowned upon as it is done in quantitative research. They add more value to the research. This also goes along well with the inclusive character of social work. Each individual is important and no one can be rejected.

Inductive

Qualitative researchers do not begin with a theoretical framework or a theory base. They first start with the field reality from where they get the data. The data gives rise to concepts. All the concepts are then related in a web of hypothesis and from this emerges field-based grounded theory. This is an inductive process. This approach has been developed by Strauss and Corbin (1998). This appears to be a more meaningful way of looking at life events of clients, rather than start with a theoretical framework into which our subjects are artificially inserted and studied. Often, theoretical frameworks are borrowed and adapted to suit our subjects. Starting from field reality lends itself to originality. We must also remember that the hypothesis in qualitative research is not a linear bivariate one as in quantitative paradigm, but a web of hypothesis where several concepts are interrelated. This would be the best way to understand human problems which are usually complex and multi-layered.

Reduced Distance between the Researcher and the Researched

Qualitative research involves getting into the life space of the researched. The researched or the subject is not merely a respondent. Quantitative researchers may be able to do surveys without direct contact with research objects. They can collect data by using hired and trained interviewers or by mailing out questionnaires. Qualitative researchers, on the other hand, often enter into the natural fields of people whom they study, and have face-to-face interviews with them. The researcher acts as the "human instrument" of data collection. Frequently, observational techniques are used, where the researcher is a participant or non-participant observer in a real-life setting. Patton (1987) points out the experiences of Piaget's closeness to his children, Freud's proximity to and empathy with his patients, Darwin's closeness with nature and even Newton's encounter with an apple, are instances where closeness to the subjects made key insights possible. Social work would greatly benefit from such an approach as it gives the inside view of the problem.

Multiple Methods of Data Collection

Qualitative researchers believe that the researched comprise of various stakeholders. To obtain varied stakeholder perspectives it is necessary to use multiple methods of data collection.

Observation, semi-structured interview, in-depth unstructured interview, focus groups and documentary analysis are some of the prominent methods of data collection used. Qualitative researchers use different methods for different stakeholders. Social work practice involves interacting with various systems with the objective of helping the client. We use multiple ways of reaching these stakeholders and working with them to reach our objectives.

Iterative

The qualitative research process is a non-linear one. Unlike quantitative researchers who progress linearly from start to finish, qualitative researchers go back and forth. They get back to the researched to clarify fill-up gaps and reach new insights. This process of iteration makes the data rich, thick and descriptive. This is a natural process in social work practice which is non-linear. Though we go from session to session in working with our clients, we do iterate by clarifying with the client and by asking for more information pertaining to an issue discussed earlier, while simultaneously interacting with other stakeholders on behalf of the client.

Assumptions of Qualitative Research

Some of the premises on which qualitative researchers build their inquiry reflect the assumptions of social work. Qualitative researchers believe that all meaning is subjectively created and contextual. The meaning is created through the perspective of the one who experiences the social reality. As such, there is no universal truth of human experiences of social reality. And, Lincoln (1990) goes on to say that, because there are no enduring, context-free truth statements, and all human behaviour is time and context bound, "we began to doubt seriously the possibility of generalization (of research findings) from one site to the next".

It is also believed that meaning, in qualitative research, can only be understood through the processes used to enact and create social reality. This requires the participation of the researched in a self-reflective process of data collection. Similar, but not so intense, processes exist in social work practice. Social work interviews are intended to facilitate this process of reflection where the client reflects on life events and helps the social worker gain insights that help collaborative problem solving.

Following the earlier assumption, a self-reflective process of data collection requires an 'interpretive' rather than a 'normative' approach to research. A normative approach looks from the perspective of what is wrong and what is right, while the interpretive approach requires a non-judgemental and non-censored view of the data. We may or may not agree with what we see. But, the purpose is to understand. The interpretive approach recognizes that knowledge and understanding is context-specific and that the lines of enquiry followed during the research process shape the knowledge derived from the research.

Another key assumption pertains to the role of the researcher. In qualitative research, the role of the researcher is that of an instrument, exploring, uncovering and making evident the varying stakeholder perspectives and interpretations.

Values of Qualitative Research

Social work practice is governed by certain fundamental ethical principles and values. These have been considered inviolable and never been contested despite the myriad approaches social work has adopted and evolved. If social work research has to be seen as a method of social work, then it has to subscribe to the fundamental social work values and principles. The methodology of social work research has to align itself and conform to these values. In this context, social work needs to actively align itself with qualitative research approaches which follow principles similar to that of social work practice. This consonance of principles makes it not only easier but also more appropriate and contextual for qualitative research to be an integral part of social work research.

There are two important values of qualitative research that align closely with that of social work. One is the non-hierarchical relationship between the researcher and the researched. The researcher in qualitative research is not the 'expert' who has the know-how to do research and hence is up on the hierarchy. The researched is not down the hierarchy because he/she is a subject of study and does not have the skills held by the researcher. This value has a direct bearing on research in the context of social work practice. Social work grew out of humanitarian and democratic ideals, and its values are based on respect for the equality, worth and dignity of all people. Extending it further they involve in a relationship that is purposeful and that which is non-hierarchical.

Qualitative research values a non-judgemental approach to understanding social reality. The researcher may not agree with what the researched believes, but considers that belief as valid in the context of the latter. This requires an empathic understanding, as is required in social work practice. This is the capacity to step into another's shoes and thereby move beyond the realm of their own experience or transcend the limitations of what they know and accept as valid forms of behaviour (Dominelli, 2004).

Quantitative vs. Qualitative

A summary of the aforementioned points have been succinctly presented by Glesne and Peshkin (1992). They have made a useful comparison between the characteristics of quantitative and qualitative modes of enquiry as under:

Predispositions of Quantitative and Qualitative Modes of Inquiry

Quantitative Mode	*Qualitative mode*
Assumptions	**Assumptions**
• Social facts have an objective reality	• Reality is socially constructed
• Primacy of method	• Primacy of subject matter
• Variables can be identified and relationships	• Variables are complex, interwoven, and
• Measured	• Difficult to measure
• Etic (outside's point of view)	• Emic (insider's point of view)
Purpose	**Purpose**
• Generalizability	• Contextualization
• Prediction	• Interpretation
• Causal explanations	• Understanding actors' perspectives
Approach	**Approach**
• Begins with hypotheses and theories	• Ends with hypotheses and grounded theory
• Manipulation and control	• Emergence and portrayal
• Uses formal instruments	• Researcher as instrument
• Experimentation	• Naturalistic
• Deductive	• Inductive
• Component analysis	• Searches for patterns
• Seeks consensus, the norm	• Seeks pluralism, complexity
• Reduces data to numerical indices	• Makes minor use of numerical indices
• Abstract language in write-up	• Descriptive write-up
• Researcher role	• Researcher role
• Detachment and impartiality	• Personal involvement and partiality
• Objective portrayal	• Empathic understanding

The detached, sterile and structured approach of quantitative research has not really blended well with the practice of social work which is a helping profession governed by humanistic values. Life events are complex, unstructured and non-linear. It appears that qualitative research is better equipped to help social workers understand such life events in greater depth and enable them help clients more effectively.

Attempts at Integrating a Qualitative Method in Conventional Research

Emerging mixed method models suggest a prudent mix of qualitative and quantitative methods, though qualitative purists aver that methods from the two different paradigms cannot be mixed within a study.

For a study on the Determinants of Participation of NGOs in Inter-organizational Networks, I included semi-structured interview as a method of collecting data from the NGO network convenors who are key stakeholders in the networking process and outcome. I situated this study in the macro-practice context of social work practice which engages in working with communities and public policy. Networking and advocacy are now seen as important tools for influencing public policy. The main source of data for the study were NGO representatives, who answered a highly structured mailed questionnaire. However, to understand the issue from the point of view of the convenors, I interviewed 15 of them personally, using an interview guide. I found certain significant advantages in using the semi-structured interview method.

One of the important advantages in the semi-structured interview is the flow of questions. In a structured tool, respondents have no control over the order of questions they have to answer. They cannot change the order. However, in a semi-structured interview, the flow of questions can be altered in accordance with the responses of the interviewee. For instance, I had wanted to ask about the impact of network activities at the end, after discussing the processes of networking. Some of the convenors spoke about the achievements of the network first. Listening to this and putting forward associated questions helped the interview proceed smoothly. Aligning with the thought processes of the researched becomes easier with the semi-structured interview.

The interviews also helped in clarifying concepts related to networking, that existing literature failed to cover. Several advocacy networks in India are pitted against powerful agents of oppression. Fighting against them requires a strong backing of organizations in terms of sheer numbers. The large numbers provided the requisite physical security to the network members when they stood up for the cause. This was stated as one of the important reasons for NGOs joining networks. However, this did not appear in any of the available network assessment tools or in the literature. A structured tool would have missed out on this very important point.

It is also tremendously practical to use the semi-structured interview in some contexts. The network convenors I interviewed were persons with enormous responsibilities. They were heads of their own organizations apart from convening these statewide networks. Though some of them interacted with me for over two hours, it would be impractical to expect them to answer a structured questionnaire with about 150 items to tick. The drudgery associated with filling up structured tools of data collection is so strong that it is very difficult to convince persons with huge responsibilities to do so.

The semi-structured interview also offered me the opportunity of subject validation of the data. I sent the interview transcripts to the convenors, who were able to fill up the gaps, correct factual errors and more important, provide additional information. This iteration process has enriched the data.

And, finally, the semi-structured interview helped me build relationships with some of the key actors in the voluntary social development sector in the state. It also broke some of the assumptions I had about some of the convenors, some of whom were larger than life, and a few others 'eccentric' and 'tough' until I met them.

Conclusions

The debate over the merits of quantitative and qualitative approaches in social research has been continuing for the past several decades. It is unlikely to be resolved soon. Attempts at a compromise are being made by advocating the use of mixed methods, while the purists on either sides hold their fort. It is also recommended that qualitative approaches can be used to generate hypothesis that can be tested using quantitative approaches. The role of quantitative research cannot be discounted. It has its place. However, as argued in the earlier paragraphs, qualitative approaches needs, to gain a predominant place in social work research as there is a significant convergence in the characteristics of both. Social work practitioners in most developed countries have moved over to qualitative paradigms and we cannot be far behind.

References

Bogdan, R.C. and Biklen, S.K. (1982). *Qualitative Research for Education: An Introduction to Theory and Methods*. Boston: Allyn and Bacon, Inc.

Dominelli, Lena (2004). *Social Work: Theory and Practice for a Changing Profession*: Cambridge: Polity Press.

Eisner, E.W. (1991). *The Enlightened Eye: Qualitative Inquiry and the Enhancement of Educational Practice*. New York: Macmillan Publishing Company.

Glesne, C., and Peshkin, A. (1992). *Becoming Qualitative Researchers: An Introduction*. White Plains, NY: Longman. Lincoln, Y.S., and Guba, E.G. (1985). *Naturalistic Inquiry*. Beverly Hills, CA: Sage Publications, Inc.

Lincoln, Y. (1990). *The Making of a Constructivist: A Remembrance of Transformations Past*. In E. Guba (ed.)., *The Paradigm Dialog*. Newbury Park: Sage Publications.

Patton, M.Q. (1987). *How to Use Qualitative Methods in Education*. Newbury Park, CA: Sage Publications, Inc.

— (1990). *Qualitative Evaluation and Research Methods* (2nd ed.). Newbury Park, CA: Sage Publications, Inc.

Strauss, A. and Corbin, J. (1998). *Basics of Qualitative Research: Techniques and Procedures for Developing Grounded Theory* (2nd ed.). Thousand Oaks, CA: Sage Publications.

16

Case Study Method in Social Work Research

B. Vijayalakshmi

Most social work research adheres to quantitative methods. These methods are based on a view of the world called 'positivism'. According to this view, there is an objective world which exists independent of the observer and that it is governed by universal laws that can be understood by scientists using positivistic methods (Mark, 1996).

In recent years, social work researchers have criticized this positivistic approach because "quantitative research is not synonymous with scientific reasoning" (Gambril, quoted in Riessman, 1994:viii) and it was also held that this view distorts and trivializes reality.

> "In applied settings particularly not all problems lend themselves to quantification and computer manipulation. .... Social workers deal with living human beings. (Therefore) ... human, experience, initiative, and emotion need greater attention in our research reports .... yet we privilege the abstract statistical aggregate in social work research: and average

tendencies, not individual lives in context" (Riessman, 1994:viii-ix).

Riessman (1994: ix) further pointed out that as a result of this orientation for quantification at the expense of individuals in context, social work has witnessed a hiatus between practice and research. The practitioners say that social work research presents depersonalized accounts that do not help at field level. Whereas the researchers complain that social workers do not use empirical findings to select interventions or evaluate them. Thus, this division between research and practice is effecting the growth of the profession the most, as the development of any profession is dependent on the close collaboration between practice and research. This is because in qualitative research, the subjective nature of reality is recognized and the point of view of the researcher becomes part of the research findings.

From this perspective, case study assumes an important place in social work research. As one of the methods in qualitative research, it favours intensive analysis of one or a few cases using in-depth unstructured interviews, observation, and narrative rather than depending on numerical reporting (Mark, 1996: 225). The method shares with other qualitative research, the quality of developing rich insights that have direct relevance to real world behaviours. As a result, by 1980s, it became popular and gained its strength as an important research method. In fact, case study method used to occupy a long and honourable place in qualitative research (Feagsin et al., 1991; Stake, 1994; Yin, 1994) as it can draw on the maximal ability of the qualitative researcher to extract depth and meaning in context (Padgett, 1998:30).

Case Study Method in Social Work Practice and Research: A Comparison

According to some scholars, the origins of the idea of case study can be traced to social workers' using case history in social case work. Platt (1981:19) observed that the work *The Polish Peasant in Europe and America* (1918-20) by Thomas and Znaniecki, was an excellent example of case study of an immigrant group where social case work records were extensively used.

Table 1

Differences between Case Study in Social Case Work and Case Study in Social Work Research

Social Case Work	*Social Work Research*
• It is the first step in the helping process with a goal to understand the client's problem so as to help the client to help himself/herself.	• Its aim is theory building and developing conceptual frameworks.
• It is typically used to instruct and advance clinical practice. Its primary purpose is pedagogic.	• It is primarily a method of enquiry and not an educational or therapeutic tool.
• The relationship is initiated by the client.	• The researcher initiates the relationship. (Schein 1987).
• There is supervision.	• No supervision, and the case study depends on the judgement of the researcher.
• Expertise and authority flows downward from the practitioner to the client.	• The locus of power and authority lies with the respondent. The researcher enters the relationship to learn from the respondent and not vice-versa.
• Self-disclosure by the clinician is potentially damaging to the relationship.	• Self-disclosure is not only accepted but also at times desirable as a means of enhancing rapport.
• Focus is on problems and emotions.	• Focus is on events and experiences of the respondent who is encouraged to share feelings.
• It suggests clinical interpretation to respondents.	• Clinical interpretation is seen inappropriate.
• Decision to terminate is made by the client, or the case worker or both.	• The relationship ends when the researcher has decided that enough information has been collected from the respondent.
• The case worker continues to work with the client even after the case study.	• No likely contact with the respondent after the data collection was over.

However, besides some similarities, there are important differences between case study used in social case work and case study method in social work research. Table 1 highlights some of these differences. This table is based on the observations of Stake (1994), Yin (1994), Schein (1987) and Padgett (1998).

What is Case Study Research?

The term "case study" is used to identify a specific form of inquiry, notably, one which contrasts with two other mainstream methods of social research, that is, experimental research and the social survey (Hammersley and Gomm, 2004:2). A comparative view of the characteristics of the three methods will be useful to better articulate the strengths and limitations of the case study method (see Table 2).

Table 2

A Schematic Comparison of Case Study with Experimental and Survey Approaches.

Survey	*Experiment*	*Case Study*
Investigation of a relatively large number of cases.	Investigation of a relatively small number of cases.	Investigation of a relatively small number of cases. Sometimes just one case.
Information gathered and analysed about a small number of features of each case.	Information gathered and analysed about a small number of features of each case.	Information gathered and analysed about a large number of features of each case.
Quantification of data is a priority.	Quantification of data is a priority.	Quantification of data is not a priority. Qualitative data is predominant.
Study of a sample of cases selected in such a way as to maximize the sample's representativeness in relation to some larger population.	Cases are studied where controlling the important variables is an important concern.	The primary concern is not controlling variables to measure their effects.
The aim is empirical generalization and theory building.	The aim is either theory building or the evaluation of an intervention.	The aim is to understand the case studied in itself. The building of theory is of secondary concern. The wider relevance of the findings can be brought out on the basis of transferability of the vicarious experience.

Source: Hammersley Martyn and Gomm Roger (2004), "Introduction". In Gomm Roger, Hammersley Martyn and Foster Peter (eds.), *Case Study Method: Key Issues, Key Texts*, New Delhi: Sage, p. 4.

Definition and Characteristics of Case Study Method

As mentioned earlier, case study is a type of research method that investigates one or a few cases in depth using appropriate methods. The general objective of case study is to develop as full an understanding of the case studied as possible (Punch, 1998:150). According to Goode and Hatt, "the case study is not a specific technique, it is a way of organizing social data so as to preserve the unitary character of the social object being studied" (1952:331). Stake (1988:258) viewed case study as the "study of a bounded system emphasizing the unity and wholeness of that system, but confining the attention to those aspects that are relevant to the research problem at the time".

Brewer and Hunter (1989) identified six types of units, which can be chosen for doing case study. They are:

- Individuals
- Attributes of individuals
- Actions and interactions
- Residues and artifacts of behaviour
- Settings, incidents and events
- Collectives

According to Lewis (2004:52), one of the defining features of a case study is its "multiplicity of perspectives rooted in a specific context". The multiple perspectives may come from multiple data collection methods used or may come from multiple accounts obtained from people with different perspectives using a single method of data collection.

This method has important characteristics, which distinguishes it from other methods of study. Punch (1998:153) identified four characteristics of case studies. They are:

- *The case is a bounded system*. However, Yin (1984) pointed out that the boundaries between the case and the context need not necessarily be clearly evident. It is the researcher's responsibility to identify and describe the boundaries of the case as clearly as possible.

- *The case is a case of something*. Identifying what "the case is" in the case being studied is important in determining the unit of analysis to be considered and in planning the analysis of data.
- *The need for an explicit attempt to preserve the wholeness, unity and integrity of the case*. As everything cannot be studied, even about one case, specific focus is required about the dimensions to be studied. Here, research questions help in defining the focus.
- *Use of multiple sources of data and multiple data collection methods*. Methods such as observations, projective tests, interviews, questionnaires and sometimes numerical data can also be used.

While these characteristics highlight the method, Merriam (quoted in Wimmer and Dominick, 1994:154) lists four essential characteristics of case study research the point of view of case study as a knowledge building tool. Accordingly, a case study is:

(i) *Particularistic*: It focuses on a particular situation, event, programme or phenomenon.
(ii) *Descriptive*: The final result of a case study is a detailed description of the case/unit under study.
(iii) *Heuristic*: It helps people to understand what is being studied. New interpretations, new perspectives, new meaning and insights are all goals of a case study.
(iv) *Inductive*: Most case studies depend on inductive reasoning. They attempt to discover new relationships rather than verifying existing hypotheses and through transfer of concepts may develop new understanding about the case under study.

On the basis of the perspective provided by the method, Stake (quoted in Punch, 1998:152) identified three main types of case studies. They are:

- The *intrinsic* case study, where the study is undertaken because the researcher wants a better understanding of a particular case.
- The *instrumental* case study, where a particular case is examined to give insight into an issue, or to refine a theory.
- The *collective* case study is the one where the instrumental case study is extended to cover several cases, to learn more about the phenomenon, population or general condition.

Thus, in the case of the intrinsic and the instrumental case studies, the focus is within the case. Whereas in the collective case study, the focus is both within and across the cases.

Advantages of Case Study

It can provide more valid portrayals of the unit/person under study, better bases for personal understanding of what is going on, and solid grounds for considering action (Stake 1981:32). The case studies are highly appropriate when the goal is individualized outcome. The major advantages of the case study methods are:

- A fuller understanding of a phenomenon and processes involved can be achieved by case studies (Punch, 1998:156.)
- Case study designs can build very detailed in-depth understanding by integrating different perspectives. They are used where no single perspective can provide a full account or explanation of the research issue and where understanding needs to be holistic, comprehensive and contextualized (Lewis, 2004:52).
- Case studies can be a very effective way of presenting profiles of different groups within a study population and for displaying verbatim text with a well-defined context. Therefore, they are often used in conjunction with survey research (White, Woodfield and Ritchie, 2004:306).

- Case studies provide great detail that helps us to understand the complexities of human behaviour. They are useful as exploratory studies when there is little knowledge or theory available to guide the researchers. The results of a case study may in fact indicate areas for examination, highlight critical issues, or suggest concepts that can serve as the basis for further theory building (Mark, 1996:218-19).
- The case study method is flexible and can deal with a wide spectrum of evidence. Documents, historical artifacts, systematic interviews, direct observations and even traditional surveys can be incorporated into a case study. Infact, multiple data sources can bring more depth, regiour and validity to the case studied (Wimmer and Dominick, 1994:154-55).

Patton (1990:54) brought out certain advantages of case study. They are:

- Case studies are particularly useful where one needs to understand some special people, a particular problem, or a unique situation in great depth.
- In evaluative studies, case studies are especially valuable to capture individual differences or unique variations from one programme experience to another.
- Sometimes researchers or policy makers are puzzled by certain cases – unusual successes, unusual failures, or dropouts. Detailed case studies of these unusual cases can provide useful insights about such phenomenon.

How to Conduct Case Study Research?

Before launching the case study research, there are certain preliminaries to be kept in mind regarding selection of cases, data collection, sources of data and strategies for analysis. To begin with, Lewis (2004:52) suggested the following steps to be kept in mind before and during the conduct of a case study:

- Prior understanding of the study contexts to make decisions about the criteria on which cases will be selected for study.
- Careful consideration about the number of cases and the number of participants in each case.
- Clear idea about the composition of each case, i.e., who are the key participants to be involved, and how this varies between different cases or sites.
- Thought need to be given as to how to organize analysis in a way that allows the comparison of the contributions of different members of each case.

According to Punch (1998:156), before proposing case study research, there is a need to be clear about what the case is, including identification of its boundaries, state clearly the general purpose(s) of the case study, translate that general purpose into specific purposes and research questions. Then, identify the overall strategy of the case study, especially whether it is one case or multiple cases, show what data will be collected, from whom, and how and state how the data would be analyzed.

Research Strategies

Case study researchers employ several research strategies, including triangulation, comparisons, intensive involvement and case selection (Mark, 1996:220). These are discussed below in some detail:

(i) *Triangulation:* The term 'triangulation' is used to refer to the observation of the research issue from [at least] two different points (Flick, 2005:178). Multiple sources are used to verify a concept or a conclusion (Mark, 1996:220). According to Stake (1994), triangulation is the "process of using multiple perspectives to clarify meaning, and verify the repeatability of an observation or interpretation". Triangulation is preferred because "studies that use only one method are more vulnerable to errors linked to that particular method" (Patton, 1990:188). Denzin (1978:28) stated it more emphatically: "No single method ever adequately solves the problem of rival causal (explanations) factors – because each method reveals different aspects of empirical reality, multiple methods of observations must be employed. This is termed triangulation."

Therefore, it is frequently applied as a validation strategy, as an approach to the generalization of discoveries, and as a route to additional knowledge (Flick, 2005:183).

(ii) *Comparison*: Comparisons are used in case studies when the aim is to form or test generalizations. In such situations, the researcher must be careful about which variables are selected for comparison, since the very process of selecting some variables for comparison means that other potential similarities or differences will be obscured (Stake, 1994:242).

(iii) *Intensive involvement*: It is a necessary part of case study approach. Regardless of the methods used for data collection the researchers must develop a 'feel' for the persons or phenomenon being studied, and this can occur only when researchers immerse themselves in the research setting (Mark, 1996:220).

(iv) *Case selection*. In case study research, representative sampling is not used as the number of cases studied are small. The only criterion for selecting cases for a case study should be the "opportunity to learn" (Stake, 1994:244). It means that the researcher should select those cases, which provide a learning opportunity for the researcher such as studying an atypical, or an unusual case. Sometimes, practical considerations also influence the selection of cases. Stake (quoted in Mark, 1996:221) observes that in case study research, the cases are usually hand picked by the researcher on the basis of practical needs, and the likelihood of obtaining the most interesting and useful information.

Some Methodological Issues of Case Study Design

Hammersley and Gomm (2004:5-7) point out a series of methodological issues pertaining to the use of case study such as generalizability, causal connections, nature of theory building, and authenticity of the results.

The first is *generalizabililty*. A common charge against case study research is that its findings are not generalizable as in the case of the survey research. The question raised is, as case study is based on only one case or a few cases, how far these findings are generalizable? There are different opinions about it. Some (Mitchell, 2004; Yin, 1994) say that the generalizations or inferences drawn from a case study are different from that of statistical inference. Others (Gomm et al., 2004:19) argue that case studies can make generalizations similar to that of survey research. However, Denzin argued that generalization need not necessarily be the objective of all research studies, whether case studies or not (quoted in Punch, 1998:154). According to Stake (2004), case studies may be epistemologically in harmony with the reader's experience, and thus to that person it can be a natural basis for generalization. However, Punch (1998:154) says that in two types of case study situations, generalization may not be warranted. They are, for example, intrinsic case studies where the case is studied because it is important, interesting, misunderstood or unique and hence selected for study. Similarly, in the case of instrumental case studies, a 'negative' case is studied because we want to learn about *typical* by studying the *atypical*. Such case studies may not be useful for generalization. Punch (1998:154-155) further points out that a case study can produce generalizable results by conceptualizing and developing propositions during analysis. For example, in social work, cases are studied in depth and are used to train the students to deal with similar situations they would encounter in the future. This clearly underlines the potential generalizability of knowledge built from case studies (Punch, 1998:155). Case studies may not be able to make statistically based normative statements about the frequency of occurrence of a phenomenon in a defined population. However, "if generalizing theoretic propositions is the main goal, the case study method is perfectly suited to the task" (Wimmer and Dominick, 1994:155).

The next issue is about *causal connections*. It is argued that as cases are studied in depth and overtime, it is possible to identify causal processes even by studying one or two cases (Connolly 1998). Others (Becker, 2004) emphasize that as the outcomes are the result of multiple pathways, narrative accounts of events in particular cases are essential if one has to understand those outcomes.

It is argued that the identification of causal relations through comparative analysis in case study research is comparable to 'statistical analysis' (Skocpol, 1979:35-6). Znanieckie (1934: 305-6) held that analytic induction leads the researcher to genuinely causal laws. Robinson (2004:194) is of the opinion that in case study analytic induction can be integrated with the probabilistic approach characteristic of other research procedures in modern science.

The third issue is about the *role of theory*. While there is a general agreement about the role of theory in case study research, there is a difference of opinion about the use of theory in explaining the case as a bounded system or in relating what is going on with in the case in terms of wider social context.

Lastly, about *authenticity of the results*. According to Hammersley and Gomm (2004:6), case study research is advocated on the basis that it can capture the unique character of a person, situation, or a group. Here, the aim is to represent the case authentically – "in its own terms".

Steps in Case Study

There are three steps in case study research: (a) data collection, (b) construction of case, and (c) analysis. Each step is elaborated in this section.

(a) *Data collection*: Data for case study can be collected on aspects such as the nature of the case, its historical background, physical setting and about other contexts such as economic, political, legal etc.

Case data consist of all the information one has about each case. At the individual level, case data can include information about the unit of analysis/person – background information, clinical records, statistical information, life history profiles and diaries and so on (Patton, 1990:385-86). The interview data, observational data, impressions and statements of others about the case will be the additional information that needs to be gathered. Further, information obtained from biographical sources carry some special characteristics. For example, Denzin (1989:129) highlights the significance of certain existentially problematic moments in the lives of individuals or organizations, which are termed *epiphanies*. He classifies these moments into four types, viz., the *major*, the *cumulative*, the *illuminative* and the *relived* epiphanies: (a) The major epiphany refers to those moments which touch every fabric of a person's/organization's life and whose effects are both immediate and long term; (b) the cumulative epiphany is that which go on for a long period of time; (c) the illuminative is the minor epiphany is symbolically representative of major problematic moments in a relationship; and (d) the relived epiphany, whose effects are immediate but their meanings are only given later. The researcher needs to keep in mind these aspects and use them appropriately in the construction of a case study.

(b) *Construction of case:* After the raw case data have been accumulated, a case record is written using this raw data. In writing the case record, the researcher pulls together and organizes the voluminous case data into a systematically arranged record of data called case record. Thus, the case record includes all the major information that will be used in doing the final case analysis and case study. The case study is constructed using the case record. The steps involved in constructing a case study are shown below in Table 3:

Table 3

Steps in the Process of Constructing Case Studies

Step 1	:	Assemble the raw case data. The data consist of all the information collected about the person/unit for which the study is to be written.
Step 2 (optional)	:	Construct a case record. Condensation of the raw case data – organizing, classifying and editing it into a manageable and accessible record.
Step 3	:	Write the case study narrative. The case study is presented as a holistic portrayal of a person or a unit. It is a readable, descriptive picture of a person/unit making accessible to the reader all the information necessary to understand that case. It can be presented either chronologically or thematically or sometimes both.

Source: Patton, M. (1990), *Qualitative Evaluation and Research Methods*, New Delhi: Sage, p. 388.

Now, in the preparation of case study, the researcher must present solid information about the case. Denzin (1989) calls it 'thick description'. Such descriptions enable those who read the results to easily understand and draw their own interpretations. Patton (1990) further adds that while there could be guidelines for the preparation of a case study, these are flexible enough to permit the researcher to use judgement and creativity while putting the information together.

Next, to ensure reliability of interpretation and presentation, two evaluators shall review the material in the case study to independently make judgements and interpretations about its content and meaning. In addition, an external evaluator may also review the raw data to check out any biases or unwarranted conclusions.

(c) *Analysis of case study data:* Finally, the data collected have to be analyzed, interpreted and presented in such a way that significant patterns are identified. As in other qualitative methods, in case study too, there are few agreed upon rules for data analysis (Miles and Huberman, 1984:16). Further, as Patton (1990:372) pointed out, there were no formulas for determining significance, no ways of perfectly replicating the researcher's analytical thought processes, and no straightforward tests for ascertaining reliability and validity.

Once the data about the case studies are organized and written down, analysis follows by using strategies such as inductive analysis. It means that the patterns, themes and categories of analysis come from the data, rather than being imposed on them prior to data collection and analysis (Patton, 1990: 390).

After the development of themes and categories from the data, the next stage is using typologies. According to Patton (1990:393), these include the indigenous typologies, and the analyst constructed typologies. The indigenous typologies are the result of the *emic* approach, which means the insider's view or actor's definition of human events is captured (Pelto and Pelto, 1978:54). In the second category, the analyst-constructed typologies, the analyst looks for patterns, categories, and themes and constructs a typology to elucidate the findings.

Yin (1989) suggested three broad analytic strategies, namely, pattern matching, explanation building and time series to analyze the case study data:

- In *pattern matching*, an empirically based pattern is compared with a predicted pattern or several alternative predicted patterns. If the predicted pattern did not match the actual one, then, the initial study proposition would be questioned.
- On the other hand, *explanation building* means making statements about the cause(s) of the phenomenon. In a typical case, an investigator drafts an initial theoretical

statement about some processes or outcomes; compares the findings of an initial case study against the statement, revises the statement, again compares the findings of a second case, and repeats this process as many times as necessary, until a full and satisfactory answer is achieved.

- In the case of *time series*, data are compared to some theoretical trend that was predicted before the research.

These are some of the important steps involved in the preparation of case studies. The next important issue in case study method is the investigator and his/her qualities.

Characteristics of a Case Study Researcher

The case study method requires the intensive involvement of the researcher. The researcher gathers much of the data through observation, participation in the respondents' activities, through taking notes, or by recording on tape. Similarly, the researcher may also interview informants and examine documents such as newspaper accounts and other secondary sources. Regardless of the sources consulted, a case study researcher must develop a 'feel' for the persons, group, or the phenomenon being studied. This is otherwise called as *verstehen,* i.e., empathy which means understanding the meaning of actions and interactions from the respondent's point of view (Eckstein, 2004).

Therefore, for a large part, the preparation of the case study depends on the skills, training, insights and capabilities of the researcher. Some scholars pointed out that the qualities required of a researcher to prepare a case study are similar to those of the qualities required of a clinical social worker. Gilgun (quoted in Padgett, 1998:13) brought out a comparison between the qualities of a qualitative researcher and a clinical social worker. A clinical social worker starts "where the client is", view clients as part of a wider social context and favour individualized assessment and maximum detail in chronicling the lives of clients. In the process, they think inductively and flexibly, examine information from a variety of sources before drawing conclusions about client's problems and in designing a treatment plan. Similarly, they modify the treatment plan in response to new information. Case study researcher uses similar strategies in the preparation of outcomes of a case study. Moreover, the case worker's ability to listen through third ear and see through third eye goes well with the requirement of a case study researcher though in case study research the researcher should remain a passive observer and listener of all they see and hear.

Padgett (1998:19-21) lists out some important traits and skills required of a case study researcher. They are:

1. Creativity and original insights in pursuing research goal and good scholarship in the relevant literature.
2. Ability to maintain professional poise and a cheerful disposition even in the most exasperating circumstances.
3. Ability to maintain a critical distance, which involves the ability to exercise restraint and a non-judgmental attitude.
4. Flexibility and reflexivity are required. Flexibility pertaining to both cognitive and theoretical aspects is necessary to appreciate different perspectives. Reflexivity means the ability to examine one's self, which is an important quality of a case study researcher. In fact, knowledge about one's own biases and prejudices is essential to know about how far these interfere with the findings of the study.
5. Glaser (1978) adds another important attribute called theoretical sensitivity. It means the ability to think abstractly and give meaning to the data, which will enable the researcher to create new conceptual frameworks. Padgett (1998:21) considers it as the *sine qua non* of qualitative method.

To sum up, it can be stated that the case study research is gaining popularity among social work researchers in spite of the criticism about its limitations for generalization and to establish causal relationships. This is because of the increased recognition of its use in capturing emotive aspects of human behaviour, which is crucial in social work research and practice. As a result, case study is assuming greater importance as a method, which could reduce the divide between practice and research.

References

Becker, H.S. (2004). "Cases, causes, conjunctures, stories and imagery". In Gromm, R., Hammersley, M. and Foster, P. (eds.), *Case Study Method Key Issues, Key Texts*, pp. 223-233, New Delhi: Sage Publications.

Brewer, J. and Hunter, A. (1989). *Multi Method Research: A Synthesis of Styles*. Newbury Park, CA: Sage Publications.

Connolly, P. (1998). "Dancing to the wrong tune ethnography, generalization, and research on racism in schools". In Connolly, P. and Troyna, B. (eds.), *Researching Racism in Education*. Buckingham: Open University Press.

Denzin, N.K. (1989). *Interpretive Interactionism*. Newbury Park, CA: Sage Publications.

— (1978). *The Research Act: A Theoretical Introduction to Sociological Methods*, New York: Mc.Graw-Hill.

Eckstein, H. (2004). "Case Study and Theory in Political Science". In Gromm, R., Hammersley, M. and Forter, P. (eds.) *Case Study Methods: Key Issues, Key Texts*, pp. 119-164, New Delhi: Sage Publications.

Feagsin, J.R., Orum, A.M., and Sjoberg, G. (eds.) (1991). *A Case for the Case Study*. Chapel Hill: University of North Carolina Press.

Flick, U. (2005). "Triangulation in qualitative research". In Flick, U. Kardorff, E.V. and Steinke, I. (eds.), *A Companion to Qualitative Research*, pp. 178-183, New Delhi: Sage Publications.

Glaser, B.G. (1978). *Theoretical Sensitivity*. Mill-Valley, CA: Sociology Press.

Gomm, R. Hammersley, M. and Foster, P. (2004). "Case Study and generalization". In Gomm R., Hammersley, M. and Foster, P., (eds.), *Case Study Method: Key Issues, Key Texts*, pp. 98-116, New Delhi: Sage Publications.

Goode W.J. and Hatt P.K (1952). *Methods in Social Research*. New Delhi: McGraw Hill Book Company.

Hammersley M. and Gomm, R. (2004). "Introduction". In Gomm, R., Hammersley, M. and Foster, P. (eds.), *Case Study Method: Key Issues, Key Texts*, pp. 1-16, New Delhi: Sage Publications.

Lewis, J. (2004). "Design Issues": In Ritchie J., and Lewis J. *Qualitative Research Practice : A Guide to Social Science Students and Researchers*, 47-76, New Delhi: Sage Publications.

Mark, R. (1996). *Research Made Simple: A Handbook for Social Workers*. New Delhi: Sage Publications.

Miles, M.B. and Huberman, A.M. (1984). *Qualitative Data Analysis. A Source Book of New Methods*. Beverly Hills, CA: Sage Publications.

— (1994). *Qualitative Data Analysis* (2nd ed.), Thousand Oaks, CA: Sage Publications.

Mitchell C.J. (2004). "Case and situation analysis". In Gomm R., Hammersley M. and Foster P. (eds.), *Case Study Method: Key Issues, Key Texts*, pp. 165-186, New Delhi: Sage Publications.

Padgett, D.K. (1998). *Qualitative Methods in Social Work Research: Challenges and Rewards*, New Delhi: Sage Publications.

Patton M.Q. (1990). *Qualitative Evaluation and Research Methods* (2nd ed.), New Delhi: Sage Publications.

Pelto, P.J. and Pelto, G.H. (1978). *Anthropological Research: The Structure of Inquiry*, Cambridge: Cambridge University Press.

Platt, J. (1981). "Case study in American methodological thought", *Current Sociology*, 40: 17-48.

Punch K.F. (1998). *Introduction to Social Research: Quantitative and Qualitative Approaches*: New Delhi: Sage Publications.

Riessman C.K. (ed.) (1994). *Qualitative Studies in Social Work Research*. New Delhi: Sage Publications.

Robinson, W.S. (2004). "The Logical Structure of analytic induction". In Gomm, R., Hammersley, M. and Foster, P. (eds.), *Case Study Method: Key Issues, Key Texts*, pp. 187-195, New Delhi: Sage Publications.

Schein, E.H. (1987). *The Clinical Perspective in Field Work*. Newbury Park, CA: Sage Publications.

Skocpol, T. (1979) *States and Social Resolutions: A Comparative Analysis of France, Russia and China*. Cambridge: Cambridge University Press.

Stake, R.E. (1988) "Case Study methods in educational research: Seeking sweet water". In Jaeger, R.M. (ed.), *Complementary Methods for*

Research in Education, pp. 253-300, Washington, DC: American Educational Research Association.

— (1994). "Case studies". In Denzin, N.K. and Lincoln, Y.S. (eds.) *Hand Book of Qualitative Research*, pp. 236-247, Thousand Oaks, CA: Sage Publications.

— (2004). "The case study method in social inquiry". In Gomm, R. Hammersley, M. and Foster, P. (eds.), *Case Study Method: Key Issues, Key Texts*, pp. 19-26, New Delhi: Sage Publications.

Stenhouse, L. (1977). *Case Study as a Basis for Research in a Theoretical Contemporary History of Education*, East Anglia, England: University of East Anglia, Center for Applied Research in Education.

White, C., Woodfield, K. and Ritchie, J. (2004). "Reporting and presenting qualitative data". In Ritchie, J. and Lewis, J. (eds.), *Qualitative Research Practice: A Guide for Social Science Students and Researchers*, pp. 287-320, New Delhi: Sage Publications.

Wimmer, R.D. and Dominick, J.R. (1994). *Mass Media Research: An Introduction* (4th ed.). Belmont: Wadsworth Publishing Company.

Yin R.K. (1994). *Case Study Research: Design and Methods* (2nd ed.). Thousand Oaks, CA: Sage Publications.

— (1984). *Case Study Research: Design and Methods*. Newbury Park, CA: Sage Publications.

— (1989). *Case Study Research: Design and Methods (Rev. edition)*. Newbury Park, CA: Sage Publications.

Znaniecki, F. (1934). *The Method of Sociology*. New York: Farrar and Rinehart.

17

Research and Action in Field Action Projects

An Example of *Ankur*

Anita Panot

Research is systematic and rigorous inquiry or investigation that enables people to understand the nature of problematic events or phenomena. Research can also incorporate actions that attempt to resolve the problem being investigated. The success of a scientific approach to research is embodied in the technical achievements that continue to transform our modern world.

Less successful, however, have been the attempts of the social and behavioural sciences to emulate the accomplishment of the physical sciences. Despite a profusion of theory, the application of scientific method to human events has failed to provide a means for predicting and controlling individual and social behaviour. Teachers, health workers, and human services practitioners often find that the theoretical knowledge of the academic world has limited relevance to the exacting demands of their everyday professional lives (Stringer, 1996).

Pressure has emerged, therefore, for approaches to research that are more directly relevant to the ongoing work of social work practitioners. In recent decades, new research paradigms, known as action research, have sought to provide researchers with new ways to understand the nature of social world (Stringer, 1996).

Research and Action Research

Formal research operates at a distance from the everyday lives of practitioners and although it provides interesting theoretical perspectives about the nature and complexities of social life, it largely fails to penetrate the experienced reality of their day-to-day work.

The objective and generalizable knowledge, embodied in social and behavioural research, is often irrelevant to the conflicts that practitioners encounter or has little impact on the difficulties they face (Stringer, 1996).

In recent decades, action research is considered as an option by the practitioners who are engaged in community development programmes. As Tierney and Taylor (1991, cited in Stringer, 1996: 506) have pointed out, there is no one best way of bringing research and practice into closer alliance. Action research is designed specially for bridging the gap between theory, research and practice (Holter and Barcott, 1993, cited in Stringer, 1996: 299).

Action research is based on the assumption that the mere recording of events and formulation of explanations by an uninvolved researcher is inadequate in and of itself. A further assumption is that those who have previously been designated as *subjects* would participate directly in research process and that process would be applied in a way that benefits all participants directly. Community-based action research is a derivative of this approach to inquiry (Stringer, 1996).

Action Research as an Approach

Action research recognizes explicitly that it is concerned about change and that the people who need to implement the change would be directly involved in investigating the issue surrounding it. Traditional research operates at a distance from the everyday lives of practitioners. It includes research questions, field research analysis, conclusion and recommendation for action, whereas action research includes data collection, analysis, reflection, recommendation for action. Action is a key element in action research. It is fundamentally different from the classic approach of defining variables and generating explanation for why people behave as they do, through hypotheses and tests (Stringer, 1996).

According to Stringer (1996:16), it is a simple routine of look, think, act that serve as a framework to guide the research process. The "look, think, act" routine is one of a number of ways in which action research is envisaged.

Kemmis and McTaggart (1988), for instance, present action research in terms of a spiral of activity: plan, act, observe, and reflect. Different formulations of action research reflect the diverse way in which the same set of activities may be described, even though the processes they delineate are very similar. Similar methodology is being utilized by professional social workers, who are engaged in community development programmes. Here, the roles of social workers include collecting relevant information, defining and describing the situation. It further explores and analyzes the situation by formulating objectives, hypothesis and act through planning, implementing and evaluating. As participants work through each of the major stages, they explore details of their activities through a constant process of observation, reflection and action.

Rapid Assessment Survey

In this paper, an attempt is made to present *Ankur*, a research and field action project initiated by College of Social Work, Nirmala Niketan, to work with children with mental retardation (special children) in state-run schools in Mumbai, and their parents. In this project, traditional research was followed up by action with the stakeholders, resulting in their further empowerment. Though not a typical example of action research *per se*, this project can be considered as a unique model of intervention, based as it is on research followed by action. An initial rapid assessment survey was undertaken to ascertain the backgrounds of 18 municipal schools working only with these children was then followed up an ongoing research to provide an holistic understanding of the problems of children and their families. This then enabled the project in its further intervention with all stakeholders.

The Problem

The institution of family is considered essential for the existence of society. Family serves as a shock absorber in times of crises and stress. On the other hand, family itself can precipitate conflict and generate stress among the family members. Having a child with disability in family is not same as having a child without a disability. Presence of mentally retarded person in a family is known to impact families in varied ways generating special needs not only for the mentally retarded person but also for the different members of the family including mother, father, brother, sister and grandparents.

Mental retardation is not only a psychological or medical problem, but it is also important from the social and cultural point of view. It is a social problem of great magnitude. It is met with in the families of the rich and poor alike, educated as well as the illiterate and in all castes and communities.

A vast majority of parents of defective children, either consciously or unconsciously, suffer from ambivalent feeling towards their disabled child. A great number of these parents have some form of guilt, anxiety, tension and frustration resulting from the realization that caring for the retarded child means a long time responsibility, and a feeling that they are responsible for child's retardation. Parents need help in extricating themselves from their emotional involvement with their defective child (Peshawaria, et al., 1995).

There is no precise information available on the prevalence, degree and kind of disability in India. However, for the first time in many years, the Census of India (2001) has included a section of disability, and authentic countrywide data and the incidence of disability. There is five per cent of the population affected by some disability - physical, sensory or delayed mental development. The number of affected people are around 50 million (Government of India, 2002).

An NSSO (National Sample Survey Organization) sample survey on children with delayed mental development (1999) found that among children up to 14 years of age, the incidence of delayed development was 3 per cent. About 2.5 per cent of children are mildly and moderately retarded, and 0.5 per cent are severely retarded. The NSSO survey (1991), covering 4,373 villages and 2,503 urban blocks, found that 29 out of 1,000 children (2.9%) in rural areas and nine out of 100 children (0.9%) in urban areas have development delays.

Statement of the Problem

Special children need special schools, training and proper vocational and rehabilitation education. The benefit of family-centred intervention is being greatly recognized even now more than ever before. Efforts are being directed towards involving parents, teachers and other family members in the training and habilitation of the mentally retarded individuals. The plight of the mentally retarded children has been attracting the attention of educators and social workers in India for a few decades now. It may be gratifying to note that India is not very much behind the countries in the West in the field of education of mentally retarded child. The interest has been growing, but slowly, to judge by the services, private and public, available for the education of these children.

The education cell of the college initiated work in state-run municipal schools in Mumbai on the issue of compulsory primary education. In the year 1999, a non-government organization (NGO), Pratham, found out that more than 763,000 children attend the 1,234 primary schools run by the Municipal Corporation of Greater Mumbai (MCGM) housed in approximately 500 buildings and spread over 23 wards, with the medium of instruction being in eight languages. Only 18 of them were special schools for mentally challenged children. These 18 schools catered to approximately 840 children, cared for by only 60 teachers and 27 support staff, with a single teacher being required to handle more than 20 special children in some schools (Pratham, 1999, cited in Bal Krishnan, 2001).

The underprivileged special children, due to their significantly sub-average general intellectual functioning and poor adaptive behaviour, are neglected and regarded as a burden by the family and society at large. However, when adequate facilities are available for their education, these children can master some skills and achieve a socially adaptive behaviour, which can help them to develop individual capabilities and become useful members of society. Recognizing the potential need for intervention in this area, the College of Social Work, Nirmala Niketan, conducted a rapid action survey of the 18 special schools in order to gain an insight into the problems faced by these schools and provide recommendations based on the finding so as to enhance the level of functioning of these special children and integrate them into mainstream society. Based on the finding of the survey, an action-cum-research project named *Ankur* was initiated in 1999 to work for the underprivileged mentally challenged children of the MCGM special school. The ultimate aim of this study was to understand the problem for effective action based social work intervention.

Objectives of the Study

The principal objective envisaged for conducting the rapid assessment survey was to study the profile of special children studying in special schools of MCGM. That included the profile of special schools, teacher-student ratio, their qualification, curriculum they teach, physical structure of the school, grouping of children, networking with other schools, teaching aids and vocational training facilities available to them. The second objective was to study the perception of teachers about the role played by the parents and the third objective was to identify the areas for social work intervention.

Research Design

The undertaken research was descriptive in nature. The survey research design was chosen to collect the quantitative information on this issue.

Area of Study

The universe of the study consists of all 18 special schools for children with mental retardation of MCGM. It involved the census method of data collection covering all 18 special schools of MCGM in which 18 head teachers/in-charge were interviewed.

Methods and Tools of Data Collection

The interview method was used for data collection, as it provide sufficient space for rapport building, interactions and clarifications. A comprehensive interview schedule was formulated after much reading and study of significant literature. A semi-structured schedule, consisting of open and closed-ended questions, was formed so as to effectively obtain objective and descriptive data.

Data Processing and Analysis

After collecting the data, each schedule was checked for its consistency and completeness. The responses were edited and closed, ended questions were coded. The open-ended questions were initially categorized both explicitly and exhaustively and then coded. A code book was prepared and later the coded data was transferred to the master sheet. The numerical data was then summarized using frequency tables and percentage. The Statistical Package for Social Sciences (SPSS) was used to analyze this data.

Major Findings

The following were the findings of the rapid assessment survey conducted by the college: There is a low student-teacher ratio (20:1) in these special schools. There is improper grouping of children with insufficient networking with NGOs and other schools. There is a lack of appropriate teaching aids and physical facilities in classrooms. It also highlighted the poor facility for vocational training for children and special program for parents and low motivation of parents to collaborate in the child's learning was also marked in the study.

These special schools are situated on the same premises as the MCGM schools for the normal children. Fifty per cent of the special schools are situated on the ground floor while the remaining are located in the first, second and third floors. (Bal Krishnan 2001).

Conclusions

Education, training and rehabilitation of all these mentally retarded children in India are essential, rather imperative. Parents of these children can do a great deal in helping the society in imparting good education and training to these children. For strengthening the families having mentally retarded children the intervention need to be directed both towards meeting the needs of the child, and parents, siblings and extended family members. Thus, the society can only be benefited when all the parents are aware of their role in proper bringing up and education of mentally retarded children.

There is an urgent need to work with the parents' group to make them aware about their rights and various services provided by the government for special children and their family. There is also a need to enhance the capacity of teachers and staff members of schools for special children. In order to bring about effective change in various systems working with special children, social work intervention can play an important role.

Strategies of Action

In response to the above findings, the college in 1999 initiated *Ankur*, a five-year, time-bound research and action project. The goal of *Ankur* was to demonstrate the strategies and techniques for a multipronged intervention, using special schools as an entry point to empower parents of mentally challenged children. The strategy involved promotion of awareness on mental retardation through exhibition, distribution of handbills, conducting street plays and session with normal children from MCGM schools.

Another strategy involved was resource mobilization of both human and material resources such as working with professionals, networking with NGOs, vocational training centres, government and private residential institutions, private schools for special children, government departments, local mandals, corporate groups and donors, parents of MCGM special schools and work media. Advocacy was also an important strategy adopted by *Ankur*, which included empowerment of parents through information and knowledge on legal procedures.

Objectives

The objective for the first phase envisaged for the intervention ranged from work with the school system, introduction of a training module, training teachers, parents and staff, mobilizing resources and increasing awareness about existing government policies to facilitate their proper utilization/implementation..

Ankur's objectives were reformulated in the second phase based on the changing need of the participants. It included strengthening of parents' group, developing systems for sustainability through awareness and networking, and developing a module for demonstration.

Action Taken

During the initial phase of work, *Ankur* worked with different stakeholders like teachers and staff members, education officers, administration officers, beat officers and community development officers as a part of the MCGM system. This helped the project to understand the internal functioning, services and dynamics existing in the MCGM system.

Ankur also conducted ongoing research with parents of 200 special children. This was an attempt to draw up a profile of mentally challenged children based on indicators for immediate and long-term interventions.

A major finding of this baseline study helped the project to create a focused approach in its intervention. It was very depressing to know that 58 per cent of the parents had neither made any rehabilitation plans for their children nor used the facilities and government provisions existing for them. During the baseline survey, the team established a good rapport with the parents. Focus group discussions, meetings and training programmes helped parents to understand not only the problems of their children but also the various facilities, schemes and services available for people with disabilities.

A series of programmes based on the research findings and group discussions helped *Ankur* plan out programmes to strive towards its goals. Parents' meetings were held to create awareness about the rights of children as well as matters related to their health. This was in addition to educational sessions for community development officers, vocational training for children and parents, as well as refresher courses for special teachers. Alliance building with the larger community helped team members promote awareness and co-ordinate with other systems for resource mobilization.

Through programmes and interventions, an attempt was made to make parents aware of schemes, legal issues and other avenues to help build their child's future. The concept of parent ownership came into existence as a result of this intervention.

Ankur's intervention was based on the conscious understanding that being social workers and not special educators, the focus was less on direct intervention with children and more on work with the external environment. Ankur shared a two-way relationship with the environment. An effort had been made to select the knowledge, resources and other inputs from the environment, transform them into output through programmes, campaigns and services and return these to the target group (Bal Krishnan, 2001).

Outcome

Ankur gained a positive image among relevant stakeholders such as parents, children, teachers, staff and like-minded organizations. It made optimal use of information, knowledge, commitment and experiences of external experts, parents, officials of the Municipal Corporation and teachers. One of the most crucial outcomes was the formation of eight Parent Associations (PAs), of which five have been registered with the Charity Commissioner. Many members of PAs have been conducting sessions on mental retardation and various schemes for children in schools and others have turned master trainers. Members of PAs now independently visit government departments to avail of various government schemes and are now able to fight for their rights. All PAs now function outside the school, in communities, and in premises offered by individual donors and NGOs.

Some tangible outcomes are the mobilization of identity cards for children, concessional fares for state transport and railways, getting educational scholarships, professional tax and income tax deduction for parents as well as vocational training for children and parents.

In April 2006, the PAs with the help of the team released a book on Frequently Asked Questions about mental retardation and two directories related to organizations, schools, institutions and residential shelter homes for special children. *Ankur* has also developed a resource manual for intervention with special children and their parents. *Ankur* has planned its intervention in alignment with the philosophy of the college to work with the poorest of the poor. It has attempted to respond to various situations keeping this philosophy in focus. The project has been able to define strategies keeping in mind the need to demonstrate non-traditional social work interventions. Attempts have been made to enable people establish linkages and interact with resource systems as well as enhance interaction with their social environment. The project felt the need to enhance people's capacity for a greater access to resources and information for framing issues when the system factor interferes with people's rights (Balakrishnan, 2001).

The entire project was implemented in two phases. In the first phase the focus was to work with the special school system and to identify and work with other stakeholders. In the second phase *Ankur* shifted their attention to work with parents. The objectives in the second phase were reformulated based on the outcomes of the project in the first phase. In the beginning of the project *Ankur* started their work with eight schools and reached out to all the 18 schools in a phased manner.

As *Ankur* worked through each of these phases, details of their activities were explored through a constant process of observation, reflection and action. Review of the intervention, reflection and modification of the action plan was carried out on completion of each set of activities.

Ongoing evaluation and baseline research helped *Ankur* identify areas for intervention. Constant and continuous interaction with children, parents, teachers and others in the system helped them to understand the need of the special children and their parents. Regular meetings, discussions, training and focus group discussions helped them plan out the strategies to work towards the goal. A close look at some of the programmes showed that they originated as a set of activities with clear-cut goals, resulting in avoidance of overlapping of activities. *Ankur* had also drawn up flow charts with each objective, suggesting alternatives in the event of failure to achieve its mission. Both short-term and long-term planning was a crucial component of the action project. Baseline research conducted by the project helped them to understand the profile of the special children, their day-to-day living, problems faced by them and their parents, rehabilitation and future plan for the children.

Participation and involvement of parents in the second phase of their work resulted in empowerment of the group. *Ankur* field action project was evaluated by an external evaluator. This provided them regular feedback about their activities. The evaluator drew out all the positives of the project based on the needs of the second phase and helped them evolve new objectives. The external evaluator helped the research team to evaluate functioning of project work both in quantitative and qualitative terms. The external evaluator was an important component of *Ankur*. Being a time-bound project all the stake-holders were well informed about the goals of the project. As a result, parents were mentally prepared to cope during termination and continued to function in the form of parent bodies. The registration of these parent bodies was the planned outcome of work with them. Success of any project depends on the role and contribution of the researcher and the team member. The team's involvement, commitment and determination to continue for the full term was the major reason for success of the project.

Conclusion

The pressure experienced in professional practice reflects tension that exists in modern society. Professional social work educators and field practitioners are increasingly held responsible and accountable for solutions to problems. These problems have their roots in deeply complex interactions between the experience of individual people and realities of their social lives. Hence, there is a need to change our vision of social work practice. It is a unique method of human inquiry which advocates the use of contextually relevant procedures, formulated by inquiring and resourceful practitioners. The entire process in action research involves collecting and assessing information, as well as drawing action plans, based on the felt need of the participants. The relevance in identifying

Ankur as a research-cum-action project lies in its use of the educative, empowering and participatory approach to enquiry as well as encouragement of personal and cooperative relationship.

This kind of research and action project, which requires facilitators to work in close collaboration with stakeholders, provides a process in a context through which people can collectively clarify their problems and formulate new ways of envisioning their situation. In this process, the project establishes a close relationship with participants, thus enhancing its meaningful contribution to the society.

References

Alphonse, M. (1999). 'Evolution of Field Action research Projects', *Perspectives in Social Work*, Vol. XIV No. 2 May-August, Mumbai: College of Social Work.

Balakrishnan, Geeta (2001). Ankur: A Research and Action Project for Children in Municipal Special Schools, *Perspectives in Social Work*, Vol. XVI No.2, May-August, Mumbai: College of Social Work, Nirmala Niketan.

Hart, Elizabeth and Bond, Meg (1995). *Action Research for Health and Social Care: A Guide to Practice*, Buckingham: Open University Press.

Kemmis, S. and McTaggart, R. (1988). *The Action Research Planner*, Australia: Deakin University Press.

Laws, Sophie Harper, Caroline and Marcus, Rachel (2003). *Research for Development: A Practical Guide*, New Delhi: Vistar Publications.

NSSO Survey (1991) India, Ministry of Social Justice and Empowerment. *Annual Report 1999-2000*, New Delhi, Government of India.

Peshawaria, R. et al., (1995). *Understanding Indian Families: Having Person with Mental Retardation.* National Institute of Mentally Handicapped (Ministry of Welfare, GoI), Hyderabad: G.A. Graphics.

Royce, A. Singleton, J.R., and Brace, C. Straits (1999). *Approaches to Social Research*, Third Edition, New York: Oxford University Press.

Stringer, Ernest (1996). *Action Research: A Handbook for Practitioners*, New Delhi: Sage Publications.

Tandon, Rajesh (ed.) (2002). *Participatory Research: Revisiting the Roots*, New Delhi: Mosaic Books.

The India Child: A Profile (2002) Department of Women and Child Development, Ministry of Human Resource Development, Government of India.

Thomas, Maya and Thomas, M.J. (2000). *Asia Pacific Disability Rehabilitation Journal, Selected Reading in Community Based Rehabilitation*, Series 1.CBR in Transition, Bangalore, National Printing Press.

Contributors

Sushma Batra, Professor of Social Work, Delhi School of Social Work, Delhi.

Tushti Bhardwaj, Lecturer, Aditi Mahavidyalaya, Delhi.

B. Devi Prasad, Professor, Department of Social Work, Andhra University, Visakhapatnam, AP.

Murli Desai, Professor, Tata Institute of Social Sciences, Deonar, Mumbai.

V.V. Devasia, Professor and Principal, MSS Institute of Social Work, Bajaj Nagar, Nagpur 440 010.

J.S. Gunavathy, Lecturer, Department of MSW, The Madras School of Social Work, 32 Casa Major Road, Chennai 600 008.

Mary Venus Joseph, Vice Principal, Rajagiri College of Social Sciences, Rajagiri, Kerala.

D.K. Lal Das, Director, Research Centre, Roda Mistry College of Social Work, Pan Makhta, P.O. Golkonda, Hyderabad 500 008.

Anna Mathew, Principal, R.M. College of Social Work, Panmakhta, P.O. Golkonda, Hyderabad 500 008.

Anita Panot, Faculty, College of Social Work, Nirmala Niketan, Mumbai.

Sudershan Pasupuleti, Assistant Professor and Director of Service Learning, The University of Toledo, College of Health Science & Human Service, Toledo, OH 43560 USA.

Nagmani Rao, Faculty Member, Karve Institute of Social Service, Karve Nagar, Pune.

S. Raja Samuel, Lecturer, Madras School of Social Work, 32 Casa Major Road, Chennai 600 008.

Kalpana Sampath, Executive Director, Arpitha Associates Pvt Ltd, 302, II Floor, Santoj Cottage, 107, Surveyor Street, Basavanagudi, Bangalore 560 019.

Ranjana Sehgal, Associate Professor, Indore School of Social Work, Indore.

Surendra Singh, Director, J.K. Institute of Sociology and Human Relations, Lucknow and former Vice-Chancellor Mahatma Gandhi Kashi Vidyapith, Varanasi.

T. Saraswati, Faculty Member, Department of Social Work, P.G. College, Osmania University, Hyderabad.

B. Vijayalakshmi, Professor, Department of Social Work, Andhra University, Visakhapatnam, AP.